THE
AMERICAN ENTREPRENEUR

The Success Stories behind Today's
Top Fast-Growth Companies

KATHLEEN TRACY

The American Entrepreneur

Graphics and layout: Abraham Obafemi

ISBN: 978-0-578-68281-552995

Printed in the United States of America

Table of Contents

Introduction

It's been said the key to entrepreneurial success is finding and choosing a niche. For one thing, it makes it far easier to describe to potential customers what service or product you provide. It creates a targeted market. And becoming known as the specialist in a particular product or service makes a business more likely to be recommended by its customers, which in turn can help a young business more confidently expand their offering into new, broader markets.

There was a time when *niche* was equated with *small*. But that limited view evaporated with the rise of digital technology. No longer are businesses constrained by size or geography. Thanks to e-commerce and virtual offices, a one-man shop in Missouri can spearhead a global, fast-growth business worth millions using independent contractors the world over. IT systems can coordinate the most complex supply chain intricacies across regions and countries with ease. Teleconferencing allows instantaneous and simultaneous communication with stakeholders across the globe.

Despite all the digital advances changing how business is conducted in our modern economy, success in the marketplace still requires forward-thinking, innovation, and calculated risk-taking, qualities that will never become obsolete. It demands a nose to-the-grindstone work ethic that never goes out of style. It feeds on an eagerness to push the envelope and implement new perspectives. It thrives when there's a willingness to really hear what consumers want and need. And mostly, it depends on a vision of what is possible if you believe.

Each of the dynamic American entrepreneurs profiled in this book embody the special combination of skill sets, personality, and determination needed to succeed, especially during more challenging economic times. Their leadership and ability to navigate the whitewater rapids of entrepreneurship not only underscores their professional achievement but will also inspire the next generation of business leaders to follow.

As hackers of all stripes become ever more sophisticated, small to mid-size businesses (SMBs) are increasingly popular objects for cyber-attacks, primarily because they tend to have limited budgets for IT security compared to their larger corporate brethren. IBM estimates that up to four thousand smaller companies are targeted every day, accounting for 62 percent of all cyber-attacks and a third of all ransomware attacks, which can cost as much as $1 million in recovery fees.

5thColumn, established in 2012 as a boutique information security company centered on next-generation cyber threat protection and enterprise data security, provides response management that helps companies deal with any current malicious activity as well as develop strategies to protect against future attacks.

Founder Ray Hicks says, "Our team can effectively stop an existing attack, identify and eradicate the source of a breach, properly document the impact of the activity, and ultimately assist in mitigating the financial and reputational impact from the attack."

Ray, considered an innovative IT security visionary by his industry peers, believes that effective cybersecurity efforts must engage the entire company. "As the IT security industry is evolving into a more mainstream function, there is a loss of expertise," he explains. "That trend is leading to the development of procedures and methods that increase associated risks. 5thColumn has brought the expertise back into the equation to quickly and accurately identify risks within applications, systems, procedures, and operations that in most cases the business was unaware of."

Ray also notes that the flexibility of the company's platform enables its experts to use it as an assessment tool. "Deployed within hours and effective within minutes, our solution benefits clients because of its simplicity and its ability to accurately identify advanced progressive threats. It not only alerts clients about the threat but mitigates it as well."

Headquartered in Chicago, Illinois, 5thColumn's stated mission is to "ensure that clients data are always available, resilient, and accurate. Taking security operations to the next level helps businesses thrive by resolving threats to productivity as they happen." By delivering IT security as a service, Hicks has streamlined the process, eliminating the need for maintenance fees, support contracts, or advanced training, using open source tools to control their clients' IT costs.

Ray says his company's mandate is the same whether dealing with a small start-up or foreign government agency: to "deliver a solution addressing defined requirements and ultimately transform clients into high-performance businesses, organizations, institutions, and governments."

For Ray, 5thColumn is the culmination of a career that has taken him from corporate IT consulting to top-secret levels of government. As director of computer and telecommunications security at Science Applications International Corporation, which provides government services and IT support, and Northrup Grumman, Ray became the chief architect of the US Department of Homeland Security's IT, security, and application infrastructure and created the first US Computer Security Incident Response Center.

One might think that Ray grew up a computer geek, visions of bits and bytes dancing in his head. But for as distinctive as his professional résumé is, his path to IT rarified air took an equally unique path.

Ray Hicks

"I ended up where I am very serendipitously. In my senior year of high school, I hit puberty and discovered girls and partying, and I didn't do as well academically as I should have. My parents were not thrilled about that. It was suggested I do a semester or year at a community or junior college and then transfer to a four-year college."

Ray had other ideas. He wrote to the Colorado Dude Ranch Association for addresses and phone numbers for their various members, then called around looking for a ranch that needed some help.

"Several responded that they hired college kids through the summertime to help staff and whatnot," Ray recalls. "You'd get free room and board and a salary. I thought it was a great way for me to get residency status for Colorado, and the big plan at that point was to go to school in Boulder."

Ray found a job at a picturesque dude ranch located adjacent to the Arapaho National Forrest in north-central Colorado.

"You wouldn't make a ton of money, but you didn't have a whole lot of worries. Everything was taken care of. And you were sixty miles from the closest paved road. So even though you didn't get paid much, by the end of the summer, you'd have quite a bit of money saved up because you had nowhere to spend it."

Despite the idyllic surroundings, he says working on a dude ranch was no vacation. There were up to 150 new guests every week, and it was up to Ray and the other workers to make sure they had an enjoyable time.

"You realized early on that in the weeks where there were a lot of wildlife sightings, which were tangible memories and stories these people could hold onto, you received much better tips, and the guests would rebook for the following year before they left."

Even though there was plenty of wildlife living in the area, their natural inclination was to avoid people.

"We had bears and other animals coming through all the time but never when you really wanted them to," Ray says. "We had this unlimited playground, and you started to realize you could use it all to your advantage and make sure that everybody had an amazing experience. So I started to engineer stories and scenarios to make their stays more interesting if needed. Riding around the property I'd find animals that'd been struck by lightning or had died naturally and would drag them near the trail so that when our riding group later approached it, I'd stop the group then ride up really quickly and jump off to inspect it, just to add some drama. I'd cut out a tooth or a claw and give it to one of the guest, and they just loved it."

Ray says he found that interacting with more than a hundred new people every week from all over the United States and from varied backgrounds offered him a unique education on several levels.

"Over the course of time, it was a great education in terms of the experience you got in learning what motivates people. To some degree you were always selling or marketing the ranch experience although most people didn't realize it."

He says it was also his first real experience of personal growth and developing the skills to figure out problems.

"It was actually pretty awesome. I got to learn a lot about working with horses and how to do basic veterinary work because you're not going to have a vet run at the first sign of a problem. So we had to deal with it ourselves. I learned everything from suturing up cuts to setting bones. Being that isolated was like stepping in a time machine, and you were either going to do it or it wasn't going to get done. That *must-do, can't fail* lesson I learned there stuck with me, and it's something I continue to carry with me to this day. That attitude is the difference between having a roof over your head and eating a hot meal that night or being out in the elements cold and hungry. That gets lost for a lot of people along the way."

Ray says he attributes many of his successes—and failures—to that very lesson.

"I've always tried to roll a lot of that into the operating philosophy we hold near and dear to our hearts. Using trial and error to refine the process of what makes for a good company, what makes for a good business. The subtle differences between a business and a company or a company and a product, and everything that goes into starting a company and developing a product and bringing it to market. And differentiating that service and product from whatever else was in market—much of that came from those lessons-learned of being self-sufficient—or else—at the dude ranch."

Indirectly, it was Ray's enjoyment of horses that led to his foray into IT, with a little encouragement from others. After spending several summers training horses at the dude ranch while studying business at the University of Colorado at Boulder, he moved back east and went to work on an English riding Farm in Great Falls, Virginia, right outside DC.

"Several of my customers were in IT sales and executive management, and one of them in particular was very persistent that I should get into technology or technology sales. And someone I'd gone to school with was in tech."

Ray's first job in the IT industry was at a customer service call center, which he likens to a boot camp. "You go in and for the first seven weeks, you're completely saturated in all the various systems you'd be utilizing to service customers."

Fifty percent of trainees wouldn't make it past the first two weeks. And out of that only another 25 percent actually made it through to the end of the instruction and start earning a decent salary. Ray got through without breaking a sweat.

"I didn't have a formal education in IT or any other directly relevant experience," he says. "But it just makes sense to me. Math was always an area where I just didn't have to try. I remember knowing more than my teacher did in my high school AP calculus class, which created very interesting challenges. But the call center became an opportunity for me because it quite serendipitously introduced me to a company called Cable & Wireless, which provided telecom services to most of the Caribbean and was looking to get into Internet services."

In 1998 Ray became an engineer for Cable & Wireless and worked on the assimilation of MCI's Internet division into Cable & Wireless' Internet service center in Reston, Virginia, while also heading up product and service delivery related to the secure web hosting services. During that time, Ray interacted a lot with the UUnet team. Short for *UNIX to UNIX network*, UUnet was the first commercial Internet service provider. The company was founded in 1987 by Rick Adams, one of the original developers of ARPAnet, the precursor to the Internet.

"A lot of guys I went to high school with were over at Uunet," Ray says. "So I was scooped up after about six months by UUNet and was dropped into their security research and development team as an engineer, working on early stages of Internet security, like developments of secure protocols. At that time there were really no Internet firewalls or any of the technologies we take for granted now."

Ray says after his regular working hours were done, he'd stay up late into the night online learning his craft and honing his skills. Much of it through his introduction to Berkeley Software Distribution, better known as BSD, an open-source software and Unix-like operating system. Ray explains the value he found in BSD.

"Linux was an open-source operating system modeled on Unix. When Linux came out it had broader appeal, and you didn't really have to be an expert in Unix to be able to harness the power that operating system. So I gravitated to free BSD because it was like the hacker operating system of the time. That's where I met a lot of the guys who taught me a lot of my early tradecraft."

Ray says his learning curve accelerated quickly from there, the pieces of IP and IT security snapping into mental place.

"We were doing quite a bit of advanced security protocol developments, and I remember the first time somebody explained IP to me along with subnetting, supernetting, and CIDR notation. I don't know if any of it makes a lot of sense to anybody the first time they hear it, but it didn't take me very long to master it. I saw it clearly in my head."

Ray's move into government work came about thanks to a cyber attack that occurred while he was at UUnet when a computer at their lab was compromised by a system they determined originated in North Korea. At the time Ray was working in the security research and development division, and they were about a year into the implementation of the IP security protocol and networking.

"And our compromised computer turned around and attacked some of our customers and took down part of the old AOL dial access network as well as the old at home cable network. I found out it was also responsible for attacking some federal computers as well. I campaigned against it for a month or so before it finally found a way on to that computer. I put all my typical wears on it and grabbed all the data off that I could. When I came in the next day, the Feds were waiting for me, wanting to know what I'd uncovered and how I did it. They made it clear pretty quickly that they were there to offer me an opportunity. Cyber attacks were ramping up against the government, so they were very keen on recruiting talent to help across civilian-, intelligence-, and defense-related organizations within the government."

In March 2002 Ray became director of engineering and operations IT security at the Science Applications International Corporation (SAIC), which provides government services and IT support. A year later he went to global aerospace and defense technology company Northrop Grumman as the director of computer and telecommunications security, overseeing the engineering and operations of the Department of Homeland Security's (DHS) security operations center and computer incident response center. Ray notes that once you are in the government IT security pipeline, most people stay in it.

"There are two paths or tracks, I'd say. There were people who wanted to be Feds, and their motivations were all over the place. A lot of the time it was at least initially driven by the power or the authority that the position or role afforded. Then you have the path that I took, which is to stay a consultant and not become a Fed. That way you tend to move more freely within the various departments if you're a consultant."

That said, very few civilian consultants have ever had the type of security clearances Ray enjoyed, such as when he was the chief architect at the DHS.

"It was unheard of really," he says. "I was the sole civilian participant in homeland security day one at working group meetings. I had multiple clearances, which is often the case when you're working with multiple agencies. It starts with a Public Trust and moves up from there. The highest in civilian clearances is a 6C."

A Public Trust Security Clearance refers to a status granted to individuals that allows them to gain access to classified information such as state secrets and military classified data. They also may gain access to restricted areas after a background check. A level 6C security clearance is a

Public Trust Position clearance required for federal employees and contractors who will have access to classified information, computer systems, or restricted areas where the risk and magnitude of damage that could be done by the employee is high. When you get into intelligence and defense matters, information security is called compartmentalization, which limits access to information on a need-to-know basis to perform certain tasks. Then there is top-secret clearance with sensitive compartmentalized information (TS/SCI) access.

"When you get to the TS/SCI access," Ray says, "you know you're going to be looking at some stuff that not a whole lot of other people are looking at."

With the demand for his consulting skills increasing, in 2005 Ray started his first company, Looking Glass.

"It started with me, and then I was like: *Well, this is scary; I need a partner*," Ray says with a laugh. "So I brought on Jeff Ahlerich, who was my deputy at DHS. It was a pretty interesting chain of events. I had met the guys who founded a company called Urchin, which Google later bought, and it became Google Analytics. Those guys gave me the whole lowdown on running your business plan, forming your hypothesis, raising capital, and jump-starting a company. That always stuck with me, but I hadn't had that burning feeling in my gut relative to some product idea or service. That changed when I started carrying around a notebook and pencil so that I could write down ideas when I had them. Ideas tend not to come at the most opportune time. I don't care how smart you are; if you don't write them down right away, they just go away. It got to the point where I had notebooks everywhere—in the car, in my pocket, in a bag. It became part of my routine every day."

Ray was transferred to Boulder, Colorado, to take over the DHS security operations center. "It was like: Holy cow. We had an unlimited budget. We could buy the best of the best within IT, and we did. We tested every product out there and bought the best ones that were available to us. That was when the lightbulb first went off."

At the time, Ray says the cost and complexity of managing IT risk was spiraling upward, and multiple stovepipe systems were becoming increasingly complicated, difficult to manage, and more costly to operate. His intent was to start a company that would develop a comprehensive security management platform based on simplicity and modularity. The Looking Glass technology would then act as either a middleware to existing security systems and/or provide functionality such as anti-virus and spyware detection among many other features.

"Out of the gate we raised $3.5 million, with just an idea on a napkin," Ray says, so the future looked bright. Then in 2008, Ray says he got forced out of the company he founded. "It was an expensive lesson, but a lesson none the less. I know now that it was a good idea decently executed, not great, but it was my first entrepreneurial endeavor. That experience really shaped the future because if I was ever going to start a business again, I would do things very differently. But at the time, I really didn't think I would ever start another one—until I got the idea for 5thColumn. Once that happened, there was no way I couldn't start the business."

After leaving Looking Glass, Ray took a job as chief technology officer and technical product director for TerraEchos, a security solutions firm in Missoula, Montana. His job was to commercialize fiberoptic sensor technology developed at the Naval Undersea Warfare Center. He stayed with the company for two years before his personal life prompted a move to the Midwest.

"I was working for those guys out of Montana while living in Boulder. They took an investment that was going to require me to move to

Missoula full-time. I love the outdoors, and I love Montana, but it would have been a bit much to be there twelve months out of the year. It's a long winter. Plus, my fiancée at the time had planned to move to Boulder, but Missoula was a stretch. So I moved to Chicago where she's from."

"The winters in Chicago are brutal too," Ray says. "But I didn't expect to be here very long. I figured we'd be here maybe a year. But her family has deep roots and ties to the city."

He also discovered the wonders of Michigan's Upper Peninsula. "That was like a whole cherry on top of the cake in terms a place to explore whenever I needed a break from the city. So I consulted for about a year when I first moved here, and from the security technology perspective, there just seemed to be a real opportunity in Chicago and the whole Midwest. Then the idea for a product started to crystalize, and that's when I started my current company."

Ray founded 5thColumn, which specializes in providing cybersecurity to high-risk, high-stakes organizations, in May 2011, and says the idea was to methodically grow the service aspect of the business.

"And that continued to substantiate and fortify the hypothesis behind the product idea. In the early years I was reinvesting all the money back into the development and refinement of our initial product, BOSS. We had sales that were all coming in word of mouth. We had a couple of large technology partners that approached us. We got great feedback about what we were doing right and where we needed to change what we were doing a little bit. It enabled me to take ownership of our infrastructure, our brand, and our identity. It also drove a level of operational accountability in the organization that allowed us to attract and entertain top talent. And it just snowballed from there."

In 2017 5thColumn made the Inc. 5000 list of the nation's fastest-growing private companies, ranking 1246, with a three-year growth rate of

328 percent. 5thColumn was ranked #31 out of all the companies in Chicago and #16 out of the sixty-eight cybersecurity companies that made the list.

At the time Ray said, "We knew we were taking the longer, windier road to success, but we never predicted that it would happen this quickly. This is a pure testament to how hard everyone on our team has worked." Today he adds, "We're now sitting at a crossroads where we're a disruptive business in a $300 billion-dollar industry."

While 5thColumn is poised to be a long-term cyber-security leader, Ray indicates he may be stepping back from the company sooner rather than later.

"I am more aligned to the earlier stage and creative aspects of the business, and I'm constantly hunting for the right person to lead the day-to-day operations of the business. When you get beyond, say, twenty-five employees, you can no longer what I call brute force your way through things by mental horsepower. You need processes and scale, which come through organizational alignment and dissemination of responsibilities to trusted individuals."

While Ray notes that it's important for employees or staff to know from a hierarchical perspective the chain of command, and the superior they go to when they have issues, 5thColumn's culture is very much egalitarian.

"I'm also a huge believer in empowering all employees to try and solve an issue if they believe they can, those same kind of principles instilled in me back on the dude ranch. So it's part of our culture to question and challenge. It's not okay to subvert, undermine, or indirectly challenge somebody. You've got to walk that walk. I tell people all the time. If any of our competitors truly want us to succeed, they should just tell us we can't do something. It's the greatest motivation. I don't know why, but telling a very capable group that they can't do something is very unifying."

When asked what advice he would give any young entrepreneur just starting out, Ray focuses on a frequently overlooked aspect of a start-up.

"I think the smartest thing that I ever did was become close personal friends with a very good accountant and a very good attorney. Those are your two must-haves, and they need to be people you can count on to keep you honest. Surrounding yourself with good legal and financial representation and providing transparency to the other people you have entrusted your business to is only going to serve your interest in the end. The speed your business is going to move is not always something you can predict. You need somebody that's going to tell you the realities of what you can and cannot deliver on because when you're staring at a seven-figure opportunity early on in your company's evolution but there's a chance you can't deliver on it, there's no way you can sign that contract."

In addition to having solid professional advisors, Ray says knowing and accepting your start-up's capability takes emotional discipline.

"Unfortunately that gets lost on a lot of would-be entrepreneurs. I don't even think that concept is really fully embraced or understood by many modern executives. But the scenario where we had to turn down a huge, massively attractive contract paid off in spades in the end. By managing to sidestep some of those grenades, 5thColumn has been able to persist where others would have fallen short."

According to co-founder Michael Niggel, Advanced Concepts and Technologies International, LLC (ACT I) "provides total program and acquisition management for customers like the Department of Defense, Homeland Security, and space, intel, and cyber communities. Every day in locations across the country and in tandem with global customers like the Unites States and Allied governments, we support the planning and execution of complex program systems that require holistic thinking to solve their acquisition and operations challenges to achieve success. These programs are as diverse as our customers and range from platforms like aircraft, ships, satellites, and sensors to operational capabilities, including information technology, electronic warfare, information operations, and increasingly, cyber security."

More simply put, it's a knowledge-based management and consulting firm. Michael says when he and Dr. Harold Rafuse founded the company in 1998, they originally positioned the firm to perform acquisition management.

"Over the past twenty-plus years, we have developed and expanded our technical expertise and services to cover total program and acquisition management, operational and technical support, intelligence support and cyber security, health care, and foreign military sales management support. This year our staff will grow to almost four hundred technical and management experts based in the United States and overseas."

Successful companies tend to be defined by their bottom line and market share, and by those metrics, ACT I checks those boxes. From 2017–2019 ACT I was a finalist for both the prestigious Small and Emerging Contractor Advisory Forum (SECAF) Contractor of the Year award and the Washington Government Contractor of the Year award. In 2018 ACT I was recognized as the twenty-fourth fastest-growing company on the *Washington Business Journal*'s 75 Fastest Growing Companies in Washington and was also listed again in 2019 as the twenty-seventh fastest growing company in Washington as well as being listed in the 2019 Washington Technology Fast 50.

But for Michael and his employees at ACT I, a more integral measure of success is how they excel at executing their work, which is reflected in ACT I's stated code of business ethics.

ACT I is committed to the highest degree of integrity and honesty. The company is dedicated to the delivery of quality products and services which contribute to national security. We believe high ethical standards are essential to our mission.

We also believe that fostering a climate that encourages exemplary behavior, includes a comprehensive approach beyond often-punitive legal compliance stances. Organizational ethics means more than just avoiding illegal practice.

ACT I pursues an integrity-based approach to ethics management that combines adherence to the law with an emphasis on managerial and personal responsibility for ethical behavior. ACT I will continue an environment that reflects our values, supports ethically sound behavior, and instills a sense of shared accountability among our employees.

Michael notes that the emphasis on ethics when dealing with clients is balanced by an equal laser focus on providing a company culture that empowers employees. "We have created a customer knowledge base, an

Michael Niggel

HR support system, and a technical developmental center that drive our employees to succeed because without finding, nurturing, and incentivizing great employees, ACT I could not find and keep the great customers we have."

That Michael's career path would be in some way government related was essentially preordained when he applied to the federal Presidential Management Internship/Fellowship (PMI/PMF) program that competitively selected only two hundred graduate-level students per year for fast-track federal service opportunities. While an internship is essentially an opportunity for students to gain work experience in a field they are interested in pursuing, a fellowship is more about professional development that will help people succeed in their chosen field. The two- to three-year program is focused on rotating fellows around the federal government in increasingly senior technical and management positions to build future federal executive leaders.

"At the time most people stayed in the program for two years, moving around as a government civilian through different agencies to build program management and functional expertise," Michael says. "I was a Reagan presidential management intern for three years with the Air Force and Secretary of Defense's office, where I started learning and mastering increasingly complex technical and management functions."

Michael says he started on the financial side and then moved into program management. At the three-year point he could have stayed as a federal civilian but decided he wanted to get additional technical skills and a balanced industry perspective, so he went to work at Science Applications International Corporation, better known as SAIC. Headquartered in

Reston, Virginia, the company provides government services and IT support.

Founded by J. Robert Beyster in 1969, SAIC split off from the parent company, which was renamed Leidos. The primary reason for the SAIC spinoff was the conflicts of interest provisions in the Federal Acquisition Regulation, which prevented SAIC from bidding on some new contracts because of existing contracts.

"Dr. Bob Beyster, who passed away a few years back, was one of the most entrepreneurial people," Michael says. "His legacy includes not only SAIC and Leidos, but he also started the Foundation for Enterprise Development in 1986 and spun off the Beyster Institute in La Jolla, California, which both focus on advancing entrepreneurship and employee ownership. Working in SAIC for ten years enabled me to master the technical and management skills needed to build and run a company that assists the US government. And I also learned how to be entrepreneurial and employee-focused. That's part of the reason I chose SAIC over competing firms because there were plenty of successful SAIC spin-offs. That's the way Bob thought about things, not *I have to control everything and everyone,* but *I want to build and propagate an entrepreneurial philosophy and mentality.*"

After honing his skill sets for a decade at SAIC, Michael was ready to branch out on his own. The timing of the move was based on several drivers.

"When I started, SAIC had annual sales of maybe $500 million. By the time I left it was around $2 billion," Michael says. "We were experiencing organizational conflict of interest (OCI) challenges where pieces of SAIC wanted to develop hardware or software and other pieces on the services side wanted to provide advice and services to the government. But you can't do both for the same customer on the same program."

Because of those kinds of OCI cases, Michael says the service sector was often seen as secondary to hardware and software since there was greater profit in that work. "We wanted to start a firm that focused our knowledge and capabilities on providing services and operations to the US government and our allies."

Another reason for choosing the entrepreneurial route was more logistical. Michael's wife was a senior Air Force officer, so like most military families, they were moving every few years.

"I had three divisions working for me at SAIC. One Air Force, one Navy, and one Army, and it was getting hard to find a career path when you're moving so frequently. There were two centers of gravity at SAIC: Washington, DC, on the East Coast, and La Jolla on the West Coast, with some other places like Wright-Patterson Air Force Base in Dayton, Ohio, or Los Angeles Air Force Base in El Segundo, California. I thought: *Okay; I can build a new company and have flexibility when we move around the US.* We could still develop and grow the company while I developed my own career ladder."

Michael and Harold opened ACT I for business in early 1998, establishing the company as an OCI-free firm—organizational conflict of interest-free. Meaning it doesn't build any hardware or software. The initial staff included the two founders, Harold's daughter and son-in-law, and a chief engineer—all who had worked at SAIC. Now all they needed was clients.

Unlike industries where you build a client base by calling or meeting potential clients in person to pitch your value proposition, government work is more paper intensive because work is typically awarded based on open competitive bids. Each prospective customer provides a set of requirements every bidder must meet. To win a contract you have to meet or exceed all the technical requirements, have talented personnel, and offer the best or an affordable price, depending on the selection criteria.

Michael says bidders are usually required to have a management team that knows how the customer operates, so getting close to the customer, understanding their requirements and their evaluation criteria is crucial. "The government competes most of its work, so you write a lot of proposals and try to go back to customers who know you, like you, and trust you. The first contract we targeted in early 1998 was a cost reimbursable contract, where the final pricing would be determined when the contract was completed. Cost reimbursable contracts are one of the more difficult types of contracts to comply with as far as government regulations."

ACT I bid against six other companies. Getting work awarded through the federal government's source selection process is not a fast or simple process. Eleven months passed and all they could do was wait.

"That first year we made $160," Michael says. "And that was only because one of our neighbor companies down the road needed their computer fixed, so our IT guy, Harold's son-in-law, went down to fix it, and we billed them $160. The life of an entrepreneur," he says with a laugh.

Harold and Michael paid the salaries of their three employees and spent their days submitting bids. He admits the first year was emotionally and financially challenging.

"We wrote so many proposals we were sick of it. We were worn out and not sure we were going to make it to 1999. Fortunately just before Christmas 1998, we won the big contract that we'd bid on back in January, a five-year contract worth a little over $1 million annually. We honestly might not have made it to New Year's if we hadn't."

It was a task order contract, meaning they would be sent work statements then ACT I and the customer would agree on how many hours it would take for ACT I to solve each task/problem. "We did about a hundred task orders over the next five years for about $6 million."

While Harold executed that contract, Michael went out to find other customers. He found a diamond in the rough when he secured a small piece of work as a subcontractor with the Joint Strike Fighter program office in 1999. The program was tasked with developing an affordable next-generation fighter jet for the Navy, Air Force, Marine Corps, and US allies.

"The F-35 program was very small at the time, and as it grew, we grew," he says.

Once the work started coming in, Harold and Michael grew into their respective roles. He says they called themselves working managers.

"We both billed direct time and worked on contracts constantly. We did as much business development and marketing work as we could on the side. I worked a high percentage of billable hours for the first fifteen years. Not only were we founders and managing directors, we were also program managers, engineers, finance guys, and janitors. I built a lot of financial models for the F-35 team when they were selecting final suppliers. I was also traveling all over the world. If it doesn't wear you out, it makes you really strong."

When they reached their ten-year mark, the company was generating about $3.5 million a year in sales. Harold, who was a decade older than Michael, decided to retire. It was a drama-free transition.

"It's interesting to me that a lot of people will bring in an outside lawyer or accountant for advice about how to do it," Michael says. "But we basically just split the company in half. I worked with Harold to write a loan document that said: *I'll pay you out your half plus interest over the next five years.*"

While ending the partnership went smoothly on a human level, it did slow corporate growth between 2008 and 2013, the five years when

Michael was paying off Harold. On top of that, the Department of Defense went through sequestration—automatic budget cuts—during 2012–2014. While always financially solvent and never in financial trouble, ACT I did not have extra funds to grow and scale rapidly.

"We grew to about $9 million, got hit by sequestration, and went back to $7 million," Michael says. "Then in 2014 we came back up to $10 million. So we were a reasonably-sized small business. But once we had more discretionary funds in 2014 to invest in growth, we grew rapidly, and by the end of 2019, we'd grown to a $50 million company. Those years were the most dynamic period of the company so far. We hired excellent, committed technical and management talent. We counted on them to do their jobs and worked with people as a team to think about the next big target, how to win and execute work, and how to make our customers successful."

Michael says a lot of the work ACT I does now is "helping the government understand all technical, cost, schedule, and management risks. And sometimes complex outside variables like working with Congress and with our allies under international agreements raise the stakes too."

At least from the public's perspective, governments are known for an excess of red tape. Michael doesn't deny it comes with the territory but says there are good reasons for it.

"Our firm and other firms like us tend to be about good government for the public benefit. The government needs to make a satellite or an airplane or defend a network, and we have to deliver mission-critical capabilities for our customers. And there are

F-35 Lightning II

critical safety issues involved. You want to accomplish the mission, but you also want to bring everybody home safely, so you're always balancing that. And we have a lot of bad guys trying to impact our ability to operate. So, yes, sometimes there's red tape, but it's needed for consistent system performance and safety."

On the other hand, Michael points out that in emergencies the government can cut through a lot of red tape to produce some dramatic outcomes the average citizen never sees, such as in space and cyber defense.

"The US government and contractors defend many national systems every day, and most citizens don't have a clue because the systems are behind the scenes. Even people in our business are unaware when the US government and its contractor support teams thwart something from happening. You're only aware of it when the bad guy actually breaks through our security; then the public becomes aware of the threats out there. We can knock down a thousand threats, but it's all about the ones that get through."

Since its first crew of five, ACT I has grown to employ more than three hundred in 2019. Michael says that from the day they started the company, he has always focused on ACT I's number one core value: the employees.

"I think the first thing that discriminates ACT I from other firms in our business is we're very focused on employee satisfaction, which is our number one metric. And we've had long discussions about what is more important, employee or customer satisfaction? We're certain the right answer is employee satisfaction first. That drives customer satisfaction, sales, partnerships, enterprise value, and all the other key metrics down the food chain. So we spend a lot of our time focusing on driving up employee satisfaction and improving our employees' experiences as well as identifying top talent, recruiting them, onboarding them, training them, and most importantly, incentivizing them."

Michael says he often hears people say: *I need to motivate my people.* That's not a problem ACT I has encountered very much.

"We generally don't have to motivate our people because we hire people that are self-motivated. When it comes to their customers' mission—whether it's the Defense Department, Homeland Security, space, intelligence, cyber, or operations—they've got the mission at the core of their being. The programs ACT I supports tend to be big and complicated and need holistic thinking, which is what we've tried to build into our teams. We don't have three hundred engineers or manufacturing experts. We have five or ten subject matter experts in aerospace engineering, mission systems, aerospace manufacturing, or logistics, and we incentivize people to solve problems using a teamwork approach. That's what makes us special and effective."

Michael is quick to point out that when he says they hire the best, he doesn't necessarily mean the smartest person in the room or even the most talented because they are not always the right person for his business. The best employees fit the culture and demands of their customers.

"The people we hire need to have a mission orientation, a mission motivation, and be able to work in teams. Think about a car dealership; you want the top salesman. A lot of times those people are not the most likable. But you go get them because you need ten individuals who can go drive business and go sell cars. But I can't take ten people like that and put them together as a team because that's not how we are oriented. We must find the right kind of people—self-motivated who are incentivized by working as a team to deliver a successful mission. You have to know what you're looking for, and then you have to focus and train them in specific skills: taking care of their customer, treating other employees with respect, and driving ACT I objectives, where employee satisfaction is the number one goal and metric. It flows down from the CEO to all the other people in the company."

After a moment, Michael corrects himself. "Actually, it flows *up* because the CEO is at the bottom of the company. It's the people sitting directly alongside our government customers who are the top of ACT I. In between are managers who are trying to help those employees be successful by incentivizing them to do outstanding work to help our government customers achieve their missions."

One of the obvious challenges in recruiting is that competitors in the industry want the same people. So job candidates tend to always have options. But Michael says that more often than not, they get their candidate.

"I think it's our culture, our metrics, and the way we think about and approach life and the work that sets us apart. We attract people based on our culture, processes, systems, and the way we treat our employees. A lot of firms put sales as their number one metric. You know they're going to grow from X to Y to Z. Obviously sales are important to us, but sales is our third metric, behind employee satisfaction and customer satisfaction. Sales is on par with partnerships and enterprise workflow, which are important to scaling for the future and providing for our staff's growth and customer support."

Jason Yaley, ACT I's chief of staff, explains why he chose ACT I. "I did my own homework and found that ACT I is dedicated to its employees and the customer mission first. They believe if you hire the right people then incentivize them and focus on that mission, everything else falls in place. Another thing that sold me was Michael saying he wants the company's legacy to be about people with a purpose and a mission. That vision is the same today as it was when they started the company. That's the enduring key to ACT I's success."

Michael tells a story about Dr. Beyster, who he says never really got upset when one of his employees told him they wanted to start their own company. Something he learned first-hand.

"Harold and I traveled out to his little office in La Jolla, which was so packed full of papers you could barely see him across the desk when we sat down."

Sir, we'd like to start our own acquisition management business. Because of OCI rules we can't bid services when the bigger guys want to do hardware and software, and we're really very good at this.

Well, I just bought Telcordia in Europe; how'd you boys like to go run that?

"We weren't expecting that, so it was like wow! But it wasn't what we wanted."

Sir, you have a lot of confidence in us to go run that type of communications business, and I'm not sure I have that capability. But I know we're really very good and passionate about acquisition and program management work, and I think we'd like to try that.

Okay. Can I buy a piece of you guys and help you get started?

Oh, yes, sir. Absolutely.

"So Dr. Beyster assigned it to our boss to make that happen. Our boss offered us almost nothing for 10 percent of ACT I, and we told him that wasn't going to work. I don't think Dr. Beyster ever knew he didn't really get a piece of ACT I," Michael laughs. "But the thing I learned was he had no problem with someone else going out and trying to build a better mousetrap. And I don't either. I enjoy watching and helping other people get more responsibility, learn more things, achieve heights they had no idea they could accomplish."

Michael is equally sanguine when an employee gets poached. When somebody tells him they've gotten a better job offer, he often encourages them to take it.

"What I don't tell them is: *Odds are you'll be back later because the other companies likely won't have the same kind of positive employee-oriented culture.* Sometimes people need to leave to figure out what a good deal ACT I is. We once had our best recruiter leave because another firm offered him twice the money."

Of course, you have to go.

"Six months later he called, saying how much he disliked the processes and culture of his new company."

Well, you can come back, but I can't pay you twice what we used to because our business model doesn't work that way.

I don't care. I want to be happy. I want to feel like I'm contributing.

"Obviously we want to keep everyone we've got focused and happy," Michael says. "But when people have opportunities, it's good for them—and for ACT I—to go see what they can do. Sometimes we'll get them back. If not, we'll get their son or daughter later."

And if one of his employees or any of his peers ask for advice as they embark on their own entrepreneurial journey, Michael's advice goes to the heart of his overall business vision.

"In former Secretary of Defense James Mattis's book, *Call Sign Chaos*, he says you must be super competent at whatever your job function is. Well, there's competency, and then there's mastery. In Japanese culture it is known as *shokunin kishitsu*, which means *spirit of the artisan*. An artisan works at a certain speed and accuracy, and there's a beauty to it. I think when Secretary Mattis says *competent,* he means more than competent; he means you need to be a master."

The second piece of advice is to care about your people and others—the people you're working for, the people you're working with, your partners, the community, and so on. The third is you must have a set of core values.

"General Mattis calls it conviction. To know where your red lines are. *We're not going to do that because it's illegal. We're not going to do that because it's unethical. We're not going to do this because I just don't feel good about it. I wouldn't want to be treated like that.* You're going to bump into cases where you have to say: *I'm sorry; we're not interested in that,* or *That's not the right way to do this because it's not helping anyone.* At ACT I we try to be like doctors: do no harm. So if you follow those three things—mastering your skill, caring about the people you're doing business with, and having a set of core values and principles so you know which side of the line you ought to be on—you pretty much can't go wrong."

By staying true to his vision and company culture, after twenty-plus years, Michael admits he still loves his job. He looks forward to coming in early in the morning to get a good start on the day's work.

"There's always a lot of interesting work to be done," he says. "Though I do need to start thinking about delegating more responsibility, especially if we reach our goal of growing ten times our current size over the next five years. I think the key is to keep moving forward, keep learning, keep pushing yourself in directions you never imagined you would go."

F-35 Lightning IIs

Michael says that as he looks back across his successful and diverse career, there is one fact that is more important than any other. "It all comes back to your people. They are the key to success for the company and for the customer. True entrepreneurs take care of their people because they know it will ensure customer and mission success. As I've told my team time and time again: *We know that if we deliver for you, you will deliver for our customers*."

The Internet has become an indispensable tool in nearly every facet of modern life, from students doing homework to the military protecting a nation. In business it's been nothing short of transformational, capable of turning local companies into global enterprises. In today's business world companies of all sizes have integrated the Internet into almost every aspect of their operations, marketing, and supply chain management.

While the positive economic impact of the Internet is undisputed, so are its growing security risks from all manner of cybercriminals. Reports of massive data breaches have become commonplace, black hats are developing ever more sophisticated malicious apps such as ransomware that blocks access to a computer system until a sum of money is paid to the hacker, and various nations across the world are engaged in acts of cyberwarfare on a daily basis. A July 2019 *Forbes* article revealed that Microsoft had notified about 10,000 customers that they had been "targeted or compromised" by nation-state attacks the previous year.

Cybersecurity is clearly a concern shared by the entire business community, but small to medium-sized businesses (SMB) are particularly vulnerable. Since they tend to have limited resources for security, SMBs are increasingly becoming the main targets of cybercrime, and the results can be devastating. The average data breach can cost a company over $3.5 million, and more than 60 percent of SMBs go out of business within six months of a cyber attack. And even those that survive can suffer irreparable damage to their brand's reputation and consumer confidence.

Benjamin Dynkin

Cybercriminals can also use SMBs as an indirect gateway to infiltrate larger companies and organizations. The supply chain is an increasingly important vector for cyber attacks. For example, the hackers responsible for the massive breach of Target's system back in 2013, which led to the theft of seventy million individuals' personal information, gained access by penetrating the network of the small business that Target used for heating and air conditioning services. Since any large company is an interconnected network that includes vendors and partners, the risk of a cyberattack is ever-present, which can lead to criminals accessing, changing, or destroying sensitive information; extorting money from users; or interrupting normal business processes.

To protect individual companies specifically and the larger economy as a whole, the need for cybersecurity grows every year. That need is what prompted Benjamin Dynkin in November 2017, along with his brother Barry, to found Atlas Cybersecurity, a managed security service provider located in Long Island, New York, which helps protect businesses and homes from all cyber threats. Atlas's team is constantly on the road partnering with companies that need security for their computer operations.

"We catch advanced, persistent threats," Benjamin says. "There are groups of well-funded, well-organized cyberthieves who engage in sustained campaigns against companies. Our services will be increasingly important as the bad guys become more sophisticated."

Ben is also the executive director of the American Cybersecurity Institute, a nonprofit policy think tank, working with federal policymakers to develop policy and law on a variety of cybersecurity- and cyberwarfare-related topics.

Unlike many IT security experts who spent their formative years holed up in their parents' basement learning code and developing computer skills, Ben comes from a more hybrid background—an academic who is tech-savvy. He says he was always a technically-oriented person, which could have something to do with the fact that he's the son of a scientist.

"My father was a Russian theoretical astrophysicist who worked as a quant on Wall Street when he immigrated to the United States, so I always had that kind of edge," Benjamin says. "But I also fell in love with law and policy and political science, which led to a really interesting duality."

Benjamin went to law school at the Benjamin N. Cardozo School of Law at Yeshiva University in New York City, and he says that while there, "I saw there was a lot of activity in some of the related areas of law that started brushing up against technology—e-discovery, digital forensics, and of course cybersecurity. Being someone who had a little bit of technical understanding definitely put me on that path. I did a couple of fantastic internships with a United States federal district court judge and got to work with some great folks who were just brilliant in the field. After that, cybersecurity emerged as my calling pretty quickly."

While in law school Benjamin also started working with the *Journal of Law and Cyber Warfare*, which he says looked at cybersecurity at the most macro of levels, such as how do nation-states relate to each other in cyberspace? How do they enter into cyber conflict? What are the laws governing it?

"This was right around the time that there were several efforts in the United States and internationally to clarify and develop domestic and international law governing cyber warfare, cybercrime, cyber everything,"

Benjamin says. "And it's still in its nascency today. There are a lot of unanswered questions, but at least we're getting better at asking the right questions."

After Benjamin graduated from law school May 2017, he looked for a way to combine his law degree with his strong quantitative and technical background. So along with his brother Barry, who is also a lawyer, they founded the American Cybersecurity Institute, a non-profit

Barry Dynkin

dedicated to educating, advocating, and raising awareness of cybersecurity and cyber warfare issues for government policymakers.

"We saw a really interesting opportunity to start a non-profit think tank related to American policy around cybersecurity, cyber warfare, cyber conflict," Benjamin says. "At the institute we get to discuss and tackle some really fun policy issues with federal policymakers. We've done congressional briefings and have the privilege of regularly talking and walking with national and international thought-leaders both in and out of government. What I like to say when talking about the institute is, we don't try to give you the answers; we try to help you ask the right questions."

To get their foot in the door of government agencies, Benjamin says they used the same approach any start-up would to get clients or customers. They made calls, knocked on doors, and basically pitched their product.

"The institute was, and still is to this day, purely a passion project. We essentially self-fund everything. Luckily, we have a really great and motivated board, and everybody's willing to do online conferencing. So you get an email address, a website, design a few things, and you're good to go. Then we started calling congressional offices and some contacts we'd made on the conference circuit."

Benjamin says they set about a dozen meetings then went to Washington, DC, and made their pitch. Which was, cybersecurity is a really big issue in need of more attention and engagement.

"We had no clue as to the reception we were going to get. We had no clue what anything was going to be. But we were prepared. We put a lot of time and energy and effort into conceptualizing the issues, thinking about what kinds of policy issues we wanted to get involved with. We made it clear: we are non-partisan, we are apolitical. What we are is concerned about security. We'd tell people: *We are looking at this from a we-care-about-national-security perspective. We're here to help. We'd love to engage you; we'd love to work with you; we're happy to do briefings on interesting issues; we're happy to discuss legislation and emerging issues with you. We want to be a resource. And all this can be yours with no obligation. We just want to be part of the conversation. We want to help move it forward. We want to be a resource and put great stuff together for you guys to be better educated around issues that you're going to face.* And it worked. I think the biggest thing was our obvious passion. We received tremendous feedback and haven't looked back since."

Benjamin says people's knowledge about cybersecurity ranged from a deep understanding of the contours of cyber issues to those with a more focused and narrow understanding of specific issues. "In Congress you can have someone coming from the Department of Defense who is still a commissioned officer but is embedded in the congressional office as a policy analyst. We met a couple of those people who were literally cyber operators for our military, so they were incredibly well-informed. Other people we met had less of a background in the field and needed more guidance. One of the key issues we came to realize was that congressional activity in this space tended to be reactive and worked to solve specific problems, which yielded a piecemeal approach to cyber. That kind of knowledge tended to be very siloed. Cybersecurity is just so new and changing so fast that knowledge bases really haven't had a chance to develop into a grand cyber strategy."

While the institute is a nonprofit, Benjamin realized that one of the problems of running an unfunded passion project organization is that it doesn't really pay for itself. So he decided to start exploring how they could build a company around cybersecurity and servicing the industry.

"We started Atlas Cybersecurity with the goal of providing consulting services," Benjamin says. "We were lawyers, but we didn't want to provide legal services. We wanted to take the knowledge that we had, apply our technical knowledge, and provide a really robust advisory service to our clients. *Hey, you need to write these policies, so we'll help you write them.* Or tell a client what tests, analyses, assessments, or whatever it might be that they needed to do, primarily around compliance."

Benjamin says through a little serendipity they made a contact at Wells Fargo. At the same time there was a new Department of Defense cybersecurity regulation coming down that would apply not only to defense contractors, but to all their sub-contractors as well.

"So Wells Fargo engaged us to go on a speaking tour to local business associations up and down the East Coast to help educate them about the coming regulation. Obviously, Boeing doesn't need any help with cybersecurity, but the small, independent, machinist that machines the components that go into the F-16 does. And that kind of client—small manufacturers—were not ready to handle the new regulation. Obviously, this was going to be our entree into the world of compliance services."

While the brothers' original idea was to provide compliance services, another opportunity soon became apparent. The businesses they were working with were very appreciative with the policies the brothers were writing for them. But many had no way to implement the cybersecurity practices that the policies mandated. Many of the businesses, even some that might be considered fairly substantial by revenue, didn't have an IT person, or the IT person they did have was their relative who did it part-time.

"They wanted to know who was going to do the implementation for them," Benjamin says. "Trying to be good advisors, we looked for companies whose quality of service we could recommend and found that that the market was incredibly divided. On one hand you had very large cybersecurity companies like IBM and Dell providing excellent services but at a high starting price, and really only pursuing the larger end of the market; on the other hand you had IT companies that were basically buying and reselling some kind of affordable cybersecurity product but weren't really providing enough security to satisfy our clients' needs. We thought we saw a gap in the market, so we said: *Can we do this?*"

They contacted a colleague, Eric Stride, who had spent twelve years on active duty in the Air Force and is now a Lieutenant Colonel in the Air Force Reserves. He had also spent five years at the National Security Agency, leading an elite hacking group as a deputy chief of a field site.

"We called him and asked, *Hey, can we do this? Does it work? Is it viable?* And turns out, it was. That happened in late 2017, and we spent more than a full year planning, building out, working on partnerships, and developing our conceptualization of operations, making sure everything was perfect. And Eric is now our chief technology officer."

They launched their security operations center and managed security service in January 2019, which dovetailed with the advisory services they'd already been providing.

"So after Atlas Cybersecurity opened its doors, the one thing that was really important to us was that we weren't focused exclusively on selling customer to customer. We were primarily focused on finding good strategic partners that could enhance their own offerings by layering in our cybersecurity solutions. We talked to several different kinds of companies—AV/IT companies, accounting firms, law firms—basically every place under the sun that would make sense to layer in a cyber offering to their service. We wanted to become a distributor of cybersecurity services rather than run a full sales organization, particularly around cybersecurity, which requires a lot of trust between the parties and takes a lot of time and energy. It was much easier to just help other people that already have a strong relationship supplement it with additional, critically needed services."

Critical to this approach was working with our partners, Eli Alcalay and Benjamin Alcalay, who joined Atlas to build these lines and develop the support channels to enable our partners to succeed.

Atlas offers clients a menu with different options, depending on the needs and the existing posture of the business. It can be as simple as basic security functions like monitoring and managing a firewall or antivirus, or something more advanced like log management, security information event management, and vulnerability management.

"Our solution is software as a service although we often call it *security as a service*," Benjamin says. "Our clients get a hardware sensor from us, they deploy our software-based agent, and then we provide them the security, management, monitoring, response, and detection as a service. But the thing is, in physical security, it's binary. An alarm goes off, you call the police, and they respond. In cybersecurity we actually have to investigate. When we get an alert, we have to figure out what's going on. Is it a false positive? Is it a real compromise? And if it's a real compromise, how bad is it? We do a lot of very manual, human-based intelligence-gathering, based on the activity we see on the systems that we have deployed to, which allows us figure out what actually happened. We then do the work to ensure that any threat is quarantined, contained, and remediated. It's not just: *Hey, here's a problem; go deal with it.*"

Atlas runs its 24/7 security operations out of its headquarters in New York and Texas, where CTO Eric is based. Benjamin notes that Atlas is a Department of Defense authorized SkillsBridge employer, which allows companies to provide job skills training to service members during their last six months of their military service.

"Because Eric is still an active reservist with the Air Force out of Lackland Air Force base in San Antonio, we were excited to make the SkillsBridge program a big piece of our talent pipeline," Benjamin explains. "We have the chance to work with them to get transitioning veterans cycled into the program, both to get them experience in the private sector and to also, hopefully, get some great operators ourselves."

While cybersecurity is a growing industry, Benjamin says Atlas has carved out a niche where they don't have a lot of competition.

"At least in terms of what we actually do, but I think the competition that we face is primarily in what other people claim they do. For example, IT service companies that resell other people's cybersecurity products, don't provide an internal security operations center but rather leverage their downstream vendors. If you look at their marketing collateral and our marketing collateral, there's a tremendous amount of overlap. But the difference is we're actually providing the service side of cybersecurity. Their personnel are focused on IT, and maybe have minimal cybersecurity training. We have very serious cybersecurity experts who have all the certifications, decades of military and intelligence experience, and Fortune 500 experience and expertise. So when we go to a business and they say: *Oh, my IT guy is providing cybersecurity*, we need to overcome that. We have to explain: *No, actually he's reselling you some solutions, but he's not really giving you the robust protection we can.* That is the real competition. For us, selling cybersecurity is very often not really about selling; it's much more about educating the consumer."

As the company grows, Benjamin acknowledges the distribution of responsibilities on his team will have to evolve. "I'm technical, but I'm not a veteran operator," he says with a laugh. "Eric's in charge of the technology side, and I take many of the other functions. That's built into our model already. We haven't gotten to a point where we've needed to add a whole additional layer of delegation, so everyone still touches everything a little bit. But we are moving in that direction, and while we're laying the groundwork for that evolution now, I'm anticipating some growing aches there."

Benjamin says they have created certain metrics to help them control how fast Atlas grows to maintain quality control and service.

"Something we like to do frequently with prospective partners and clients is trials. When we started, we'd send test trials to anybody who asked, anywhere in the world. But now we're trying to be more discerning and implement some limitations. We say: *Hey, if you're going to be a partner and want to sign on the dotted line here, great. But until you bring me real clients, you only get two trials a month. Once you bring me a certain number of clients, I'll get you to do four trials a month. And once the next tier is reached, you can do eight trials a month.* We never really thought about return on investment. We were just thinking about returns and how to hit bigger numbers. Now we're trying to mature our thinking to say: *What's the return on investment? How much effort do we need to put in to earn that marginal dollar?* By building out those key performance indicators and metrics, we can use that data to measure all the facets of our service delivery pretty granularly."

But Benjamin admits that getting a start-up off the ground and guiding its continuing growth has been a big learning curve that's encompassed a lot of trial and error, picking other people's brains, and learning as they go. "We also have some really great mentors from a variety of backgrounds. But ultimately experience is the best teacher. No matter all the advice and guidance that we had, every business is unique as are the failures and challenges that it will face. You have to get through them to reach each next stage of growth. We're very fortunate to have a great ecosystem of people who we can go to for advice and guidance and who can help us through our specific trials and tribulations, rather than a more generalized guidance. And whenever we come to one of our mentors with a question, we get some truly great feedback."

One of the things Benjamin says he learned that he would pass on to other entrepreneurs starting out is the importance of understanding a prospective client's business cycle.

"Hurry-up-and-wait drills is the name of the game. Someone calls and says: *I need this,* and you go spend the whole day making it the number one priority because hey, this is going to be a great client. You get more material, and then they go dark for three weeks. Understanding that cycle and how to operate within it is really important. You don't want to lose a lead, but you also can't always make everything the number one priority; gleaning insight from the prospect is critical to understanding the reality of the situation. You need to adjust to people's business cycles and expectations so that you can pace yourself with them. If someone operates on a three-month buying cycle, that's fine. You just need to know it and plan for it, so if you get a phone call, it doesn't come out of the blue and interfere with other opportunities. You have to respect the business cycle of the industry that you're in."

Benjamin recalls how when they started, they would assume each call meant immediate business. So the tendency was to jump a little too high.

"You've spoken to the CEO or CFO of the company and get really excited and very hopped up because you think: *Oh my God, this is an amazing opportunity. It's going to be awesome. We're going to leapfrog our projections by a month or two months because they're really interested.* And then you find out they need three, five, or ten weeks to evaluate. That's just the nature of the beast because of the bureaucracy of most businesses—big and small. Particularly in this industry, when people aren't really sure what they need and what's out there. Everyone understands they need to address their cybersecurity risks, but they often don't know what their needs really are."

One of the more common types of cyber-attacks that has been growing in popularity is ransomware, which is designed to encrypt a victim's file system, potentially causing an irreversible loss of data. An increasing number of cybercriminals are utilizing ransomware to extract money out of their victims. Some surveys from *Forbes* have shown that losses for businesses can average upwards of $84,116 for each incident, with some businesses willing to pay upwards of $1 million to decrypt their data. Benjamin says that there are ways to help clients who have been attacked such as working with them to restore data from their back-up solutions.

"We are also now talking to a start-up that's doing some very cool things in ransomware rollback. Because we're service-focused and not product-focused, I can update my stack for all of my clients in an afternoon to get them all protected by new solutions, just like this one."

Currently about three-fourths of the solutions Atlas deploys are third-party, and one-fourth are proprietary, but the company hopes for the ratio to be 50-50 by mid-2021.

Like most start-ups, Benjamin says they had a five-year plan when they organized the company, but because of its growth, they've had to adjust it a couple of times.

"Things have evolved pretty dynamically. For example, in the last several months, we've become one the leading companies in superyacht cybersecurity. We happened to find the right partner in the space, and we really tripled down on it as a focus industry for us. And that's meaningfully affected how we view our five-year plan now versus in January 2019. So while we do have plans, we understand that nothing can be set in stone, and the key to success is openness to opportunities as they arrive and dynamism in their pursuit."

For both Dynkin brothers, founding a start-up and seeing it morph into a fast-growing company has been gratifying because it was based on a personal passion for promoting security.

"I really believe in what we're doing," Benjamin says. "I think the most important thing is that you're passionate about what you do and that you actually believe that what you do serves an important purpose. I studied economics in college. I never wanted to be someone who just seeks profit for profit's sake. Obviously, profit is critical to the business, and that's why I'm doing all this work and have not taken a salary in over eighteen months. But it's also important for me to know I'm actually doing something important. I'm protecting businesses from threats. I am protecting people. I'm protecting information. I believe in our mission to provide security and stability to the businesses I work with, the supply chains that they're in, and the economies they're a part of. I'm very proud to play my part in the ongoing struggle.

"In the realm of cybersecurity, we are all risk vectors and the majority of our threat surface lies in the private sector, so what we do isn't just important in terms of protecting our individual clients, but playing our role in upholding a broader shield against hostile activity in cyberspace. Also, I really love the fact that unlike almost any other business in the world, we get to wake up every day and fight bad guys. We fight criminals. We get to work with law enforcement. There's obviously nothing wrong with being an accountant or a banker, but we get to be essentially a private defense force that serves our clients. And that's really fun, fulfilling work."

There are quite a few advantages for businesses that extend payment terms to their customers, which is effectively extending short-term credit, similar to how a credit card would function. Consumers and businesses alike are generally willing to buy something now if the payment is delayed so by extending payment terms, businesses are likely to increase sales. Consider a logistics company that delivers goods on behalf of a shipper that is given thirty days to pay, a practice sometimes referred to as net-thirty billing that has helped businesses incentivize their clients.

It's a model that's been around for much longer than it's even had a name. As far back as 2000 BC, merchants in Mesopotamia allowed businesses to purchase now and pay later. A couple of hundred years later the first official rules around payment terms were chiseled onto the black stone stele containing the Code of Hammurabi.

As long as the merchant gets paid per the stated terms, offering payment terms works great. But offering payment terms also has disadvantages as well. Not only does it affect cash flow but when payment terms are not met, owners are forced to chase down payments, fielding time-honored excuses: *The check is in the mail. I didn't receive the bill. We're switching banks. The person who authorizes payments is on vacation. We sent it last week; can't imagine why you haven't received it.* Every minute spent chasing a customer to pay money that is owed is one less minute spent where the time counts: growing the business.

Enter Biller Genie, which has innovative SaaS technology that helps businesses collect outstanding balances and gain back valuable time by automating the entire accounts receivable workflow. Founder and chief executive officer Thomas Aronica says that the platform helps businesses work smarter, save time, eliminate administrative expenses, and improve cash flow by standardizing and automating invoice procedures and follow-up initiatives.

"Historically, enterprise level accounts receivable automation has only been available to the biggest companies in the world that have the resources to develop their own internal systems to manage these processes. Our goal is to democratize accounts receivable automation technology by making enterprise-level automation technology affordable and accessible to small and mid-sized businesses throughout the United States and Canada."

So far, so good. The Miami-based company has quickly emerged as an industry leader. In 2019 Biller Genie was singled out as one of the year's top fintech start-ups at the Money20/20 conference. Biller Genie was also a recipient of the Electronic Payment Association's NexTen Award and the CPA Practice Advisor's Technology Innovation Award.

Prior to founding Biller Genie, Thomas had been in the merchant services business for more than a decade. Many of his customers had routinely asked for a solution that would help them get overdue invoices paid faster.

"We knew there was a big need for a solution like Biller Genie before we started building it. We didn't set out to be a game-changer," he says. "We just wanted to help our clients save time, get paid faster, and succeed by automating their accounts receivables. But after we went live it was evident that the problem was universal, and others outside of our small portfolio could potentially benefit from our solution. So we opened it up to the general market, and the response was beyond anything we could have

Tom Aronica

dreamed of. It's nice that we've gotten the recognition that we have, but it's the feedback we've received from our customers telling us how much Biller Genie has helped them streamline their business and improve cash flow that's truly game-changing for us."

Biller Genie's fully automated platform features integrations with popular accounting platforms such as QuickBooks, Sage, and Xero; electronic bill presentment via email, SMS, and paper mail; automated payment reminders with custom messaging, cadences, and style; multiple payment options (credit/debit cards, ACH, Apple Pay); a hosted, merchant-branded customer portal that drives self-service; and additional features like a late-fee manager that alerts customers about penalties associated with delinquencies that help to expedite payments.

"In recent years there has been a proliferation of automated accounts payable solutions that use artificial intelligence to automatically code transactions to the proper expense categories," Thomas notes. "But a void remained in the marketplace for accounts receivable automation. To me the priorities seemed backward. Shouldn't businesses be more concerned with improving the processes around receiving payments from their customers than automating payments to their vendors?"

Although Thomas seems completely in his element as a rising star in fintech, it's not a career path he anticipated taking as a youth growing up in Long Island, New York. His parents had more traditional dreams for their son.

"I grew up in a European household, where the environment was one where I was always told that I had to become a doctor or a lawyer when I got older. So I always thought that was going to be my path. I left New York after I graduated from high school and moved to South Florida to attend the University of Miami. I originally had plans to study medicine, so I enrolled in pre-med courses. But I realized shortly after classes began that it wasn't for me. Since I was already enrolled in the College of Arts and Sciences, and the pre-law program was in the business school, I shifted gears toward what my parents argued was the next best alternative: computer science. I always had an affinity for computers and programming as a child, and it was the field I was destined to study."

After graduating with his computer science degree in hand, Thomas mulled over his options. "I had received job offers from Microsoft and Google, but much to my father's dismay, I didn't want to sit behind a desk writing code my whole life; that wasn't my personality."

Probably to his father's even greater dismay, Thomas spent the next two years working in fine dining restaurants while he tried to figure out what he wanted to do with his life. A touch of serendipity showed the way.

"A buddy of mine from high school had started working as a sales representative for a well-known credit card processing company," Thomas says. "I remember going to a meeting that he set up for his boss to recruit more salespeople. It was your typical dog and pony show, he threw the keys to the Ferrari down on the table, telling us how he could turn us into millionaires. I wasn't impressed by the show, but the content landed. I don't know why, but it all made sense to me; it just clicked. I understood the math. I understood the technology. I understood the network. Even though I certainly had never thought: *Okay, I'm going to own a credit card processing company* while growing up, it was an industry that just made sense to me."

After that meeting Thomas began selling some accounts as more of a side hustle than full-time endeavor, mostly trying to build a portfolio in his spare time while still working in the hospitality industry.

"A year later, a college friend and his father had started a health insurance agency and recruited me to be one of their salespeople, but I was acting very much like a partner," Thomas says. "Not taking a real salary, building all their sales protocols, managing the books, and even letting some new recruits live with me. I was supporting them through the growth of that company. After a year and a half of pouring my heart and soul into helping to build the business—and commuting an hour and a half each way, every day—I approached them with a demand; it was time to either pay me a real salary or make me a partner. I was all in and had already done all the work to help set them up. This was somebody I was really, really close with that was a good friend of mine."

But his friend and his father opted not to make him a partner, nor were they willing to pay Thomas an appropriate full salary. It was a stinging personal rebuke and professional lesson.

"I walked out that day and vowed to never work for anybody ever again. And that's how I got into the payment processing business full-time."

By then he had already built a small portfolio in his spare time, but by the end of 2007, he was ready for his first entrepreneurial endeavor: a payment processing business that he named PCI Professionals

"When I left the health insurance agency, I spent the next six months identifying and negotiating a contract with a major national processor. I had just turned twenty-five years old and was trying to figure everything out as I went along. My father had given me $15,000 to get started, $10,000 of which went to our Visa/Mastercard registration on day one. I was this one-man show starting what was to be a big business. And I had no idea what I was getting myself into."

Thomas admits that the processor he was working with probably shouldn't have set him loose. "I was in way above my head," he says. "I was under-capitalized with no real-world experience, no help, and no guidance, starting a residual-based portfolio from scratch. My first check was less than ten dollars, and I thought: *What did I get myself into?*"

But Thomas was undaunted. He says the day he signed the contract with the processor he went back home to his condo, ripped the cabinets out of his master walk-in closet, and that became his (very small) first home office.

"I had CRT monitors on TV trays in this twenty-square-foot walk-in closet. I rented out the second bedroom to supplement what little income I had started to generate. Over time I outgrew my closet and moved the "office" into the second bedroom. A few months later I hired a salesperson to work with me, so we moved the office into the master bedroom, and I was living in the guest room."

For all the office space musical chairs, this was not an overnight success story. It was more a cautionary tale of just how difficult it is to build a start-up on limited funds.

"The worst years of my life were 2008 to 2010—by far," Thomas says with a rueful laugh. "I was working 9:00 to 5:00 trying to sell. Then from 5:00 p.m. until midnight I was performing all the maintenance on the accounts: building the procedures, writing the policies, and putting together the infrastructure of the business. From midnight until I couldn't keep my eyes open anymore, I would build the website and the customer and agent portals. Then I'd do it all over again the next day. Twenty-hour days were common. It was like that for years, seven days a week—the story of any young, budding entrepreneur."

Thomas admits he came close to throwing in the towel several times. In addition to the physical and emotional wear and tear, his finances were precarious.

"The bank foreclosed on the my condo because I couldn't afford to pay the mortgage. I was paying other people's salaries and couldn't afford to pay myself. I would go days eating just rice and beans because I didn't have money to go food shopping. I wasn't able to see my family for holidays because I couldn't afford to travel. It was a crazy, really unhealthy couple of years. Looking back, I don't know how I did it."

He finally visited his family for Thanksgiving in 2009. He was at his lowest point, ready to wave the white flag.

"I was out of money. I knew I had a good business, and no one could argue that I wasn't putting in the work, but I was basically a one-man-show and just wasn't generating enough revenue to pay the bills. When I went back to my mother's house that November, I was basically in tears. I had gotten to the point where I physically just couldn't do any more. It wasn't for lack of effort; I couldn't possibly work any harder. My father used to tell me: *It takes money to make money*, and that's the point I was at. I just needed to put some money behind it to build it. That Thanksgiving, sitting on the edge of the bed in tears, I told my mom I was going to give up."

Not on her watch. That night she wrote Thomas a check for $20,000—her last $20,000. To this day, he calls it his lucky money. It was what he needed to get down off the ledge and over the hump. Thomas returned to Florida revitalized and took steps to further grow the company.

"I was in a networking group at the time, and I went to the financial advisor for help: *You know how hard I've been working, and I know you see*

my potential, but I need help. I can't pay you for this, but if any of your clients are interested in small business, I'd love to talk to them."

The advisor introduced Thomas to a few people, and that led to his first business partner. "It was really a bet on me," Thomas says. "Looking back there was no real business to invest in. We were losing money, had a tiny client base, and only a promise of future growth. He was really taking a chance on me. We split the company 50/50 in return for a cash investment spread out over the course of the year. He was a commercial real estate investor, so part of the deal was him giving me office space for free. The investment and the office enabled me to recruit and hire better support. All of a sudden I had a little bit of cash flow, so I could start to make and execute better decisions. That little investment had a serious impact very quickly; we tripled revenue that year."

But it was too little, too late. Despite the eventual growth the company was still behind and had fallen short of the minimum volume they needed to generate per their processing agreement that was coming up for renewal. Thomas needed $70,000 or else the processor was going to cancel the contract, so he made the case to his investor to keep pushing forward. But his investor was much closer to the end of his career than the beginning, so the investment was akin to a game of chance, one that came with a tax break.

"I let him know what was going on and that we would need more money to keep the doors open," Thomas says. "But he had lost interest after the first few months. While the business was growing, it was still pocket change compared to what he had accomplished in his career. He said: *Well, I took a bet, and I lost. We'll have to close the business because I'm not giving you any more money.* After three years of putting everything I possibly could into starting a business—all the blood, sweat, and tears—and just as we were finally hitting our stride and starting to grow, my business partner was willing to just use me for a tax write-off. I wasn't about to let that happen, so I went on the hunt to find new investors."

Coincidentally, that same week there was an industry conference in town that Thomas was attending. The keynote was the owner of a competing office based out of Washington, DC. "I listened to him talk about the growth challenges for new companies in the industry. It was like he was speaking directly to me. I would have followed him into war by the time he was done. He got off the podium, and I latched on to him. He couldn't shake me for the remainder of the conference. I started telling him where we were and asked if he could help."

Serendipitously, one of the advisors for the keynote's company happened to live in Miami. Thomas says they spent the next few months getting to know each other, going through due diligence, and trying to figure out how the company might be able to invest.

"We took a liking to one another, and I soon learned that the advisor also had a small processing company in Miami and was also looking for opportunities to invest in. After courting each other, we eventually said: *What are we doing here? Why don't WE do a deal together now and position this for a bigger opportunity together in the future?*"

The advisor had another partner who was also a serial entrepreneur, and they were both interested in the payments industry. So for the second time in his career, Thomas found investors who were willing to bet on him as much as they were betting on the business. By early 2011, less than a year since the original investor had come in, another deal was in the making. Thomas's new partners paid off the original partner, paid off the minimums that were due to the processor, and each made a small cash investment on top. They merged the two processing companies together and rebranded to SkyBank Financial, with Thomas as CEO.

"Within a year we tripled the company, just by being able to invest in leads and with the guidance of engaged partners who helped me make smart decisions. We started to build a reputation in the industry. We started to build a reputation in the community. A year later we were cash flow positive and a year after that we became an acquisition target." Thomas jokes, "My five-year-old little engine that could became an overnight success."

In 2013 Thomas and one of the partners, the original advisor, went back to the processor that originally put them together. They structured a deal to sell part of the portfolio and used the proceeds to buy out the third partner.

"He had put about $150,000 into the pot in the middle of 2011," Thomas says. "Eighteen months later we bought him out for almost 10x. Needless to say, he was pretty happy with me and the results we created for him."

Thomas and the remaining partner continued to grow SkyBank, and by 2017 it was a multi-million-dollar company. As the business matured, so did their strategy. Thomas says the traditional door-to-door sales model and being everything to everybody wasn't scalable. And with new players entering the market, there was more margin compression than ever before.

"We had turned SkyBank into a very profitable business, but I was never able to position it for the scale that I sought to achieve. It was very much dependent on me. In essence I was the business. Sure, we had employees and sales people and all the processes in place, but if I wasn't driving forward, the business would stay stagnant. I had a vision of creating an enterprise that could function and live on without me, which would be very meaningful for everybody involved. That's what my dream was before Biller Genie, and that's still what it is today."

Around 2015 Thomas started to recognize a shift happening in the credit card processing industry. Companies such as PayPal, Square, and Stripe were coming into the market and changing the way small businesses looked at processing payments.

"I read the writing on the wall and knew that we would have to adapt if we were going to last," he says.

He realized the future of the industry was in the software and the technology, not necessarily in the transactions. Luckily, technology was right in his wheelhouse.

"I recognized the additional value we could create by combining transaction processing with integrated software solutions. So from 2015 to 2017, on top of all my other duties, I spent the majority of my time working with other software companies. We would help them build payment technology into their software, and I would consult on design and business logic. At times I would even dust off the old college notebooks and write code so we didn't have to wait on other developers getting back to us."

Thomas says he also helped set up their go-to-market strategies, provide all the back-office support, and consult with them on how to put it all together. "We turned into a boutique processor focused almost exclusively on supporting our software partners, and because of my background, I was really, really good at it."

Thomas credits his success to having a technology background in computer science that allows him to talk tech. And as a CEO himself, he understands how to run a business and had been doing so for many years.

"At the end of the day, at the true heart of it all, I'm a sales guy," he says. "I had this unique set of capabilities that made me very effective at structuring the integrated software deals. I could speak to a CEO, a chief marketing officer, and a chief technology officer, and break the opportunity down in a way that each of these different business segments understood the opportunity and the value we could create for the other."

Thomas explains that his new strategy was a supplement to what they were already doing and it allowed him to drive scale. "It's the one-to-many model; I could only walk into so many places in a day, but if I did one integration to a software company, and they had thousands of clients, we had an easy way into their entire distribution channel. So it was a way to drive up transaction volume faster while having a more sophisticated conversation that added a lot of value beyond the transaction."

Then he thought: *What if we can also assist with getting the payments?* With the next integration he went a step further and built logic to help send invoices. Another integration later the ability to send reminders was added. As he sharpened his skillset with each integration, he noticed that the clients using the system were happier. Fewer payments were delinquent. Cash flow was improving. There were fewer questions about price and more about value.

In the middle of 2017, Thomas had his eureka moment. He was getting out of the shower one morning and thought: *Why am I enabling other software companies when I could just build my own software exactly how I know people want it?*

"And that was how Biller Genie came about," he says. "After I got out of the shower, I looked at myself in the mirror, and it hit me like a ton of bricks. I could visualize exactly what I thought it should look like and how it should perform. My idea was to take all the strategies I had developed, which I knew worked, and build a solution that could connect to any other software application and make it even better."

At the time of his epiphany, Thomas had just bought out his remaining business partner, and once again owned 100 percent of the company. Initially he thought his new software application was simply going to be a better way to grow his payments business and make it more profitable.

"I never thought that it was going to be its own company," he says.

Thomas started the research and development in 2017, intending to build the app from cash flow. He hired his first developer. Then his second. Then a third. Fifteen months later the first version of their application was complete, which they named Biller Genie.

"The first product was a QuickBooks desktop integration that we launched at the end of 2018," Thomas says. "Within two weeks, I knew I had something bigger than I had originally thought on my hands. All of a sudden we had social influencers, banks, and major payment providers reaching out to us eager to get involved. Customers couldn't believe how well it worked, and how simple it was to use. They started to refer us to their friends who in turn referred us again. I knew I had finally found the growth engine that would get me to the scale I had envisioned nearly ten years before. I soon realized that I had landed on a segment of the market that was largely unrepresented. Competing solutions were designed for enterprise clients that were costly to implement and not accessible to the small business owner. And there was no one servicing that lower to middle market."

Thomas was making enterprise-level automation technology affordable and accessible to the small business owner, the ones he says needed it the most.

"It was the first time in the dozen years I'd been in business for myself that the vision I had set out to achieve was accomplished," he says. "And as with any other successful entrepreneur, as soon as the vision is achieved, the vision changes. I now believe that with Biller Genie we can do something even bigger, something that's more meaningful for the people who work with and for us."

Thomas says that Biller Genie is just getting started, and he has big plans and a long-term vision for how the software will evolve in his pursuit to help business owners get paid faster. He plans to secure additional funding and is actively building the executive management team to position the business to achieve greater heights.

"I believe we have the opportunity to fundamentally change how businesses collect payments from their customers. The global e-invoicing market is set to grow by 20 percent between now and 2026, and we are on the leading edge of this growth. There is a tremendous growth path with different verticals and opportunities that we can expand into, ultimately getting into financing and factoring as well as third-party collections management, blockchain, and more. I see myself continuing to drive innovation that we can bring to the market and make available to small and midsize businesses."

One of Thomas's goals is to democratize automation technology that is typically only available to enterprise businesses that have the means and the time to implement it. "If we can have a small impact on the way consumers interact with their vendors, then we could have a small impact on the economy. And any small impact goes a long way."

Thomas would also like to have an impact on other entrepreneurs through mentorship or even just offering some hard-earned advice. Number one is to be prepared for it to take much longer than you project it will to build a business.

"Regardless of how strong the vision, how well-planned the execution path, life is always going to throw curveballs at you. In business you need to pivot quickly when you're in start-up mode. Ask questions, be inquisitive, and learn from everyone. Being an entrepreneur is not easy, but it sure is fun."

According to statistics from the International Civil Aviation Organization, over the past twenty years or so, the aviation industry has seen dramatic growth. Passenger numbers have ballooned from 1.467 billion in 1998 to 3.979 billion in 2017, driven by cheap airfare and a decade of global economic growth. Industry experts predict the number of passengers traveling by air will surpass eight billion by 2037. While that might be good news for major commercial airlines, one of the challenges faced by the aviation industry as a whole will be having enough pilots to meet flight demand, especially for regional airlines, many of which are already experiencing a pilot shortage.

In order to meet the looming pilot training demand, it is estimated that 66,000 training aircraft will be needed over the next twenty years to meet Boeing's estimated global demand of new pilots.

Another issue facing the industry is the cost of training those new pilots. A study released by North Dakota and the University of Nebraska-Omaha found that the high cost of training is preventing many aspiring pilots from pursuing their career choice. In years past many airline pilots came from the military, but as those numbers have decreased, there has been more reliance on civilian-trained pilots. Would-be pilots unable to secure a place on the limited number of airline-sponsored training initiatives need to pay large sums for their training before an airline will consider them employable.

George E. Bye, founder and CEO of Bye Aerospace, believes an answer to both issues can be found by producing a new generation of electric training planes. As the company reports: "According to the FAA in 2008 there were 10,800 two-seat trainers in use, with an average age of forty-eight years. These old aircraft are difficult and costly to maintain, burn expensive leaded avgas producing carbon dioxide (CO_2) and are nearing obsolescence. The clean, all-electric eFlyer 2 trainer is ideal as it dramatically reduces the ops-cost for flight training while replacing a small, obsolete training fleet of 10,000 conventional aircraft that averages nearly fifty-years-old."

He also notes that his e-plane could easily reduce the hourly cost of a training aircraft to as little as $3 in electricity costs versus more than $50 for a traditional avgas powered machine, and estimates the e-plane will be able to cruise for up to three hours on a single charge with a 450-pound payload.

Founded in 2007, Denver-based Bye Aerospace is a global innovator of electric and solar-electric aircraft, focusing on advances in energy and design efficiencies. Although the electric plane industry is only now on the cusp of commercial scale, George notes aviation engineers have been working to on the technology for decades.

"When we first identified electric propulsion as a possibility, we studied the electric aspect, did some market analysis about potential opportunities for both electric and solar electric, then about twelve years ago we sharpened our pencils and began to drive engineering concepts around solving market problems using electric. As our understanding of technology trends and market trends grew, those concepts have been refined, and now we're to the point where we have a threshold about to be achieved of market-ready products designed with innovative, zero-CO_2 electric and solar-electric propulsion systems, that will be certified inside the next two years. It is a gigantic business opportunity because the

George Bye

problem with pilot training needs to be solved most urgently. And we have the right product, the right market, and a strong compelling differential with electric."

Named one of the Top 50 Colorado Companies to Watch in 2017 and the *Denver Business Journal's* Small Business Award category winner for 2018, Bye Aerospace is actively developing and flight-testing prototypes of all-electric general aviation training, personal, and business aircraft. Currently the company's main project is the two-seat, all-electric eFlyer 2 (formerly the "Sun Flyer 2") general aviation aircraft, which aims to be the first FAA-certified, practical, all-electric airplanes to serve the flight training and general aviation markets.

The interest is already high. The company says it has received hundreds of pre-orders, and in October 2019 Quantum XYZ announced it had increased the amount of purchase deposits for Bye Aerospace's two-seat and four-seat eFlyer aircraft to be used as air taxis. Quantum CEO Tony Thompson says, "The additional purchase deposits are the second in a series toward an expanded agreement for a fleet of hundreds of aircraft. This transaction cements Bye Aerospace's status as the foremost electric aircraft manufacturer in the nation."

Bye Aerospace is also developing medium- and high-altitude solar electric, long-endurance piloted and optionally unmanned aerial vehicles (UAV) called SOLESA, which are designed to provide a significant reduction in operations cost and an enhancement in range and loiter time relative to current survey and patrol aircraft, and the StratoAirNet family of atmospheric satellite UAVs, which are intended to provide persistent intelligence, surveillance, and reconnaissance to support commercial and government security requirements.

George notes that the integration of the advanced solar-cells "launches the initial demonstration phase of an entirely new paradigm of highly efficient solar-electric UAVs." He says the potential commercial mission applications for the StratoAirNet include "communications relay, internet service, mapping, search and rescue, firefighting command and control, anti-poaching monitoring, damage assessment, severe weather tracking, agriculture monitoring, mineral source surveying, spill detection, and infrastructure quality assessment."

The company website notes that Bye Aerospace's goal is to revolutionize the general aviation, aerospace, and defense industries. Considering his background as an author, engineer, former Air Force fighter pilot, and entrepreneur, George E. Bye seems particularly well-suited to take on such an ambitious task.

#

George's affinity for aviation was evident early while growing up in Corvallis, Oregon. He recalls that he and his brother would build Lego airplanes and would use their mom's scarves and handkerchiefs to make parachutes for their GI Joes. His parents bought a single-engine Piper airplane in the 1960s and after his mom received her pilot's license, she would take George flying, further fueling his aviation imagination.

Throughout high school he followed news of NASA's space programs and the military's development of supersonic jets. When George enrolled at the University of Washington in Seattle to study engineering, he also received an Air Force pilot ROTC scholarship. After graduating in the summer of 1980 with an engineering degree, George joined the Air Force as a Second Lieutenant, and in early 1981 he went to Williams Air Force Base in Phoenix, Arizona, to receive pilot training.

George says he vividly remembers his early flying training, calling his first solo "a very powerful memory and a profound experience."

He earned his wings a year later and was assigned to jet transport out of McChord AFB in Washington State, near Seattle.

Because of his youthful fascination with the space program, George says he considered applying for astronaut training but ultimately opted not to because it wasn't really flying.

"I'd always had that in my portfolio of desired outcomes, but being an astronaut is quite a bit different from being a pilot. You're riding a rocket into space that lofts you into an orbit which, at zero gravity is more than comfortable. Once there you're performing a task like putting a satellite into orbit. While all that's technically interesting, you don't have control of your craft; you're doing something other than flying."

After completing his initial tour at McChord, George was invited to become an USAF T-38 advanced jet trainer instructor pilot in a new NATO undergraduate pilot training program in Wichita Falls, Texas, (ENJJPT) that had a unique fighter-pilot-only oriented training syllabus, emphasizing two- and four-ship formation and tactical flight training. Successful graduates from the program were assigned to fly the most advanced jet fighters of the time. During his five-year tour at the program, George logged one thousand flight hours in the supersonic T-38 and went from new instructor pilot training student pilots to later training newly assigned ENJJPT instructor pilots arriving to the program from across NATO nations.

In 1989 George returned to McChord near Seattle, from where piloted various missions to Europe, the Middle East, Asia, Central, and South America. In 1990 George was recalled to active duty to fly missions during Desert Storm, amassing one thousand flying hours as an aircraft commander in a single year flying the Lockheed C-141B transport plane. After Desert Storm, George flew missions in Somalia. When he completed his USAF service in 1993, George had accrued nearly four-thousand flight hours.

George says the idea to start Bye Aerospace focusing on e-planes was born from both his personal passion for teaching, engineering, and aviation and frustration with ingrained aerospace bureaucracy. But flying time and a passion for aviation doesn't necessarily an entrepreneur make.

"There's nothing about being a pilot that makes you an entrepreneur," he says with a laugh. "Perhaps there are aspects of being in the military that give you character qualities that may help in business, but again, just being in business is quite a bit different than being a pioneer and entrepreneur."

What made the transition from the military pilot to an entrepreneur seamless, George believes, were values passed down through his family. He recalls helping his father on building projects, such as learning to build an electric motor from scratch. His mom, an accomplished artist, taught him about design.

"The teaching and designing aspect is also part of my family history," George says. "I have several relatives who are university professors that conduct scientific research. On my father's side there's quite a bit of engineering and military as well. All that was in my makeup already, so the transition out of military and into aerospace was easy from that aspect. The entrepreneurial, pioneering aspect was fueled by a recognition of aerospace bureaucracies and processes that made it difficult to introduce something new. In a sense I felt it was my duty, an obligation to society if you will, to do something to make the world a better place. That's what drove me to start the company."

That passion and commitment didn't make the process any easier. Like generations of entrepreneurs before him, George found that it was "an absolutely overwhelming, monumental task. Building a company and developing a product are very hard to do. In our case we weren't just improving an existing part of system, like *Hey; let's make a better flap ... Let's improve the landing gear ... Let's reduce the drag on the plane.* Or even: *What about a new plane?* We were creating a new type of aircraft, so you're literally having to create all of the resources, the staff, the design and engineering teams, the leadership board, financial structures, legal structures, the business plan. You have to organize the company. Being a private C corporation allows us to invite potential stockholders to the company where they can participate in ownership and help provide the resources to help make the vision become a reality. You talk to people, associates, and you go step-by-step to achieve milestones. It was a huge endeavor for sure."

Despite the time and effort and challenges, George's belief in the viability of his idea never waivered. While some might see it as blind faith, he says it was much more grounded in engineering and aviation knowledge.

"It was an absolute, deep understanding of the market and of the technology, coupled with the ability to organize and motivate a team to bring it to pass. And of course with that motivation and understanding, you can talk to a potential interested person and say this is what we're going to do and would you like to join us and have some ownership in this opportunity? That's what selling stock is."

Before Elon Musk's Tesla brought the idea of mass-market electric cars to the mainstream consumer, e-cars seemed like a fad or niche vehicle, like glorified golf carts. Today nearly every major car manufacturer is developing e-cars, e-trucks, and e-SUVs. But to the general public e-planes might seem like a

more daunting technological challenge, although the concept of using electric motors to power airplane systems dates back at least to World War II when the B-29 Superfortress bomber used electric motors to power its gun turrets. Since then, other airplanes have replaced hydraulic and pneumatic systems with electrical power to control such things as stabilizers and brakes, which can save significant weight and reduce fuel burn.

Using electrical power to actually propel planes, however, is a more complicated challenge, mostly related to battery limitations—in other words, you probably shouldn't expect a electric 787 taking you from Los Angeles to Tokyo anytime soon. But as Richard Anderson, director of Embry-Riddle Aeronautical University's flight research center and a professor of aerospace engineering told the *Los Angeles Times* in 2016, "A lot of the technical advances that happen start in smaller airplanes, so there will be a market that stands for smaller, fully-electric airplanes."

In a conventional jet airplane, the engine sucks air in through its front, a compressor squeezes it, and fuel is sprayed in and lit, creating burning gases and forward thrust. Electric plane power is much simpler, with batteries powering an electric motor that spins a propeller. It's more efficient but involves far less thrust, which is why electric planes tend to be slower. But the big payoff is a less expensive, quieter, more environmentally-friendly way to fly.

The advances made by his company and others have helped to start changing public perception of what might be possible with e-planes.

"There's great skepticism still, but it's much reduced compared to five or ten years ago. When we first started out twelve years ago, maybe a little bit more than that, the idea of an electric plane was profoundly dismissed as a serious research project. The consensus was that the batteries were too big and too bulky."

So naysayers questioned the potential benefit of even pursuing electric aircraft since there were so many challenges to overcome.

"Of course we understood those challenges very well," George says. "But we could also see the industry trends of batteries evolving and getting more efficient and lighter, which were being utilized in electric vehicles. That was true for hybrids like the Toyota Prius, which evolved greatly when comparing its first and second models and the fourth and fifth generations. Also, Tesla was born in that time frame. Looking at the big picture, we saw all those trends as very favorable to our view that aviation would be able to capture those benefits. So we stayed at it, and we persisted, and we pioneered, and we shared the vision. As we began to collect more employees and more stockholders, people in the market began to respond, and some early pioneers contacted us and said, *Hey, you know what? We'd like to sign up.*"

George acknowledges current battery technology may limit plane size and range but points out that aviation in general has limitations.

"There's a size limit on how big a plane can be, period," he notes. "Physics, structural weights, aerodynamics are all a reckoning to a configuration whether it can balance and fly. Right now, a Cessna-sized e-plane can fly; we're doing it, and we'll be bringing it to market in the near term. The next step will be a larger plane that can fly a little faster as the technology matures. The bigger the plane and the faster it goes, the harder it is to do. It doesn't get harder on a linear basis; it gets harder on an exponential basis. There is a radical increase in drag the faster you fly."

George explains that even if you point many planes straight down at the ground, they can't go faster than the speed of sound because of the drag on the airplane. So of course a propulsion system must overcome the drag to have a cruise speed, and the amount of energy needed to do that goes up very fast.

"You often hear people talk about concept planes and how they are going to create an electric jet," George says. "And I just smile because unless they find a way to undo the laws of physics, that's going to be a bit of a challenge at this point in time. We  are the first in the world with an airplane to be certified with the FAA, and we should have the world's first certified electric airplane in about two years time because we are grounded in reality and innovative design and engineering."

Despite his background as a fighter pilot with thousands of airtime logged over a decade of military service, George says he passed on the chance to be one of his company's test pilots.

"No, that would have been a tremendous distraction. We hired a test pilot to specifically do the very focused test flight activity that had to follow protocols and required written reports. Of course I would love to, but that wasn't my job as CEO, so it would not have been the best use of my time unfortunately. As much as I love to fly, I needed to stay focused on keeping the program moving ahead."

A truism about being an entrepreneur is that it takes one set of skills to found a business and get it off the ground, but it takes a different skill-set to be a successful chief executive officer who guides the long-term, big-picture direction of an enterprise. In George's case he relied on personal discipline to make a successful transition from founder to CEO can be a challenge

"It's absolutely correct that just because you achieve one level as an entrepreneur doesn't mean you are capable of taking it to the next. You have all these levels of personal threshold that you pass, whether it's your personality, training, character, discipline, tenacity. With me it had to do with military training, business training, and the adaptability to given circumstances. Working with people, motivating people—investors, board members, engineers. There are certain characteristics in an individual that either help you rise to the occasion meet a challenge, draw a team in around you, solve problems. All of those things come into play. There is also some organic aspect to it. There is a natural transition with the achievement of certain levels. You learn as you go and learn with each milestone you hit. So being a good CEO is part organic, part training, and part learning. Most important, it's starting every day on your knees with both humility and determination."

By current estimations, George says Bye Aerospace's eFlyer 2 planes will be five times less expensive than current gas models as far as operating costs and maintenance. The planned rollout will start with the two-seater targeting the flight training market. Next they will offer the four-seat model, targeting more current pilots, air-taxi companies, and air cargo.

"The distribution of cargo like for a FedEx or UPS could be possible," George says. "The eFlyer 4 could provide convenient transportation of people, just like with an Uber or Lyft, at a gigantic reduction in price from current air taxis. It just creates a whole new business model because it's so much less expensive. And of course it has social and community benefits such as no noise and no CO_2 emissions."

George notes that while aviation innovation comes with a certain amount of risk, safety is always top of mind.

"Current research confirms that we are on the leading edge of a revolutionary transition to electric aviation," Bye said. "The momentum is growing at an extraordinary pace. Despite the exciting progress, however, Bye Aerospace maintains safety as our absolute top priority across all of our programs. We are adhering to the discipline, focus, and maturity required to successfully implement such a sweeping transformation."

The success of the eFlyer will undoubtably prompt others to develop their own electric planes. But aviation development and certification takes time, so for the foreseeable future Bye Aerospace will likely remain the industry leader.

"At the moment we are the only soon to be certified program. I'm very confident that competitors will appear. Somebody else will come along. But just not yet."

Despite the sooner-rather-than-later impact George believes the eFlyer 2 will have on the pilot training industry, its impact on more mainstream aviation will evolve more methodically.

"We'll see it happening in layers. What we're doing now will have an immediate and profound impact all across the flight training world. Personal transportation will be the next layer. The larger, faster aircraft will take five or ten years. Over the next decades we'll see this progression of electric vehicles not just on the ground but in the air."

As the industry moves forward, George says new obstacles to overcome and problems to solve will constantly arise.

"But the key is all in the execution. At every level there will be all kinds of chaos and challenges. As you scale, as you start production. With macro- and micro-economic trends. With regional trends. Bringing a product to market. These are all the things that can play to create a challenge. You just have to solve them and keep moving forward."

In looking back over his experiences with Bye Aerospace's growth, technological advances, and design innovations, George says the best advice he could give the next generation of entrepreneurs would be to look inward before starting a business.

"One of the most important things for an entrepreneur is to really know themselves. To found and build a company, there's such a requirement for what I would call true grit and courage. You simply cannot understate the amount of tenacity you must have to be an entrepreneur. So do an honest self-evaluation. Identify what have you done in your life that demonstrates your ability to display courage, dogged determination, and persistence in the face of immense and seemingly crushing opposition and challenges."

He says the other crucial key is how you manage failure.

"One of the things I ask potential team members is how do they manage failure? What is your automatic response? Do you immediately throw in the towel out of frustration? Is it devastating for you? Or do you fail forward, seeing it as a learning experience? Do you keep your chin up and refocus? Do you internalize or externalize? If you think about people throughout history we call our heroes, people we hold up as leaders, almost without exception it's not because they had some miraculous power, or sailed through a charmed life; what we admire is that they achieved what they did despite the huge challenges they overcame in their life. They typically failed many times before succeeding, but they persisted with courage and grit. That tenacity is what we find inspiring, often more than whatever their actual success was. So what I urged any entrepreneur, regardless on the industry you want to make your mark in, is don't fear the challenges or the setbacks or even failure. Keep your eye on the prize, and you will ultimately achieve success."

Trucking has been a part of the American transportation industry since the late nineteenth century when trucks switched from steam-powered engines to internal combustion engines, which were much more powerful and enabled trucks to carry larger loads for greater distances. With the increased construction of paved roads, the trucking industry began to achieve a significant national foothold in the 1930s. Among the early trucking pioneers who helped build the industry was the Digby family.

WJ Digby ran a produce stand and bought a truck to haul his vegetables and fruit. Then he bought a couple more, and that led to the Digby Truck line. A company website notes: "He founded several trucking companies over the years and involved family members at every opportunity. These ventures advanced to an extensive trucking empire," and the Digby family became one of the leading providers of transportation in the United States, with various family members operating well-known long-haul carriers including Navajo Shippers, Inc. and WJ's Golden Arrow Route Company

So Jon Digby quite literally has trucking in his blood, and in 2015 followed in his grandfather's entrepreneurial footsteps by founding the latest transportation business on the Digby family tree.

"I grew up in the business, so a few years ago, I decided to go on my own in a totally different niche and started my own truck line," he says.

ColtonCooper Logistics is a full-service logistics company with a focus on heavy final mile with service in Colorado and surrounding states. In 2019 the company was named to the Inc. 5,000, ranked the 316th fastest-growing company in the United States, with a three-year growth of 1,449 percent and annual revenue pushing $10 million.

While Navajo and Digby are long haul truck carriers, Jon's company focuses on the final leg of the supply chain. In the context of the trucking industry, the last mile describes the movement of goods from a transportation hub distribution center to a final destination. The final mile of a delivery is often the least efficient and highest in cost, meaning Jon saw an opportunity to create a needed solution.

"I went to a convention recently where they said that our industry does a trillion a year just via truckload. And that doesn't include FedEx, UPS, and those kind of services. So it's a huge space. I came up with a model for a piece of that space. I want to be the guy that delivers a product to the person that bought it. Not necessarily residential. We deliver to Walmart stores, to Safeway stores, to Kroger stores—big box delivery."

While he had a general idea for a business model, what Jon didn't have was much capital. "I basically started this company with no cash," he says with a laugh. "I came up with the idea of employing owner-operators, so I theoretically don't own any trucks. The guys that drive them do, and they run under my operating authority and my name, ColtonCooper LLC, but they own the truck. The benefit for me is it keeps me out of the maintenance business, and I don't need to own a place to store my trucks or have a shop."

In other words, it's like a franchise for trucking. Once he had the model, he approached the businesses he wanted to work with.

"I went out to all the heavy grocery companies because my target market is consumables; if you eat it or drink it, that's what I want to haul because to an extent it's recession-proof. So I went after the Albertsons and

Jon Digby

Safeways and those guys of the world and asked them to try my service. I'll have an owner-operator come over pick up your trailer and deliver it to your store. And the business just started growing and growing from there. And it's what's carved me into the industry in a niche capacity."

One of his biggest challenges was finding truckers in the Denver area. "It's very white-collar, very high tech in Denver. You know it's like Silicon Valley. And to get a truck driver here is very difficult, especially with the cost of living here. So I cover a five-hundred mile circle around Denver and do store deliveries under contract for large grocery store chains. Basically everything we do is dedicated. So a customer comes in and says: *I want ten trucks to haul every day for the next four years,* and I'll put them under a contract. That's how we're building our business."

Jon is also building it by being one of the highest-paying employers in the state. According to industry data, the average ColtonCooper Logistics truck driver earns about $240,000, which is 225 percent above the national average.

"They say I'm the highest payor in Colorado for trucking. That's because compared to a lot of my competitors, I'm gracious with the franchisees' commissions. We do a percentage of gross revenues split with the owner-operators, the guys who own their trucks. That was by design because I had to scale quickly to establish what they call lane density if I was going to get anybody's attention. How was I going to get Walmart or Amazon to notice us? How would Albertsons and Kroger know I have a truck line? So if you look at all the highways in a five-hundred-mile radius and locate one of my trucks, I've got another truck five miles behind that truck and another ten miles in front of it because I'm so consolidated in my market. It's creating a niche. What happens in lane density is instead of us going and chasing Walmart, they are now chasing us."

Coming from a family of truckers would seem to have given Jon an entrepreneurial leg up, but he says he probably had more of a learning curve to tackle than most founders.

"I have always been more of the visionary guy than a day-to-day grind guy, so scaling the business this quickly was challenging. Prior to starting ColtonCooper, I ran a piece of the family business but had no experience in financials, data analytics, operations, purchasing trucks—I never did any of that. My dad, my uncles, and my brothers handled those things. So I had to learn it myself as I went along."

And then there was still that matter of no capital. "My big claim to fame is I did this with no outside money. No investors, zero Digby money, zero family money. Nor did I take any customers from family. It was all me starting with $600, which I've been told is mathematically impossible. People ask me how I did it, and I say God. I remember when I went to lease an office at a nice building in central Denver. I went to the landlord, who said he needed the rent upfront. It took an hour of begging to convince him to let me pay in thirty days. And somehow I was able to make the payment. I'm not even sure how."

Jon chalks a lot of it up to divine providence because he started the company during a particularly dark time in his personal life.

"I was going through a divorce, and it was horrible. I lost everything in my divorce, everything. I was wrecked and wasn't even working. And the truth of the matter is one morning I got up, and God said: *I want you to go and start a trucking company*. And He told me where to drive. I went straight to that office building with hardly any gas and remember being nervous that I'd run out of gas on my way home. I came here with no concrete business plan. I didn't know if I was going to run New Jersey or was going to do California."

After he secured the office space, Jon started the search for drivers by visiting maintenance facilities around the greater Denver area. "My best chance of finding owner-operators was at these shops. I looked for independent names on the side of the trucks, and when I found one, I'd stop and go talk to them."

The pitch was straightforward: *Hey, I'm starting a trucking company. Would you like to come over and lease on with me and help me start it?* Jon says he hired three drivers, then two more, then ten more came after that.

Jon's breakthrough with his customer base came about in an unexpected way. "When you have a low number of trucks, you usually have to use brokers, so you don't have direct customer relationships. And that's how I started out. Then one day I was approached by somebody who asked if I was willing to volunteer in the annual Truck Rodeo."

Kind of an Olympics of driving, the Truck Rodeo consists of several different events that challenge drivers' skill with all aspects of trucking. Spectators are invited to watch the competition, such as drivers navigating an obstacle course designed to test the driver's agility behind the wheel or how well they can pre-trip inspections. The event attracts drivers from all over—from Walmart to FedEx drivers.

"It's a real pride thing," Jon says. "So I went out and judged what's called pre-trip. Before a driver is allowed to leave with the tractor and the fifty-three-foot trailer, they have to know the fifty-one things to check."

For example, they need to make sure the lights work, the tires have air in them, the brakes run, the signals and the hazards work, that the fire extinguisher in the truck working, and dozens of other items.

"It's a whole process. So I was volunteering at that event, and all these trucking companies were there, and some guy comes up to me and says: *Hey, this tall guy over there that wants to talk to you.* I walked over and said: *I'm Jon Digby; can I help you?* And he says: *I'm Billy with Safeway, and I just wanted to see a Digby volunteering with my own eyes* because my family had never attended the rodeo. But I'm different, and he appreciated that. So the man says: *I like your integrity; I like what you're about. Do you want to do some business with Safeway?* And now I'm their contract carrier and do four million miles a year with him. It's crazy how that happened."

Through his relationship with Safeway, Jon then contracted with Bimbo Bakery, a multibillion-dollar company who was looking for carriers. And from that relationship, more companies hired his services.

"I just had to get the first one to start the business rolling, and the way I got it was from volunteering and not from any past relationships from the time that I was with the family business. If you put yourself out there, good things can happen."

With ColtonCooper growing so quickly, Jon has been forced to make the jump from founder to CEO quickly and admits the transition hasn't always been smooth.

"It was like the worst experience ever. And it's still happening to this day. I think one of my skills is knowing where my sweet spot is. And my brain is always thinking three to five years ahead. I have to surround myself with people that can manage the daily details because I'm not a detail guy. I'm a salesman. So that's very tough. I don't know what it's going to look like in ten years; I don't know if I'm going to be able to mold into a true CEO. That's yet to come; that'll be the next chapter."

Jon says he's found the training process particularly challenging. "I was by myself for quite a while. I didn't hire anybody until I had about twenty trucks. Training is hard because I don't have the patience. If there's a paperclip on the floor, I'm the guy that sees it and picks it up. Some people don't see it, or they see it and don't pick it up, that drives me crazy. I'm one of those guys. I can also see details from a mile away, and that's a hard thing to train."

Basically in a trucking business there are four assets: a truck, a trailer, a customer, and a driver. And Jon explains that those assets need to be touched daily.

"Some of those assets have voices; some don't have voices. Trailers do not have voices. So a driver can accidentally drop a trailer at a truck stop and not tell anybody, and it can sit there for three months. So you have to touch every asset every single solitary day. I'm very good with the labor part and the people part in terms of motivating drivers, making them excited about the work, listening to their problems, and getting them to do things they don't necessarily want to for the greater good of the company."

For example, sometimes ColtonCooper books more loads for the day than there are trucks available. "Say we book sixty loads today out of Denver but only have forty trucks. I still expect us to cover those loads. So you have to really dig deep into creativity because those logistics are highly complex. Driver A needs to take a load to Cheyenne, Wyoming, so Driver B from Rapid City, South Dakota, can come get it. And training the office operations staff to visualize that is tough. They don't innately see the solution of covering sixty loads with forty trucks. I can look at that scenario and have the logistics puzzle solved in ten minutes. But most people look at that scenario, and they simply want to go to a bar and drink as much alcohol as they can because in their heads, it doesn't make sense mathematically."

Another challenge Jon's had to balance is that the trucking business is very seasonal, which

Inc. 5000 #316 2019

peaks between Thanksgiving and Christmas, then falls off the first few months of a new year.

"When January, February, and March come around, your owner-operators still have truck payments to make. They still have to keep up maintenance. They still have alimony and other bills to play. So we also have to get creative the other way when we only have forty loads but sixty trucks available. That's when you talk customers into giving you freight they normally wouldn't. So our operations people must be able to handle those situations as well. Even when they are experienced professionals, I have a certain way I want things done, and it takes time to acclimate to it. I'm pretty aggressive on delivering service on time, that's the main item taking care of the customer, and I think our staff does that better than any of my competition."

With the exponential growth his company has enjoyed, Jon has a unique perspective on what advice he would give another entrepreneur just starting out.

"Make your first hiring an accountant," he says. "My dad told me that, and I would pass that along to anybody. Make sure your books are perfect so you know where you're operating from a profit-and-loss standpoint day by day, week by week, month by month. You've got to have the data, and it's got to be correct. That was the biggest thing for me personally."

Coming from a family with a business legacy, Jon envisions eventually turning the company over to both family and employees.

"I named the company after my two sons, Colton and Cooper, and they both work here and are both very involved in the running of it. So the legacy part is to them, but growth-wise and strategy-wise, we want to go national, but not a global scale because trucking overseas is very tough with all the different customs and regulatory issues. It's a different monster, and I wouldn't even know how to even begin a conversation about that. So Denver is the flagship store, which we call a service center. We think that if we grow to about two hundred trucks in this market, that will be ideal. If you get too big, it becomes harder to maintain your quality control."

Once he reaches the sought after saturation in the Denver area, the plan is to establish other service centers strategically located throughout the United States, using the same model Jon used in Denver—draw a five-hundred-mile circle around that city as the work area. But in addition to consumables, ColtonCooper is now also getting into medical goods.

"We go after customers that are potentially recession-proof," he explains, adding that his next service center will likely be based in Las Vegas, which would encompass Phoenix, Los Angeles, San Diego, and into Central California.

"That's a huge market that includes the Port of Los Angeles. But Arizona and Nevada are important too because you've seen a lot of companies on the manufacturing side have moved there because of advantageous tax rates and workers' comp reasons. So there's a lot of freight going back and forth Vegas to LA, Phoenix to LA, Phoenix to Vegas, Vegas to Phoenix."

If all goes as planned, after that he'll target the Southeast, the Midwest, then the East Coast. Jon says each service center will run on their own profit and loss financials and will be run by their own general manager. But that ambitious expansion won't begin until Jon feels his Denver operations is in perfect financial shape.

"Somebody once said to me that you need to take care of your own backyard first before you try to be a big shot and go everywhere else. But we already have a lot of customers asking us to go to other locations, so we know the demand is there."

Jon jokes it's easy to resist the temptation to move faster on expansion than he should because his accountant won't let him.

"I got into a little debt and am on a payment plan now to pay it off by mid-2020. I'll turn fifty in 2020, and I think that the older I get, the more I'll be the lender. I don't want to be the borrower because I don't want to be a slave to some personal guarantee that's out there. Should an economic downturn happen, I don't want somebody knocking on my door wanting money. I want to stay on a debt-free schedule that keeps us disciplined. Don't grow if you can't pay in cash. There's a lot of debt in trucking, and I've avoided it like the plague through our business model. The trailers that I haul, I don't own them. Safeway does, Albertsons does, Walmart does. I don't own the trucks, the drivers do. So my balance sheet is not loaded up except for that line of credit that will soon be paid off. And if earnings stay like they are now, we'll have zero debt. And then once we're at zero debt, we'll be able to grow with no debt."

Jon admits he's itching to start the next service center because the process of building a company is what he likes best.

"I'm your basic ADHD serial entrepreneur guy. So when it comes to maintaining an established zone like we are now in Denver, I find that day-to-day stuff boring. I've got one of those minds that just keeps going and going; I'm not built to sit around. Yes, we're making money, but the phones aren't ringing anymore like they were when I was building our base. So I'm the guy who is going to take on the job of opening Vegas. And I'm more the guy like Sam Walton, which is to say that I envision ten years from now having eight service centers across the country and see myself on a plane visiting those service centers, hanging out with the drivers, and hanging out with the customers. That's my niche."

When asked if the apples did not fall far from the Digby tree with his own kids, Jon says it's mixed.

"There is a little Digby DNA that's out there. It's a toughness in being able to make quick decisions. Both of them have that. Colton is more about the systems and processes. Cooper is too new to have carved out his niche. He just got out of college, so he's still figuring out where the bathroom is," Jon laughs. "But like me, Cooper is a salesman. So I envision one day-one running the front office and the other running the back as long as they can get along. I have my dreams but know that ego and pride, especially among family, can come into play."

Which is why it's very rare that a company can succeed as a generational business, something Jon is very aware of.

"I'm the third generation, and my kids are the fourth, so we've come further than most do. I just tell my kids that it's their names on the sides of our trucks. That can lead to pride and humility, or it can lead to ego and a sense of entitlement. So I always tell them that they need to be humble; they need to eat that humble pie every morning, which is hard to truly understand when you're in your twenties. So my prayer is that one of these days they're going to wake up and go: *Oh my God, Dad's right*. It would be nice to see the Digby legacy live on to the next generation of trucking professionals."

Cooper, Jon, and Colton Digby

E&A Worldwide Traders, Inc.

Every product has a shelf life, meaning the length of time it can be kept in a store or at home before it becomes too old, too obsolete, or too out of fashion. But just because an item is pulled from the shelves doesn't mean it ends up in the local landfill or at Goodwill. There are secondary sales channels that help manufacturers' bottom lines, provide merchandise for an array of businesses, and offer consumers the ability to purchase quality items at reduced costs. While some companies may have branded outlets stores, most rely on wholesalers that purchase, distribute, and sell brand-name closeouts.

Since 2002 E&A Worldwide Traders has specialized in acquiring surplus inventory from major brands. Founded by Elan Eliav, E&A is a national wholesale company with annual revenues of $5 million that buys general consumer goods from thousands of companies around the world that are excess, overstock, or general closeouts as well as items from package changes, buybacks, and canceled orders.

"Simply put, we purchase unwanted stocks from product manufacturers who want to turn their surplus merchandise into profit," Elan explains. "We review and buy surplus inventories or stocks that are no longer usable then sell them to casinos, hotels and resorts, airlines, travel shops, restaurants, amusement parks, correctional facilities, food banks, and vending merchants. Our customers love the deals we're known for. We also carry attractive home furnishings, seasonal merchandise, and hundreds of everyday items that consumers can buy at tremendous savings as well as put together corporate gift packs and promotional baskets for special events."

Elan says the roots of his entrepreneurial spirit can be traced back to his family's strong work ethic. He grew up in a blue-collar home and started working various jobs at a young age.

"My father was a very hard worker and a business owner. He also lost many businesses too, so I had to go out and make something of myself. School wasn't really my forte, and I knew I had to do something to live the American dream. I always wanted to be an entrepreneur. I wanted to work for myself. I didn't want to make money for somebody else," he says with a laugh. "I had the drive, the determination, and the motivation to go out and be successful."

Elan eventually got a job with a trading company that bought excess inventory in exchange for advertising media or other goods and services. Essentially it was a barter company.

"Corporate barter has probably been around a long time, and it's really for a public company that has assets on its books but doesn't want to go out to the marketplace and take a loss. So what they're able to do is take whatever asset they have and receive full value for it in the form of trade credits, which they can utilize to offset any operational expenditure that they have—outside of payroll and postage. It's a genius concept because there's no loss reported. They're just taking their excess inventory to leverage operational expenditures. It's a win-win situation for a public company."

Elan says he had to learn the business mostly through trial and error. The extent of the training offered was a handbook the company gave new employees.

"The barter companies I worked for just told us to make cold calls. They didn't really teach us the ins and outs of the business, so I had to learn

Elan Eliav

everything by myself. But I always had a knack for buying and selling. I used to do it with my baseball card collection. In junior high and high school I was always buying and selling something."

Elan ended up staying at the company for four years. Then he got the entrepreneurial itch.

"I said to myself: *You know what? There is a niche for me in the business, but there's really not much more that I can achieve here at this company. I need to go out and do it on my own.* Not so much in trading inventory for media but more trading inventory for cash," he says. "I took what I'd learned from the barter companies and just did it on my own. I had no mentor, wasn't taught the business. I began using the basics. I started E&A in December of 2002 to buy excess inventory directly from manufacturers for pennies on the dollar. Then I would resell it to discount retailers all across the country, including Big Lots, Tuesday Morning, Dollar Tree, and many of the other discounters that are out there."

Even though many companies go direct themselves, Elan says his company maintains a niche because when it comes to excess inventory and closeouts, manufacturers don't really have the time or inclination to hire someone in-house to focus their sole attention on it.

"It's the end of life for a product that they've tried to sell-through or a product going out of production, and it's not worth their time. So companies like E&A exist because of that. In addition the manufacturers we work with don't have to wait thirty, sixty, or ninety days to get paid. We pre-pay for that merchandise upfront, so that money is wired to them right away."

One advantage Elan had when starting E&A was not being burdened by a non-compete from his previous company. Even so, he started the business with just $500, no clients, and working out of a rat-infested basement office space.

"I definitely paid my dues. I left the previous company with my phone, my pen, and my notebook. I used every bit of money I had to bootstrap the company. I just put my head down and did what I had to do to learn the business and build it from scratch. I did a lot of cold calling in the beginning. I was determined to stay with it even though it was a lot of hard work. I'd leave home at eight o'clock in the morning and not come back until ten o'clock at night, hardly seeing my family. I faced a lot of obstacles, but I knew if I got past them, I was going to see light at the end of the tunnel. I believed hard work always pays off. So it was belief and faith."

Elan says that all things considered, the business took off relatively quickly. And within the first year the company was bringing in significant revenue.

"I was lucky enough to run into some inventories that I was able to flip fairly fast," he says. "I was also fortunate to find some discount retailers who believed in me, and I was able to deliver. My word is my bond, so whatever I said I was going to do, I did it."

From the beginning Elan went for the buckshot approach, targeting every category and product rather than trying to focus on any one type of vendor.

"Today we specialize in everything from apparel to sporting goods to food," he says. "Consumables comprise about 35 percent of our business because food goes short-dated; in other words it has an expiration date, so we do a tremendous amount of volume with food because of those reasons. From a manufacturer's perspective, products don't get better with age. It's not wine."

In the beginning stages of E&A, Elan says he wasn't focused on food. But over the last several years, that has changed as the number of opportunities for food deals have notably increased.

"Our business has taken a significant shift because food has become such a big commodity. A lot of these discount retailers are constantly on the treasure hunt for food opportunities. So we're out there searching for food deals that we can supply to our customers."

An interesting legal quirk is that while manufacturers have to comply with any number of rules and regulations, a company like E&A doesn't, not even with food products. Elan says it's why he wouldn't want to be a manufacturer.

"Regulations tend to be the bane of many companies' existence, but especially when food's involved. There are too many headaches; there's too much risk involved. But with us, should there be a recall on any food, it goes back to the manufacturer. We have no liability or responsibility, even though we are a third-party seller of that food."

That same principle is why E&A can move wine, beer, and spirits without having a liquor license. "We're able to provide a retailer's liquor license to buy their merchandise and sell their merchandise. There are many different facets of our business; it's really anything across the board. Our motto is: *We buy low, we sell low, and we make a profit.* There's no other business in America that can do that."

Elan says that despite the vibrancy of their industry and its importance to so many businesses' bottom line, few people are aware of what a company likes E&A does because it operates largely out of the public eye.

"My parents don't even know what I do, to be honest with you," he laughs. "It's a very underground business. Many people go into a TJ Maxx, into a Marshalls, into a Big Lots, into a Dollar Tree without ever knowing where those products come from or why everything is so much cheaper. They don't know it comes from companies like ours that can negotiate pennies on the dollar for a large quantity of goods, sell it to a discount retailer, which in turn offers it to consumers at considerable savings for them while still turning a profit. It's a win-win-win-win."

While the discount industry might fly under the public's radar, Elan has noticed that more entrepreneurs are getting into the business. He says when he first started, there was minimal competition.

"There were two, maybe three big close-out companies. But it's been growing of late. Now everybody has a niche and does it differently. We can say that we're grandfathers in this business, having started in 2002 when there weren't as many other close-out companies. Our longevity, our history, and our experience have given us many advantages and a lot of ammunition. We've learned from the best. We've had some significant mentors, and we know buying and selling. There is an art and a psychology to our business that you have to master. But once you do, there are endless amounts of money you can make. And we have mastered that psychology."

Elan compares E&A to Wall Street day traders, except of product instead of stock. "We take possession of the inventory. We have the capital, and we're risk-takers; we're not afraid. We believe the bigger the risk, the bigger the reward. And that's what we do on a day in and day out basis."

More often than not, the risk has reaped rewards. But every now and then the gamble doesn't pan out. Elan recalls the time he lost a half-million dollars.

"It was on a slipper deal that I had purchased and sold to Family Dollar right before the Black Friday. But I was a week late shipping the product, and Family Dollar canceled the order. I was left with a $500,000 loss. I was able to sell the slippers but only for about $50,000. So I took a $450,000 hit. Fortunately I was able to regroup, start again, and rebound, and we're still here today. But that loss almost crippled our company."

The near-disaster—which was self-inflicted because of a systems breakdown that led to a late shipment—was a lasting learning experience. The moral was you can never be too comfortable on a deal.

"You have to be very proactive. After that deal we became a lot more proactive in communication, in delivery, in implementing new procedures, in developing a different company culture, and in establishing a different mission statement that we cannot get comfortable. Deals come and go, and it only takes one to sever this company. So we became a lot more aware of staying on top of each deal from start to finish."

The commitment to being proactive also necessitated a significant staff overall. The slipper disaster made Elan turn a more objective, critical eye at his operations, and he realized many of his employees were not a good fit for the company culture he needed to build.

"We fixed the situation. We hired new people and let go of others. It's all about change and growth. So I was able to see the silver lining of that huge loss. I thought: *You know what? I just have to get up. You learn from failure; success comes with failure, and I can't let this stop me.* And I didn't; I moved forward."

That's not say there haven't been other risks that didn't turn out as hoped. But they were intentional, calculated risks that had no direct impact on E&A. One risk was shooting a pilot for a potential television series called *The Haggle King*. Another was an online business where Elan was selling on Amazon and eBay.

"I poured a lot of money into that, but I lost money," he says. "Then in 2013 I started my own website called Uhaggled.com that I was very close to raising venture capital for. "

The idea behind the site was to offer

a variety of products for sale—electronics, watches, sleep masks, perfume, wireless chargers, and even toothbrushes—and prior to each purchase the buyer would haggle to get the lowest possible price. Even though the site never got enough traffic to gain traction when self-funded, Elan remains bullish on the idea.

"It was actually written up in the *Daily News* and a couple of other newspapers because the concept was fun and unique," he says. "I'm still waiting for that magic person to come along and say: *I love the idea. Here's the funding for it.*"

Like any entrepreneur, Elan's role has changed as E&A went from start-up to young company to a sustainable, mature business. But his perception of himself hasn't changed much since he first founded the company.

"While I consider myself a leader, I've never considered myself a CEO. I don't come to manage. I'm not a good manager of people and the reason why is because I have a soft side to me, and my heart gets in the way. That's one of the reasons why I was never able to catapult this company to the next level; I'm not that individual to lead, to be that CEO. I consider myself an entrepreneur. And what that means for me day in and day out is that I still come for the thrill of the deal. That's my bread and butter and that's what I need to focus my attention on because without me there's really no company."

Elan says he once hired someone to function as a CEO. It didn't work out, so he decided to just have faith that being himself would work out okay for the company.

"If there's nobody I can hire who can do this job, I need to bank on myself. And that's what I do day in and day out. So I'm not necessarily that big leader CEO; I'm the thrill-seeking guy that gets the deals done. I'm a religious guy and come from a religious background. My father was a cantor in a temple. I've always believed in God, so I leave it up to Him. Listen, I've had times when I had zero dollars as the end of the month was approaching. Then on the last day, I'd get an inventory I was able to buy and sell and would make $20,000 profit. So I always have faith and believe that if you put your head down and work hard, it's going to come."

Of course, working hard usually means having to sacrifice other things like time with friends, time with family, and sleep. Elan says it's a matter of what your priorities are. His was making E&A a success.

"On Saturday nights while my friends were out clubbing and going to parties, I was at my office working. But hard work does pay off. I believe everything is up to God, but if you have faith, go out there, and are a hard worker, you will reap the benefits. I say this to every person that's come through my doors, and it works."

In the beginning Elan built the business by seeking out clients. While he still does that, he also gets business now from a combination of word of mouth, referrals, or because of their reputation.

"At the end of 2019, we bought and sold from around six hundred manufacturers. Roughly 25 percent of that was repeat business. Many of those manufacturers share our information with other manufacturers. On average we see about one hundred inventories a day, which is above the industry standard. That's because we provide cash upfront. To a manufacturer, cash is king, especially for a small- to medium-sized company. Suppose a company produced a protein bar that failed in the marketplace. They want to get as much cash as they can to move onto the next great idea. With us there are no returns, no chargebacks, and no headaches. We wire transfer the funds, we send in a truck to pick up the merchandise, and then they're done with it. They'll never hear from us again—until the next time they need us."

Besides loving to make deals, Elan says what he enjoys most about his business is that he never knows what the day will bring—or more accurately, how much the day might bring. "One day can change your life. I've made $300,000 in one day. So you never know. On any given day I might come into the office and strike a deal for $100,000. Every day is a new day."

Unlike the barter companies he worked for when starting out, Elan takes the time to train his employees but also looks for people with certain intangibles. "I only look for individuals who have a knack for buying and selling and who are street smart. It's not so much being book smart; it's having common sense because what we do is psychological. At the end of the day, we are middlemen between the manufacturer and the discount retailer. A buyer needs to be comfortable that you can really acquire that inventory on their behalf, even though 99 percent of the time when we call, we don't have physical possession of the inventory yet. So you need people who can present that assurance."

While Elan loves to wheel and deal, he says there are times you have to turn down business if the financials or terms don't meet certain standards. "We pre-negotiate a certain price, and if that price is unable to be met, we pass on that opportunity. We don't try to create a miracle. We have a certain threshold and a certain pricing structure that we must follow. The discipline to do that is the result of hard-earned experience. I try not to get into the buyer's mind. I'm not a buyer at a TJ Maxx. I'm not a buyer at a Big Lots. I'm not looking to figure out what their pricing structures are and what their models are. That doesn't concern me. At the end of the day, I just need to know that I can buy it at a certain price and then sell it. To be honest, 99.9 percent of the time I don't know what that price is; I'm just making an educated guess. You have to buy it right, but as a rule the less you pay, the better chances you have to sell it and make a profit."

Even though E&A continues to prosper and grow, Elan admits that it is still difficult for him to take time off to go on vacation. He says the most time he's taken off since 2002 was probably a week.

"And even for that week, I was still tuned in. I had my phone, I had my laptop, so I never was completely away from this business." he says. "It's just nearly impossible to turn off the phone. We're on call twenty-four hours a day, seven days a week; we're like urgent care for a manufacturer," Elan says. "You never know when a manufacturer is going to have a million-dollar inventory problem. If they need to move quickly, then we need to respond quickly. We need to look at the inventory, make an offer on the inventory, then go out and shop the inventory to see if we can find the buyer for it. These things happen very quickly, so you always have to be tuned in."

One thing Elan has learned during his years running E&A is that to thrive as an entrepreneur, regardless of your industry, you must have a passion for it. You should wake up every morning excited about going to work.

"Being an entrepreneur is about motivation, shifting out negativity, staying positive. It's about getting rid of the distractions in your life and whatever else is not serving you or preventing you from growing as an individual. It's about looking at yourself in the mirror and asking yourself how badly do you want to succeed. It's about believing you can overcome all the challenges. And more than anything, it's about hard work and faith. If you have that, you'll get you where you want to go."

frontline source group

After the 1906 San Francisco earthquake and fire, the city was brimming with residents who suddenly found themselves homeless and unemployed. Local philanthropist Katharine "Kitty" Felton, the daughter of Oakland's mayor, established the first staffing agency in the United States, not as a commercial venture but as a social service to help restore people's pre-disaster way of life. However, it wasn't long before entrepreneurial-minded individuals saw the business potential in staffing, and soon employment agencies sprung up across the country, typically offering temporary secretarial and clerical staff. The human resource industry was born.

Over the decades the industry moved beyond filling front office temp positions to providing a range of staffing needs. But while the services offered evolved, the main business model remained essentially the same until Frontline Source Group developed a new approach that has propelled the company to be a four-time Inc 5000 honoree as one of the fastest-growing placement companies in the United States. Founded in 2004 by Bill Kasko, Frontline offers direct-hire, temporary, and temp-to-hire staffing services across a variety of industries.

Bill credits his company's success to building strong partnerships with their clients and operating as an extension of the client's internal hiring team. "By learning about and understanding the unique needs of our clients, we're able to deliver personalized services and provide high-quality candidates perfectly suited for their business," he says. "We've positioned ourselves to help both hiring companies and job seekers navigate the challenges of today's hiring processes. In a cookie-cutter industry, we strive to be different."

Nowhere is that more evident than in Frontline's business model, which was inspired by a visit to a car dealership.

"My wife and I were buying our daughter her first car, and I was sitting there listening to the salesman going over the five-year warranty on the car. My daughter looked at me and said: *Dad, that's kind of what you guys do.*"

It was standard in the industry that anyone hired from a staffing agency came with a guarantee that the employee would stay for ninety days—to get a leg up on the competition, Frontline offered a 120-day guarantee. If the employee left before the guarantee period, the staffing agency would give the employer all their money back. Bill says it wasn't uncommon for an employer to use someone for three-and-a-half months then fire them and want their money back.

"I've always had a problem with the idea that the agency should somehow guaranty that this person will stay at the company," Bill says. "Nowhere on my business card does it say Red Cross or some other charity or nonprofit. Our employees are paid well, and in order to compensate them, Frontline needs to be compensated for our work."

Bill explained to his daughter that his company offered a guarantee, not a warranty—the difference being in the former you get your money back while with the latter you get a replacement. And the lightbulb went off.

"I sat there and looked at her, thinking: *Why DON'T we do that? Why don't we have a long type of a warranty? We already do something different by offer 120 days, but why is it limited to just that?* So I got all of the managers together, and we did a weekend lock-in. I said: *We're not*

Bill Kasko

leaving here until we figure out a plan of how we do this."

The result of that brainstorming-hostage session was Frontline's five-year warranty on their placements.

"It was a game-changer," Bill says, "because it's the only thing like it in the industry."

The way it works is straightforward. When an employer hires someone from Frontline, if the placement doesn't work out for some reason within the first 120 days, the agency gives the client a prorated credit towards their next placement.

Bill says, "If they come back to us after the 120 days up to five years and tell us the placement was promoted and the client needs to fill their position, we will refill that position at a fifty percent discount of our usual fee."

This model came about after an analysis found that 98 percent of the workers placed by Frontline are promoted within the first year. Plus, according to data from the Bureau of Labor Statistics, the average tenure was only 4.2 years. By offering that five-year warranty, Frontline enabled employers to hedge their bets because two out of three placements would likely leave within the warranty window.

"Our clients loved it, and the industry hated it," Bill says with a laugh. "Unfortunately the industry that we're in is very much like used-car sale; it's very here today, gone tomorrow turn-and-burn. A lot of employers and clients value what we do, but a lot of them treat us like a commodity. What we did was to differentiate ourselves from the beginning was to not do business with the ones that wanted to treat us like a commodity. We would rather walk away, so we say no to more clients than we say yes."

Bill also used the warranty as a lever to get paid promptly. "We tied the warranty to billing. In order to get the warranty, the client had to pay their bill according to terms, and it had to be paid on time—not so much as a day late. But if you pay on time, then you have this warranty as a reward. Basically, from the beginning we set out to do the opposite from everyone else and stand tall and proud while doing it."

When they first launched their new model, Bill received apoplectic emails and LinkedIn messages from other staffing company owners from all across the country asking him what the hell he thought he was doing.

"They would literally say things like *You're an idiot. This is terrible.* And then they would post it on social media. We would just respond: *Thank you.* I told everyone to expect blowback because we had discovered something that they didn't. We figured out a problem that enabled us to say: *Hey, here's real value; here's a long-term commitment. We're not going anywhere.* The feedback we get from our clients now is really incredible."

Even if the client hasn't been scrupulous about payments, they usually come away satisfied. Bill says when an employer contacts Frontline to report a worker has left or been promoted, the first order of business is to check their payment history. If they always paid on time, the warranty price kicks in. If they didn't …

"I get it that sometimes a business goes through hard times when things get tight," Bill says. "So even if an account has collection notes for being in arrears at one point, we will still give them some sort of discount. And they are happy as can be. The tone that we set is what differentiates us from everybody else. We truly have done the opposite of the industry norm; we've stepped out of that box. We've thought about things from a client's perspective, and we do not view our clients as volume or generated revenue. Whether we do one or one hundred placements a year with a client, we work to develop a relationship with them."

But, Bill notes, the consideration needs to be mutual, one-on-one relationship.

"If we feel like we're viewed as a commodity because a client is trying to fill one position by using ten agencies at the same time, we will literally say: *We appreciate you coming to us, but no thank you* and walk away. We're not interested in that."

Developing relationships with employers has been a cornerstone of Frontline's process, and it wasn't a happy accident; an intentional aspect of Bill's vision was making sure Frontline served clients the best way possible. To that end he proactively went out and talked with business leaders and others in the community about the people they surround themselves with, asking three main questions—*What do you look for? Who do you work with? What's the operation that takes place for these people?*—that focused on their processes and service. And through those questions Bill was able to develop the kind of staffing service that would best serve employers and employees alike.

"From the beginning I identified that you have to surround yourself with the best people that are out there. You need to have a process that's phenomenal, but as we found out, it also needs to be something that you can change, something you can look at and say: *Hey, we're not doing that quite right. We need to rethink this.* And then need to have that service side because we're in the service business. Essentially we sell people—in a legal way—which is not like selling a car. If your vehicle stops working, then you just bring it in to be serviced. But with staffing you're dealing with humans, and they're unpredictable. So we needed to be creative, and by listening to our customers, we saw what made sense. So after a lot of controversy over the years, I came up with an idea that made sense for our industry."

While it may seem that Bill was born with staffing in his blood, it's actually a second career. The first chapter of his professional life was spent as an IT network security expert. He also taught networking part-time at Southern Methodist University in Dallas. But in the early 2000s he was looking for a change—even though it wasn't the most opportune time.

"My wife and I had two kids and at the time aged something like three and five, but I wanted out of network security."

One of their neighbors worked for Robert Half International, a Fortune 500 staffing agency that specializes in placing full-time finance and accounting professionals, and told Bill the company was interviewing for a new IT salesperson. He suggested Bill apply.

"I told him I wasn't a sales guy; that wasn't me. I was a network guy. He said: *Man, you ARE a sales guy; you just don't know it, and you know IT like no one I've ever met.* This was around 2001 when many people still didn't really understand the Internet. They didn't understand what an IP address was and sure didn't understand how that worked. There were still fax machines everywhere. So I made the change and went to work for Robert Half. And I absolutely loved the industry."

At the time the United States was in the middle of a recession, so staffing became more than a job; Bill felt he was doing a service and helping people. One placement in particular that occurred his second week at the agency was seared into his memory.

"That night at dinner I was telling my wife and our kids how after I placed this gentleman on a job, he started crying on the phone and thanking me because now his family home wouldn't get foreclosed on. I remember my daughter looking at me and saying: *You're the best dad.* And that was it. I was done looking for my next career. This is what I was going to do."

But that didn't mean he would necessarily do it as an employee of a Fortune 500 company, even though Bill thrived the two years he was there, named the company's Rookie of the Year and a Division Director Chairman Club winner.

"Yes, I won awards, and it was a great organization. But I didn't do things the way they wanted me to. I was not inside the box, and it was a very in-the-box company."

In short, he tended to go rogue.

"I was very off the rails," Bill laughs. "But they didn't have a problem with it because of the amount of money I was generating. I was a little bit older than the other sales guys who were kids right out of college, and I had experience behind me. I understood business; I had already been very successful in a career. So I could sit down with the CEO, have a conversation with him, and understand their frustrations."

Bill left Robert Half and had to go to work for another agency located an hour away from where he lived to comply with the non-compete agreement he had signed when joining the company, which was based on geography, not industry.

"I was able to do the same work, but I had to drive more than a hundred miles a day to do it. While at the new company, one of my former coworkers asked if I had ever thought about starting a business. I said I didn't know how I would fund the business."

But the comment planted a seed, and the idea of owning his own business quickly fermented.

"I told my wife that if I could repeat my success at the new staffing agency to know I wasn't a one-hit-wonder, maybe it was something I could pursue. And within ninety days I was number three in my new company."

Frontline has dozens of office locations

When asked what the secret sauce of his success was, Bill says it was his honesty.

"I didn't treat it like a used-car sale. I approached it as a partner and a consultant. Everyone else in this industry wants to do that, but the reality is they're afraid to actually tell someone: *I can't help you. I'm not your best resource.* I was able to have those conversations."

And having an angel on his shoulder didn't help either. Through a friend he was introduced to an investor whose company funded staffing agencies. A recommendation from his friend and a phone call later, the investor floated Bill a $3 million line of credit that enabled him to get Frontline up and running. Since then in addition to his warranty model, Bill has championed other breaks from the staffing industry norm. For example, ten years ago if company ABC called looking for a senior tax specialist, a staffing agency would already have an inventory, or pool, of potential hires to select from that could start work immediately.

"Today when we have the lowest unemployment in the history of this country, I can't do that," Bill explains. "Today's recruiting skills have completely changed from where they were a decade ago. We no longer have a pool of workers; it's not even a birdbath. So the recruiting technique is much more difficult now compared to then. We have to utilize all the tools out there to find the best match."

To that end Frontline has developed an internal, searchable database of candidates they have accrued over the past fifteen years. Bill estimates that database contains about 1.6 million people. So now if company ABC calls for a senior tax director, Frontline creates a job description that details the requirements then publishes it. Individuals will see the position and apply to it. Frontline then reviews the applicants' résumés and identifies those who meet the criteria and seem like a fit for the position. A recruiter then gets them on the phone to ask additional screening questions designed to determine if they truly are a good fit. Then Frontline puts together a package for the client to look at.

"At that point the client's hiring manager determines whether or not they want to go to the next step, which would be a phone or video interview to start the process of the hiring," Bill says. "It used to be a quicker cycle, but finding available great people today is very difficult."

And some companies' internal standards can greatly decreases the number of suitable applicants, Southwest Airlines being exhibit A. Its mission statement reflects what sets it apart from the competition. *Dedication to the highest quality of customer service delivered with a sense of warmth, friendliness, individual pride, and company spirit.* Its vision statement is: *To become the world's most loved, most flown, and most profitable airline.* Lastly, Southwest's core values include to *Live the Southwest Way* (warrior spirit, servant's heart, fun-loving attitude).

"They are an incredible client to have," Bill says, "but they are exacting. Even if they bring individuals in as an independent contractor or as a temp employee, Southwest still interviews them as if they're going to be a full-time airline employee. So it's very difficult to find the right person who is a culture and personality match who also has the necessary skills. And I love it. Then if you take a company like Walmart, it's totally different. They're just looking for bodies. Walmart treats staffing like a commodity; Southwest Airlines does not, which is why we would rather do business with Southwest and have told Walmart no on multiple occasions."

Bill says each staffing request essentially starts from scratch, and that process is one reason they are so successful in their placements working out well and adding value to the employer.

"Because we're not shotgunning people out there to companies—here's five people; take a look and let us know what you decide—the employer has a better return on their investment when they use our agency. We act almost as an extension of their HR department."

Bill estimates that four out of five HR departments have very limited hiring processes; most deal more with issues involving current employees, not securing new employees. "So Frontline becomes that extra arm for them, and it's cost-effective because we're successful."

A significant amount of time is spent educating employers on the realities of today's job market.

"It's unbelievable. You want a receptionist and only want to pay $10/hour? That doesn't exist. A lot of business owners and company executives still believe there are tons of highly qualified people out there looking for work who want a skilled accounting professional for $40,000 dollars a year—and oh, by the way, they want them to work fifty hours a week. We have to educate them that yesterday's $40k is now $60-$65K. You cannot find someone who has a college degree in accounting and Big-Four experience to accept that salary. It's not going to happen."

And yet staffing agencies by and large are loathe to disabuse their clients of those notions. Bill says rather than explaining the staffing facts of life to employers, they say: *Sure, we can find you that* but never do. Then the clients are left wondering why it's taking so long.

"It's because they haven't been educated about reality. I know that sounds ridiculous, but that's how many in the staffing industry roll. They just won't tell a client the truth. So how Frontline works isn't so much stepping out of the box; it's being in the box but telling the truth. We find it so much better to just say: We can help you, but here's what you're going to pay. If you don't want to pay that much, then we need to scale down some things. The requirement of having worked at a Big Four? Scratch that. A full four-year degree? Make that a two-year associate's degree with five years work experience utilizing the same type of tools that you have.

Making the effort to work with the employer to get the right fit rather than trying to force the round peg in the square hole creates a relationship we know is going to last much longer."

Which is especially important in an industry that's contingent on results. There is no upselling or verticals in staffing. "You have to have everything in order, and you have to be continuously looking at your process to make sure it's the right way to do it. If there's a hiccup, you need to embrace change to keep the whole system running correctly. You can't be static in a world that's always changing."

The employee side has its own challenges. Bill says to find the best people, you cannot keep them waiting because they have other options. The days of clients having the luxury of waiting for an agency to find three qualifies candidates they can review at the same time are over.

"We tell them that's not how that works anymore. If we wait even forty-eight hours, they'll be off the market already. So our clients have to make a commitment on the front end that when we send them a candidate, they must be ready to interview and hire."

He notes that social media and Internet sites like Glassdoor are double-edged swords. Good reviews can increase a company's profile and attract new talent. But a bad review can damage the brand.

"So if we tell candidates they're going to have an interview but the employer doesn't follow through as promised, they will go crazy and write a bad review about us," Bill says. "I've seen it happen to other agencies, and we're not interested in that. So we have processes in place to make sure that doesn't happen by utilizing every communications tool, from upfront agreements to follow-up calls. All of the processes involved are important, and once you manage and understand this accordingly, it will be much easier to find and hire the right people in the most cost-effective manner possible."

Bill's IT background has proven particularly handy. He built a system that has enabled Frontline recruiters to be highly efficient, including customer service for candidates. Part of the system includes a program provided by a company out of Spokane, Washington, that surveys both candidates and clients to come up with a net promoter score, which is a metric for determining the state of a customer's loyalty and satisfaction with a brand or product.

"We started doing that years ago, and it really helped us see what candidates and clients needed and wanted. We took what they said to heart and made changes that turned the negatives into positives, and we've been winning every year since. Today we have our own net promoter score and our own AI program that is communicating with our people all the time. We go a customer service step beyond to make sure candidates know it's important to us, that we do care, and that they're not falling into a black hole."

And just as with employers, Frontline does not deal in false hope. "If we can't help them, we tell them that. If they have a skillset for a position we don't cover, we say so. We get people all the time who call and say: *I'm a forklift driver in a warehouse.* I tell them Frontline is not the agency for them, but then I refer them to a competitor who is in their wheelhouse."

Frontline currently offers staffing services to a variety of industries, including technology/IT, administrative, human resources, accounting and finance, oil and gas, customer service, engineering, and legal. Bill says diversity, including providing direct-hire, temporary, and temp-to-hire helps make staffing recession-proof. And he says not all industries are a good fit for Frontline.

"At one time when oil and gas tanked, we looked at jumping into healthcare because it was a hot market. That lasted about three months. We failed miserably. It wasn't the right thing for us. We can work in the medical side doing front office or records, but nursing was a mistake. We did not have our database built with résumés; we didn't have the right tools in place."

So while it was easy to see what failure looked like, sometimes it's murkier determining what success is. Bill acknowledges that different people judge success on different levels.

"Is it revenue? Growth? Profit? Instead of looking at success from those perspectives, we went back to what I call the three pillars: people, process, and service. And in the middle of that is where our core values reside."

They call it C-HERE: communication, honesty, ethics, respect, and entrepreneurial spirit. And there is another unofficial core value that's emblazoned on a wall in the Frontline office—an homage to the Costanza Method. In the *Seinfeld* series, Jerry's hapless friend, George Costanza, decides that to change his life around, he will simply do the opposite of his natural inclinations. Bill has employed that method with a twist: to succeed in staffing you need to buck the status quo.

"I've often thought I should write Larry David a note because that concept was a game-changer for me," Bill admits. "And it's something that drives us here. Anytime somebody says: *Well, this is what everybody does* … I respond: *Then do the opposite.* Just because everybody else does it, doesn't mean it's right. It just means there's an opportunity for you to grab by just looking at a problem or a system or a process in a different way. And that's exactly what we've done and will continue to do."

In the eyes of the government, not all investors are created equal. There have long been legal rules for investing, depending upon what you're investing in. Suppose in 2014 you had read about an upcoming Broadway show called *Hamilton* and wanted to invest in it. The only way you could was if you were an accredited investor, which means either having a net worth that exceeds $1 million or an annual income that exceeds $200,000 for each of the previous two years, with a reasonable expectation of the same income for the current year. For a married person the threshold is $300,000 for each of the past two years. If you fail to meet those standards you are non-accredited. So your dream of investing in a musical you thought could be a hit would have been dashed.

The reasoning behind these rules is that people with that much money aren't likely bankrupting themselves by investing. In other words, the government made laws to prevent people of modest means from losing their life savings. Of course there's been no law against gambling away your money at a casino or accruing tens of thousands of dollars in credit card debt that exceeds your assets, so it seems like the biggest achievement of accredited-investor standards was keeping about 98 percent of Americans from having an equal shot at investing in a potential money-making business or enterprise.

Crowdfunding has changed that inequality. At its simplest, crowdfunding is a financing method that involves funding a project with relatively modest contributions from a large group of individuals, rather than seeking substantial sums from a small number of investors. Equity crowdfunding is raising capital through the sale of securities, such as shares, in a private company, meaning one not listed on the stock exchange. Thanks to public awareness and some favorable legislation—which includes allowing small businesses to raise up to $50 million in capital online from the general public—crowdfunding models have become accepted and increasingly popular financing strategies for a variety of businesses, including those in the hospitality industry. The new rules have enabled HotelierCo founder Nathan Kivi to develop an innovative company that uses an equity crowdfunding model to give everyday people the opportunity to own part of a hotel.

"With HotelierCo there's an opportunity to open up the hotel industry to every suitable US citizen, not just accredited investors and institutional money," Nathan says. "Having an offering circular qualified is a lengthy process to make sure investors understand all of the risks associated with the investment. There's also a loyalty side of the platform that hasn't been tested before in the hospitality space, where the large number of hotel owners also become advocates and frequent users of their investment."

HotelierCo is currently considering properties in Charlotte, Napa Valley, and Dallas. To manage HotelierCo's properties, Nathan has selected Valor Hospitality Partners, which oversees more than seventy-five hotels around the world, from boutique hotels to luxury resorts.

"This is the future of hotel investment," Nathan says. "Essentially, you're blending real estate with business operations, giving yourself more areas you can leverage. Hotels are able to work in the market at a faster pace than other real estate properties. We want people to get excited about it as we get more developments off the ground. We want everyone in the US to be a hotelier."

His current venture is blending his experience in the real estate and

Nathan Kivi

hospitality industries, which started back in his native Australia. After graduating from college Nathan got into commercial property through a fund management company.

"They had mandates to invest in certain sectors. So a group called Australia Post Superannuation invested a few hundred million in the hospitality space through Eureka Funds Management. Through Eureka we ended up acquiring a portfolio of assets from the Intercontinental Hotel Group who were offloading from their balance sheet. So long-short, there were about three of us running a billion-dollar hotel fund."

The portfolio was comprised of predominantly high-level hotels that Nathan often traveled to. He remembers thinking: *Wouldn't it be great to own a part of this?* But at the time there was no conduit to ownership except for large institutions. During his tenure at that company, Nathan earned a master's degree in property development with a focus on hospitality. He also received a certificate in hotel asset management through a course at Cornell University. After running that fund for several years Nathan decided it was time for a sea change.

"The fund was in a wind-down phase, and my partner at the time—who is now my wife—said: *Well, if you're looking for a change why don't we move to Las Vegas in the United States, and you can play poker for a living*, which was something I always fantasized about doing. I had been to the States many times because my mother is American, so I grew up having both Australian and United States citizenship. So before my future wife could change her mind, in 2012 we sold everything we owned, made the trip to the US, and bought a place in Las Vegas. I got my realtor license there and dabbled in that, but predominantly played poker for the next two and a half years."

Was it everything he's imagined?

"It was so stressful," he says with a laugh. "But it was an experience. I had always played poker on the side for money, and the game is more technical than you realize, so I learned a lot. For example, it is all about the odds and everyone's going to get lucky at some point. In general, everyone's going to win roughly the same amount of hands. So it's learning how to make the most out of the hands you're going to win, lose as little as possible in the ones you aren't going to win, and understand which hands to get away from as they aren't going to win you money in the long run—even though in the movies they do."

Another thing he learned was to frequent the casinos that attracted tourists, like the Wynn. Nathan says the Bellagio was also a magnate for amateur poker players because it's associated with the *Ocean's Eleven* film and its sequels.

"So there were a lot of bad players there. But it was mostly about just making friends with people that ran the card rooms. If there was a good game going, they'd send you a text 24/7 saying: *There are some really bad players here; get to the tables now.* You tip them for the heads up, go to the tables, and play in the good games."

Nathan says it was a good time while it lasted, but two and a half years was enough. "You can make a living at it, but you're never going to see great wealth unless you manage to win one of the big tournaments. I'm glad I did it, but it was definitely not something for the long-term."

Besides the lack of a secure future, Nathan also missed working in the hospitality space. He wanted to get out of the poker rooms and back into hotel management.

"At the end of the day, it's just playing cards. The hotel space is just a lot more complex and interesting. There is a lot more skill involved in understanding all the facets of hotel investment between someone who owns it to someone who runs it. There's a brand on it, the value of the land and how that fluctuates, and how well the business itself does because you own the business. Because I had run a fund that was predominantly Intercontinental Hotel assets and IHG has a corporate office in Atlanta, I contacted the company to let them know I was looking to get back into the hotel space. They offered me a role on their global acquisitions and mergers team. In that position I was trying to help acquire strategic brands as well as sell existing hotel assets they wanted off their balance sheet."

Nathan explains that when it comes to business loyalty, there's a tension between online travel agents and brand companies like Marriott, IHG, and Hilton. He saw it as an opportunity.

"The brands were always in this loyalty war with online travel agents, who were also a large cost for hotels. I knew about the new regulations enacted regarding crowdfunding, so I suggested: *Why don't you offer to sell the hotels to your members and use crowdfunding to break them up into smaller share pieces that regular people can own?* Not only would that successfully remove those unwanted assets from the company's balance sheet, but it would also allow people to come on the journey of ownership with IHG. Then if somebody owns $500 or $1,000 of an Intercontinental Hotel, next time they're making a decision to stay at a hotel, they will much more likely pick an Intercontinental Hotel since they have a financial stake in and personal connection to the company."

Nathan points out that while it may sound similar to a timeshare model, he was advocating something quite different. With a timeshare a developer will typically build a hotel. Then they will sell a time allocation to an individual—for example a $10,000 investment might allocate a room for the buyer to use for two weeks of the year. Some timeshare models don't offer a specific room; instead the purchaser is buying a block of time at the resort, meaning they would get a different room each stay.

"What I envisioned was owning part of a hotel. If a hotel is a $100 million property and makes a $10 million profit, that's a 10 percent return," Nathan says. "So if you invested $5,000, your return would be $500 that year. Suppose the next year the occupancy rate goes up and the profit increases. Then your piece of the profit increases proportionally. You don't get a room for two weeks; you get a monetary return on investment. It's just like owning a residential investment property—exactly the same structure. But it's a much bigger beast with more to it."

The more Nathan worked out the details about his idea, the more he saw its viability. But crowdfunding wasn't in IHG's wheelhouse to pursue.

"They basically said it wasn't their core business. *If that's something you want to do, then just quit, and go do it yourself.* I said: *Okay; done.* I quit and started looking into."

During that time the Australian SB&G Group that had acquired the Eureka FM portfolio Nathan used to run was looking to expand internationally. They reached out to him and offered him the position of chief investment officer to help them set up a platform in the United States.

"I told them I'd be happy to help but I was starting the work of creating my own company, and I wanted a stipulation that there was no conflict with that. They agreed, so I agreed and am still helping them out today on that. Then along the way I came across Valor Hospitality Partners, a fantastic hotel management company that's based in Atlanta as well. They have expertise in operating world class hotels as well as taking over distressed hotels or those with development or operating challenges and turning them around. I got on very well with the two owners. During one of our conversations, they asked if I could think of a strategy for Valor to grow its United States platform. I told them about the crowdfunding idea I had pitched to IHG then asked if they would effectively be partners in

HotelierCo. They thought that was a great idea and agreed and helped finance our start-up costs."

In turn Nathan was named Valor's chief strategy officer. That was in 2017. It took Nathan two and a half years to get HotelierCo trademarked, submit all the necessary legal paperwork, build the website, develop the brand, and get the first deal up and running.

"Initially we focused on more of a boutique aspect because as with any investment, there is risk that goes along with possible reward. But with a boutique hotel, it's more than just a potential financial benefit. There's also a cool lifestyle element to it, where during dinner party conversations you'd go: *You'll never guess what I just invested in. Now I'm a part owner of a hotel.* Then as we educate our investors about the intricacies of hotel investments, and as time progresses, then we'll look to open it up to a larger diversification of hotel type."

Using the crowdfunding model, Red Lion is looking for Nathan and Valor to help grow its boutique Hotel RL lifestyle brand. "They're trying to crack the market that at the moment is dominated by Marriott, Hilton, and IHG," Nathan explains. "That's why they're open to going down a different avenue that a lot of larger brands wouldn't contemplate. Over 2020 and 2021 we're hoping to fill three $50 million funds with Red Lion Corporation."

One of the other things that Nathan says has proven exceptionally difficult in the crowdfunding-based process is dealing with the Securities Exchange Commission. "With our initial development assemblage, from when we first executed the contract in January of 2018 to get it fully qualified for the way that we wanted to run it, ended up taking around nineteen months. It was definitely a good learning experience to understand the SEC process and what it takes to get an offering to market. We have already used those lessons in preparing our first Hotel RL investment fund. So we'll go to market showing investors the lifestyle brand we are targeting, the list of Central US markets we are prepared to invest in, and the return profile that we're expecting. Then once we have enough money in escrow, we can start targeting the first asset. The intention will be for each $50 million fund, we'll target four assets with about 50 to 60 percent debt. Once we have our first $7.5 million, we'll start looking for our first asset in those markets."

One reason the SEC filings have been so complex is precisely because investors don't have to be accredited. The agency is trying to ensure that Nathan is giving potential investors everything they need to know about the risk associated with their investment.

"We're just doing it in a formal process," Nathan says. "So if unaccredited people want to invest, we just have to verify that they're not putting in more than 10 percent of their net worth or annual income. As far as HotelierCo's business model, we put in a small sliver of equity to help get the deals up and running. But effectively HotelierCo is a fund management company, meaning we manage the assets on behalf of the crowdfunded retail investors."

For many industries, start-up growth plans are fairly straightforward: get the product or service to market, build a customer/client base, maintain cash flow for expenses, scale. With hotels it's a different formula.

"The cash-flow issues for us are more around the cost of customer acquisition and how much you want to spend on marketing. I'll tell you that no matter how deep the bucket is for marketing costs and digital space, you can spend more. It's basically balancing that out. The way that the business works is you're basically just buying real estate. But because the projects are typically larger, we would struggle with growth with extreme success; if we start pulling in $150–$200 million a year, we'd therefore have to find $400 million in assets. And with the initial funds targeting an average size of $25 million, it could be difficult to find sixteen suitable hotels to acquire in one year. It relies on remaining disciplined and not buying assets that don't meet our threshold. If there are additional funds, we will be patient and not submit anything else to the SEC until those buckets of money have been invested into hotels."

At first blush it might seem logical to target top markets such as Manhattan, Los Angeles, San Francisco, and Miami. But Nathan points out other brands are already firmly entrenched in such areas.

"Those markets are also too hard for us to crack at the moment because the cost of land is exceptionally high, so $50 million dollars doesn't get you a lot. With its first $50 million dollar Hotel RL fund, HotelierCo is going to target cities in the central United States, a strategic move with Red Lion's head office in Denver. Then the second two funds will be West Coast and East Coast funds."

Rarely does a start-up have no competition it its space; and when they do it tends not to last long. Nathan says there are a few other groups utilizing crowdfunding that do it using a slightly different model, but none in the hotel space.

RealtyMogul.com and Fundrise both target multifamily and other commercial property investments. But they have minimal exposure to hotels. Not only is HotelierCo doing the hospitality space, which those other companies don't do because they don't understand it, I'm trying to do the entire hotel. In their business model in multifamily, they'll open a $50 million fund then look for fifty $1 million developments. They'll say: *We'll put one million dollars in if you give us a 10 percent return on our money*. That's a business model I don't like at all because if you're making fifty $1 million dollar outlays, monitoring those investments is administratively intensive. You could have one person run four $25 million dollar assets, whereas you might need ten people to run fifty $1 million dollar investments. They use that model because on one hand it's easier as money comes in to just throw it into an investment. But it also becomes a bit more difficult because you have to continually find investments that are worth investing in."

While HotelierCo investors don't get free rooms for their investments, they do get perks that encourage them to come see and stay in their hotel. Each owner will receive discounts on accommodation plus food and beverage based on the level of ownership, provided they book directly.

"Essentially you're giving investors a benefit that also benefits the hotel and them. Online travel agents can charge up to 25 percent. If the investor saves 20 percent by booking directly, and the hotel makes 5 percent more profit, the investor makes more money and gets to stay at their own hotel. It's a win-win. We're also providing perks to larger investment sizes such as invites to grand opening or relaunch parties. Not each hotel will be able to do the same things for investors, but we intend to always incentivize owner/investors."

Looking into his entrepreneurial crystal ball, Nathan is optimistic that by mid-to-late 2021, they'll raise $150 million with the Red Lion Group, which will be about $300 million in assets. "We would potentially roll that out and continue down the path of doing those funds. We have had other large brand companies inform us that if our crowdfunding proves successful, that they would allow us access to their hundred million members to follow a similar business model."

While Nathan admits that sounds great, he also knows it would be dangerous territory. Too much success too fast can be a start-up's rapid downfall.

"We would need to come up with a solid business plan to address what happens if we start filling $50 million funds on a continual basis with that many members. And that's just talking about the United States. We also intend to grow into other markets that Valor's in, such as the UK and South Africa initially."

For as carefully as he planned out HotelierCo's build out, Nathan admits there were still some surprises. "My background is structuring deals and understanding what a good hotel deal is. But I wasn't prepared for the cost of digital marketing. I would see Fundrise spending millions a year on the social media side; and now that we're in it, I see how quickly that money gets spent. Yes, you can target people through age range, salary, where they take holiday, but the cost of accessing those people is a lot more expensive than I could have ever imagined. As a result we are looking to use Start Engine as our platform so HotelierCo can focus on finding and managing the hotel investments."

The red tape required to reach non-accredited investors was also much more time consuming than he anticipated, especially in how things had to be worded, including on the web site. "It's been an eye-opener how much scrutiny every single word on everything gets just to ensure you're not doing anything contrary to SEC or FINRA legal requirements and obligations that we have."

As with any investment, Nathan is occasionally contacted by people looking for a get-rich-quick scheme. They equate the crowdfunding investment with placing a bet.

"They don't understand that they're buying real estate that might have a typical return of 10 to 12 percent a year," Nathan says, "which is better than having it in the bank if you need liquidity. But don't invest thinking that a $1,000 can turn into $100,000 because that's not what we're intending to do. We offer an asset-backed investment. A hotel is like buying a home; you're not taking a pure business risk because you've always got the asset behind it. If you're looking for a fast, huge payoff, this is the wrong investment for you. Go put your money in high-yield junk bonds or a pure start-up investment."

Personalized Brewing Done Right

When compared to wine, tea, and beer, which have been enjoyed by people since the earliest civilizations on Earth, coffee is a relatively modern beverage. Its storied beginning claims a goat herder named Kaldi saw his goats energetically frolicking after eating the berries of wild coffee bushes. He consumed a few himself and declared the beans a gift from God. Myth or not, coffee's popularity has grown ever since.

A 2015 report from the National Coffee Association found that Americans drink coffee more than any other beverage—including water—spending more than $74 billion a year on their precious brew. Globally an average of five hundred billion cups of coffee are consumed every year.

That's a lot of Joe.

For centuries people have brewed coffee by adding ground beans to near-boiling water. Today whether it's the ubiquitous urn, a fancy French-press, a percolator, or pour-over, these have largely been variations on the age-old tradition—brew a pot and pass it around. Outside of espresso, the idea of personal choice usually amounted to: *Would you like regular or decaf?*

Long before the emergence of iFillSystems, this was the scenario that Edward Cai found himself facing. It was a cold December Sunday in 1992 and while attending a fellowship meeting at the Church of Ann Arbor, Michigan, Edward watched the rhythmic pulse of the church percolator, eager to enjoy a warm cup to fight off the winter chill.

"Back then the common way to make coffee was with a coffee percolator, and the church I went to had a big coffee maker, which was so bad after sitting around all day. We started talking about why wasn't there a better way to make coffee."

Questions like that can keep a newly graduated engineer up at night. It wasn't long before Edward's fruitful mind was brimming with new ideas of how to make a better cup. By the end of 1993, Edward had designed and built his first single-serve brewer, giving birth to the original company, Household Technologies Group, which later evolved into United Home Technologies and iFillSystems.

The king of home coffee brewing at the time was undoubtedly Mr. Coffee. For those who can remember, famous baseball player Joltin' Joe DiMaggio had hit a home run as the television spokesman for what would become a ubiquitous household brand. Whether by chutzpa, good karma, or just plain luck, Edward was able to arrange a presentation of his invention with Peter Howell, then the chief executive officer of Mr. Coffee. In the company's Bedford Heights conference room, Peter watched how Edwards's ThermoCell, which is the heart of the single-serve brewer, drew one cup of water and metered it through twelve grams of coffee. Peter loved the innovative technology and quality of the brew. The launch into single-serve brewing began.

Peter should be at least partially credited with starting this single-serve revolution. He and his team quickly identified many of the key benefits for single-serve, including reduction of wasted coffee, additional brewer sales, brewing just one cup in less time, and the luxury of personal choice. The development of the technology continued, and Edward received US patents on his ThermoCell and other key technologies for single-serve.

As any entrepreneur knows, the ecology of big business is always in

Dr. Edward Z. Cai &
Robert Hensley

motion, and during the development time, Mr. Coffee was acquired by a new company owner, Health-O-Meter. Fortunately Peter became the chairman of the combined companies and continued to be an enthusiastic supporter of the single-serve program. But the corporate landscape continued to shift, and by 1998 another company stepped into the picture to acquire Mr. Coffee. With the change in ownership, Peter announced he would be retiring but not before he introduced Edward to his successor, Meeta Vyas, who in turn introduced him to John Hamann, the president of the new owner, Sunbeam Household Products.

John, a former executive with Apple and consequently comfortable with new technologies, is credited with creating much of the technology in wired homes and smart appliances we use today. John and his team had seen a demonstration of the improved single-serve brewer and two months later invited Edward and his fiancée, Jenny, to a dinner at his home in Boca Raton, Florida. During the dinner party the two struck a patent license deal and the key terms for an agreement. Lawyers for both parties were uncharacteristically efficient, and the agreement was inked in just a few weeks. Immediately the Sunbeam engineering team started their single-serve brewer development as the marketing team began conducting consumer focus groups and other studies.

Edwards' single-serve brewer had survived all the CEO changes, and it looked like it was finally going to see light from its six-year (1993-1999) incubation tunnel. Under Sunbeam's new ownership it seemed the Mr. Coffee brand was destined to revolutionize the world of coffee again, twenty years after its invention of the automatic drip coffeemaker in the late '70s. Enthusiasm ran high. The marketing team's studies revealed a huge surge in the popularity of espresso drinks, and it was believed adapting the brewer to include espresso would make a great addition. While engineering the addition of yet more single-serve options was exciting, it also created delays in the market launch.

Everything seemed to be going smoothly until Edward had a startling conversation with John. It turned out that Sunbeam was on the brink of bankruptcy. As a result John left Sunbeam. After his departure Sunbeam terminated both the single-serve brewer project and Edward's patent license agreement.

Edward decided it was time to move to the West Coast and accept an offer to join Hewlett Packard's new Inkjet Business Unit at its Corvallis, Oregon, campus. Edward made HP management aware of his brewer innovations, but for now that was put on the back burner.

"At HP I met some wonderful people and future friends, including Jim and Fay Sedgwick, Rick Van Abkoude, Dave Orr, Steve Andersen, Dave Otis, Dan Beamer, and Lee Mason," he says.

Together they worked on the growth of inkjet printing from its beginnings to the $20 billion business it became over the next ten years. Edward loved his work as procurement engineering manager and later as a research and development manager, gaining valuable business experience as he thrived in the HP Way.

Part of the move included transferring his ongoing MBA education from the University of Michigan to the Oregon Executive MBA program, jointly offered by University of Oregon, Oregon State, and Portland State University. There Edward became friends with fellow students Kevin Williams, a vice president for Spectra Physics, and Scott Overson, vice president of financing for Intel.

Rising from the ashes of his previous efforts, the idea of single-serve brewer commercialization became the MBA project for Scott, Kevin, and Edward. The team traveled to Hamilton Beach-Procter Silex, West Bend, and Salton to pitch the single-serve brewer concept to their marketing and business leaders. Judy McBee, senior vice president of marketing of Hamilton-Beach, Salton's CEO, Leon Dreiman, and Peter Winstanley, president of the coffee division, were all intensely interested. The team learned a lot, successfully completed their MBAs, and everyone went back to their respective busy work schedules.

In early 2000, Hans Damen, senior vice president of business development for Sara Lee called Edward from Utrecht, Netherlands, at 5:00 a.m. He invited Edward to meet with the research and development team of Sara Lee's Douwe Egberts Coffee division and with business leaders from its top European countries to discuss the potential for developing single-serve coffee for the European and American markets. The meeting date was scheduled for just six weeks later.

Edward began burning the midnight oil, knowing he needed everything on his side to make this opportunity work. He called a former HP colleague who Edward believed could help him assure success. Rick Van Abkoude, whose family came from a small town near the Douwe Egberts Utrecht mega roasting plant, had retired three months earlier. With the help of a mutual friend, Edward convinced Rick to come out of his cozy retirement. The Utrecht meeting was less than three weeks away so Rick and Edward shifted into high gear. Rick took responsibility for the market research and preparing the presentation while Edward developed and fine-tuned the formulae—grind size, fill weight, filter pore size, brewing time, temperature, and pressures—for several different single-serve brewer prototypes.

During the day Edward was still managing a team of scientists and engineers at HP, but his nights were filled with hundreds of repeated coffee experiments. On the eve of traveling, Rick and Edward selected three of the brewer prototypes and more than three hundred single-serve pods that Edward had made by hand. With everything packed into three extra-large suitcases, they boarded their flight ready for the company's first international business meeting.

The two-day meeting in Utrecht was a success. The first two single-serve brewers and pods worked flawlessly and brewed consistent coffee with a fine, golden crema layer. The third prototype brewed both a single cup and a larger pot of coffee with small and large JumboBean pods. As a dozen excited executives stood around the machine watching the large JumboBean quickly filling a forty-ounce pot, Edward had an uneasy feeling. As he moved closer to check the pot, the JumboBean exploded, sending hot, wet grounds in all directions, landing not only on everyone's suits but across the face of a Van Gogh painting that hung on the wall. Everyone in the room was stunned.

Surveying the aftermath of the explosion, Hans said, "Glad we all survived the bomb! Douwe Egberts will pay for everyone's dry cleaning—including Mr. Van Gogh's."

Everyone had a laugh, wiped off their clothes, and the meeting continued. To memorialize the incident, Edward purchased the domain name JumboBean.com and still owns it to this day.

A license and development agreement between Household Technology Group (iFillSystems) and Sara Lee/DE was soon reached. This beginning utilized Edward's patents to create the first commercial single-serve brewing system, the Senseo. The new venture would mean extensive work, so much in fact that a choice had to be made, stay at HP or take the leap. He met with HP management, and a three-month transition plan was developed to ensure all of HP's product development projects would go smoothly after his departure.

Less than a year into the Senseo Agreement, Rick and Edward presented their new Pods at the Quarterly Project Review meeting with the Sara Lee DE team. Following the meeting, the team presented the new two-bar, low-pressure Senseo machine capable of generating a dense crema that formerly could only be achieved with a sixteen-bar, high-pressure commercial espresso machine. Hans Damen and Heidi Klemback, vice president of research and development for Sara Lee Douwe Egberts, stared in amazement as a cube of sugar floated on the coffee brewed from the new machine.

The low-cost Senseo is essentially a co-development with industry giant Philips, which was brought into the project to manufacture all the Senseo brewers. Edward's ThermoCell technology was selected because it did not need the expensive pump. Both the Philips and iFillSystems teams charted and analyzed hundreds of standard brew charts for the ThermoCell-based Senseo machines.

The launch of the Senseo system did well, especially in Belgium and France, where it remains popular today. However, the system didn't capture a significant enough portion of the North American market. A new player was on the scene, and its growth by anyone's standard was simply breathtaking. About two years after the Senseo single-serve had been launched by Sara Lee and Philips in both Europe and the United States, Keurig

introduced their K-Cup technology to American consumers. Feeding the market demand that had been clear in the introduction of a single-serve option, Keurig's launch was wildly successful and quickly took retail shelf space away from Senseo. Even though Senseo had primed the pump for this gushing onrush of consumer demand, Keurig had become the consumers' choice.

A sad day in iFillSystems' history came in 2005 when Senseo exited the US market. In retrospect there were many causes for the failure of the Senseo single-serve in the United States, including the availability of different coffee roasts, blends, and varieties under the K-Cup. Also, the K-Cup final brew phase was air-dried compared to the wet and messy used Senseo pods. Analysis and research indicated that there was perhaps a more basic reason—the perceived safety factor. Because the K-Cup is fully enclosed and the coffee can't be touched by other people's hands, it was considered more hygienic than Senseo's filter packs. Before Senseo's US launch in 2002, they compared the JumboBean with the selected filter pods, and the perceived safety of JumboBean was clearly recognized. But the environmental concern and the possible explosion of the JumboBean overpowered other concerns.

In the end iFill stayed out of the market until 2011 when their exclusivity agreement with Phillips and Sara Lee finally expired. The next time around iFillSystems set out to improve the design and implementation of Keurig's K-Cup single-serve technology. Not just in how the brew could be made better but also in terms of how the entire industry works and what it means to both businesses and our world ecology.

Tim Widmer, senior vice president of sales, explains the evolution of the iFillSystems brand. "I joined the company in 2014 to help Edward transition his business. Edward's first step had been inventing the iFillCup pod design for a richer and fresher brew. The idea was intended for the home consumer market, where people could buy from their favorite local roaster and fill their pods at home. I suggested he take a different direction."

Tim told Edward he thought there was a market in working directly with specialty roasters and providing brewing systems for the hospitality industry. His direction proved successful.

"We went to our first Specialty Coffee Association trade show, and sure enough all the roasters said they loved the design of our pod. Even Keurig loved the design," Tim says. "And all of them said: *I want to fill my own.* We immediately started developing filling systems for our iFillCup pods and thought perhaps iFillSystems was a better transition name to the community than iFillCups."

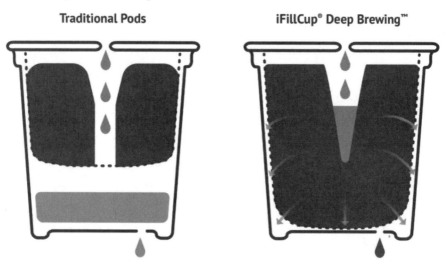

So iFillCups now refers to the company's pods, and iFillSystems refers to all the filling systems they've engineered around production of their pods.

"In the beginning the Keurig system was entirely propriety," Tim explains. "But then the utility patent ran out, and that's when everybody got into the game. However, Keurig does own the word K-Cup, so because of the licensing, everyone started looking for words they could utilize, such as pods."

But the iFillCup isn't merely a horse by a different name. It's a different species.

"Our pod design is unique," Tim says. "It has a food-grade sealant that acts as a one-way valve allowing coffee to de-gas inside the pod while not letting air back in. This is a huge advantage because we are able to take fresh-roasted and ground coffee immediately into the pod, where everyone else uses a heat seal format that requires roasters to hold the coffee for at least three days before packaging to give it a chance to degas. If they don't do that, the heat-sealed pods will burst. Immediate packing rather than waiting three days preserves a tremendous amount of coffee's nuance and flavor."

While Edward's pod technology proved it could enable roasters to provide the highest quality and flavor, his deeper intent was to go beyond simply providing a rich cup of coffee and find ways to promote sustainability, both within his company and the industry at large.

Edward says he was disturbed by what was happening in the coffee market after the K-Cup took over the world. "Knowing all these pieces of plastic were going into landfills and getting into the ocean did not make us feel good about our industry. We understood people loved the convenience and variety of the K-Cup, but environmentally it was not good because the design makes it difficult to separate and recycle the used polystyrene, paper, and foil. Unfortunately, these materials primarily go into landfill."

Edward says the problem affects waste disposal throughout the world but especially in Europe and North America. "When we came back to the industry in 2011, we got several cup engineers together to invent a new K-Cup design that might be more ecologically friendly. What we came up with had a polypropylene cup, a polypropylene filter, and a polypropylene lid, uniform materials that were 100 percent recyclable."

It took almost four years for the team to get a workable design because of the difficulty in piecing the filter, cup, and lid together using thin polypropylene. Now they hope to provide more comprehensive solutions and promote a sustainability revolution.

Robert Hensley, iFillSystem's director of business support, explains, "From the beginning our plan was to be environmentally friendly, so there's definitely a philosophical underpinning towards being Earth-friendly in our designs and materials. Taking responsibility for the lifecycle of our product is really a practical stance in terms of business as well as doing the right ethical and moral thing. Our vision began as a design evolution—how to improve the pods for single-serve coffee and beverages," Robert says. "We didn't know it at the time, but what evolved was an enterprise that fits perfectly into the concept for a circular economy. That philosophy has driven our core projects, and we believe this sensibility resonates well with customers too and will continue to carry us forward."

Simply put, the circular economy model mimics nature's cycle of life. Just as in nature where there is a cycle of birth, life, death, and return, there is also a natural cycle in business—an *ecology of transformation* —from product design, production, use, and recycling. For Edward and his team, the idea of making a pre-assembled pod of easily recyclable material fit perfectly into the responsibility of being good stewards for the earth.

"We are just one piece of a bigger puzzle," Robert says. "But we want to do our part to address the issues of our industry within the larger picture that affects us all. The other crucial component are the thousands of coffee entrepreneurs who gave birth to the specialty industry and enjoy a wealth of raving fans within their local communities."

By pre-assembling the pods, iFillSystems took a huge step in reducing the complexity of production so that smaller, specialty roasters could participate in the single-serve market. Again, having local roasters grind and fill their own pods for improved freshness and quality seems to fit perfectly with their circular economy model.

As Robert puts it, "If we look for it, there is a natural fit between global and local production. Some things are really only viable if done on a large scale. Huge economies of scale come into play. For instance, the production of filter materials only makes economic sense if done in large volumes. On the other hand, filling a pod with fresh ingredients for fresh consumption makes more sense on a local basis. Put the two together and you have a distributed manufacturing scenario that works for everyone."

The downside of single-serve has been the problem of waste. Every year more than ten billion single-serve coffee pods are disposed of in landfills across the planet along with about sixty-seven million gallons of waste coffee grounds, making it a global problem.

"It's an issue that reaches into the quality of life for all," Robert says. "And we believe that creative design and effective implementation can provide a true circular economic solution. Nature works in circles, and so should we. One of my life's heroes was Buckminster Fuller, and he made a wonderful observation saying: *Pollution is nothing but the resources we are not harvesting, allowing them to disperse because we are ignorant of their value.* Bucky is right. The plastics in our pods can be recycled into other products, and the spent coffee grounds are a rich source of nitrogen for fertilizer. The whole concept of better by design should include not just how we use something today, but what happens to it tomorrow."

iFillSystems.com

To that end iFillSystems has been hard at work on one of their latest projects. The iFillZero, a smart solution for zero waste designed to turn those billions of used pods and millions of gallons of spent coffee grounds into products and profits. The iFill team believes that a proactive stance when it comes to environmental stewardship, as opposed to a punitive approach, is much more likely to succeed in reaching the hearts and minds of consumers.

Robert observes that in the past, "We've attempted to solve the plastic in landfill problem by trying to limit or eliminate some plastics products, and put the burden on consumers—both corporate and individuals— with costly collection, shipping, and processing schemes. Both of those solutions have left the public dissatisfied and largely reluctant to participate. If an initiative is too costly or punitive, it's doomed to fail. We've seen that time and again in plastics programs around the world. When it comes to pods, if it's just too much trouble or the costs too high, they are simply tossed into the garbage with no hope of sorting them out. For any initiative to really work, it has to spring from a genuine value and offer some kind of profit incentive. If it doesn't, it will simply prove unfeasible to be implemented on a large scale."

iFillSystems believes that producing 100 percent polypropylene pods was only the first step in implementing global change to the single-serve marketplace. The second step is developing the technology that can separate the polypropylene from the coffee grounds in an efficient and cost-effective way—the iFillZero. The third step will be harvesting the plastic and grounds for profitable reuse in plastics manufacturing and nitrogen-rich coffee fertilizer compost.

"We have begun discussions with both injection molding companies and with garden supply outlets such as Lowes," Robert reports. "Opportunities abound for the reutilization of polypropylene and coffee waste."

By focusing on distributed manufacturing and local collection and processing systems, the iFillSystems' team believes they can get thousands of local businesses to participate. And while iFillZero is designed to address a coffee industry problem, the hope is it can also be applied to other landfill problems as well, such as plastic water bottles.

"The single-serve coffee market is a multi-billion-dollar industry annually and is here to stay, so opportunities abound for private sector participation," Robert says. "We are only at the beginning, but we believe this three-key solution can work socially, politically, and economically."

From a business perspective iFillSystems' single-serve technologies have applications far beyond coffee. "It's obvious that all the big players like Nestle, Starbucks, Coca-Cola, Anheuser Busch, and others are looking at the single-serve future of food and drinks," Edward says. "We saw this coming about five years ago, and that is the technology we're working on right now. For example, we're looking at building a new business for freshly-made soup. We  could also expand this single-serve coffee concept into teas, baby formula, alcoholic drinks— basically anything is possible."

Jonathan Wells, vice president of sales, agrees. "We got in on the shirttails of the coffee industry, but now you see the world evolving and expanding into new product categories such as CBD-infused products, health drinks, and pharmaceuticals. I have even heard someone is looking at spices going into a single-serve pod. Really, it's coffee to virtually everything; there's a whole new world of possibilities where this can go."

As consumers become more and more accustomed to single-serve options, Edward believes other industries will find new opportunities too. "The biggest thing single-serve has going for it is personalization. That's where we see single-serve going. Not that long ago you made a pot of coffee, and that's what everyone drank. Or you made a pitcher of iced tea and served that with dinner. Now Mom can have tea, Dad gets his diet shake, and your teenager chooses a protein sports drink that will build muscle. Anything you can put into that pod can be tailored to a specific market. Recently we were at a supply show for the health food industry, and one of the scientists there commented that he had a lot more room to work in formulating ingredients with a single-serve pod as opposed to being constrained by what can fit into a little capsule."

Because they are both manufacturer and supplier, iFillSystems looks at development from two different perspectives. "We supply to a wide variety of companies," Robert says. "As Jonathan mentioned, we've got companies developing CBD-infused products that are interested in our equipment. That's one channel that we can serve. Edward mentioned soups, and we see viability in a whole range of products there. I would say the doors are pretty wide open with potential, and we're happy to work with other companies to realize that potential."

With so many possibilities, there could be the temptation to strike out in multiple directions at once and lose control of growth. Robert says iFillSystems has so far grown organically, responding to consumer and commercial need.

"We have grown rapidly, but keep in mind that we started with coffee, and that remains our primary focus. The other areas are extensions that were added to what we do, and we've grown from there into other industries because they're coming to us for our know-how."

Edward notes that iFillSystems' manufacturing and brewer technology is helping other companies develop new markets. "Even though we don't get too directly involved in other companies' product development, we are true partners because we provide the technology that will be the foundation for the new market. What we began in the coffee industry, we are now expanding into multiple markets with new brewers, new recycling systems, and filling equipment for beverages of every type. We make innovation affordable and level the playing field with Earth-friendly solutions that make better tastes and a better world."

You might think that with all iFIll is doing with their existing business that the story would be complete. But just like George Washington Carver saw more in a peanut than anyone ever imagined, the same can be said for coffee.

If you put the two words *coffee and energy* together, you might simply think about that jolt of caffeine that gets you going in the morning and keeps you going at night. But what if that same coffee could be used to power your laptop, your cell phone, and even that brand-new electric car you've had your eye on? While on the surface that might not seem to make sense, it's below the surface where things get very interesting. As it turns out, long before iFill was even a gleam in Edward's eyes, he was working day and night as a graduate student exploring exotic materials that could be used for efficient energy storage—in other words, batteries.

Deep in the recesses of Texas A&M University, Edward was working on his doctorate with his advisor Prof. Charles R. Martin. Together they were toiling away with strange little things called nanotubes, which are one two-thousandth the diameter of a human hair. Something that small can be hard to imagine, but if we imagine the thickness of a human hair was like the height of the Washington Monument, which is some 555 feet high, a nanotube would be about four inches tall, the diameter of a tennis ball. But just because they're small doesn't mean they were easy to create. Edward's graduate school days and nights found him laboring in the lab sixteen hours a day, seven days a week, just to make a single gram of nanotubes. That single gram was barely enough to conduct a single set of electrochemical experiments, but it was worth it because it turns out that nanotubes have a very interesting quality: they possess an unusually high electronic conductivity of 1,100 Scm. That is so high that it remained the most conductive polymer known in the world until Andre Geim and Konstantin Novoselov at the University of Manchester made some equally high carbon graphene in 2004, which they were awarded the 2010 Nobel Prize in physics for. Geim and Novoselov's graphene shared a common property with Edward's little nanotubes: both are capable of storing 200 percent more energy than the best lithium-ion batteries. That kind of energy storage could mean a revolution in our energy future. But cost has been the problem. Edward's original nanotubes cost nearly one thousand times the price of gold. While still expensive, Geim and Novoselov's graphene brought production costs down enough to make some commercial applications realistic.

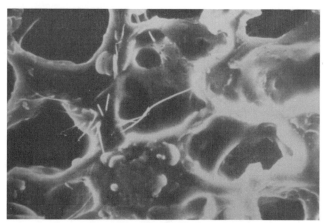

Green coffee fracture 4000X magnification

Now the process comes full circle to the little coffee bean, which Edward calls "nature's hero" because he says it will play a big role in how nanotubes will be used to spark a revolution in energy. Exactly how that's done remains proprietary but needless to say any affordable, environmentally-safe technology that can store 200 percent more energy than the best currently available lithium-ion batteries is likely to revolutionize electric cars, utilities, wearable electronics, and possibly even electric airplanes.

Keep an eye on iFill because their niche just might be getting a lot bigger.

Chapter provided by iFill

Does this sound familiar? Every year at your annual medical check-up, the doctor weighs you, looks into your ears and throat, listens to your heart and lungs, takes your blood pressure, and maybe draws some blood. Then they will likely scan your skin to identify any worrisome moles or growths. But it's likely that very, very few suggest a baseline audiology/hearing evaluation. Research over the past decade suggests that could be a crucial oversight for your overall health, especially your brain health.

Our senses aren't stand-alone processes. They are integrated with our physical, emotional, and mental health in ways we are still learning. For example, studies show that even small moments of flavor sensations can lift a person's mood. Researchers have found the sense of touch, as in touching another person, can lower blood pressure and heartrates and reduce the recovery time of patients from illnesses. Touch, especially massage, can also strengthen your immune system.

And now there is a growing body of evidence that maintaining healthy hearing is important to your overall health. Hearing loss has been associated with depression, heart disease, diabetes, and an increased likelihood of injury by falling. Perhaps most surprising is the link research has found between hearing impairment and brain health, including cognitive decline and dementia.

Researchers at Johns Hopkins University and Medical Center conducted studies with senior participants to determine how hearing loss might influence cognitive decline. In each study they tracked those who developed dementia and how quickly it progressed. They found that people with hearing loss had higher rates of dementia, including a 200–500 percent increased risk for mild to severe forms of hearing loss, respectively. Even after considering age and other risk factors, adults with hearing loss were significantly more likely than adults with normal hearing to develop dementia. In one study, people with hearing loss were 24 percent more likely to have Alzheimer's. In another, researchers found that the worse the hearing loss was, the more likely the person was to develop dementia and cognitive decline.

Frank Lin, a physician and assistant professor at Johns Hopkins University School of Medicine who authored one study noted that people tend not to give hearing loss the same kind of attention they give high blood pressure or heart disease, perhaps because it's seen as a natural or inevitable part of aging. But Lin stressed it may be time to take a more serious look at the condition and its ranking as the third most common chronic condition affecting seniors in America.

To be clear, the early treatment of hearing loss has been determined to be the single most modifiable risk factor for the prevention of dementia by the *Lancet* medical journal. Although the medical community can't say that treating hearing loss would prevent dementia altogether, research indicates treating hearing loss may slow down the progression of dementia and cognitive decline, which would have a significant positive impact on our aging population. It's also important to note that having hearing loss doesn't automatically mean you're going to develop dementia. Like all mammals, humans lose their hearing as they age, but that doesn't mean they have to experience dementia. As with most major medical conditions, the early detection and treatment of hearing loss are crucial to positive treatment outcomes.

Jared Brader

But before we can begin treating hearing loss, we have to know it's occurring, meaning that annual evaluations need to become an integral part of any health plan and wellness regimen. Providing access to comprehensive evaluations and treatment options for tinnitus and hearing loss, a progressive degenerative disorder, regardless of geographic location or financial means, is the mission of Jared Brader, founder of Intermountain Audiology and the Hearing & Brain Centers of America, as is making sure the forty-two million-plus Americans with hearing loss and tinnitus who are at an increased risk of dementia and cognitive decline receive quality treatment at an affordable price from certified specialists across the country.

What makes Jared unique is that he's not an audiologist or otologist. Jared is a problem solver, practice owner, and audiology profession leader dedicated to breaking down the barriers that keep the citizens of our country from treating their hearing loss, and the associated cognitive impact that could result in the mind-robbing disease of dementia. Jared's primary emphasis each day is growing the national message, communicating with those in need, and solving the complex problems in the audiology profession that have left audiology with the lowest treatment rates of all major medical conditions in our country. Jared leaves the patient care and treatment to his team of medical professionals and devotes his time expanding the number of Americans who have successfully treated their hearing loss, tinnitus, and associated cognitive needs.

"Our profession has had a messaging problem for many years, and unlike most practice owners and providers, I've focused my daily energy on improving our message through medical-based marketing and growing access to patient education and information to help treat more patients," Jared says. "So early on I focused my time directly on providing free educational information, symposiums, and other scientific-based marketing to seniors and their families while improving the patient experience and process for treatment in our nationwide clinics. I became serious about speaking directly to patients and their families, answering the questions and concerns they had regarding treatment. We invested in treatment team training, patient experience, and treatment outcomes using the latest in diagnostic equipment. Matching the patients' need for more information, with the appropriate patient experience, resulted in one of the most-successful audiology and hearing healthcare practices in the country, making significant contributions to our community, our patients, the profession of audiology, and the lives of our treatment team members."

His efforts also landed the company onto the 2018 and 2019 Inc. 5000 as one of the United States' fastest-growing companies among all industries, a top-50 health care company, America's highest-rated hearing health care center, and one of the few practices in the country endorsed by the only Harvard Medical and MIT-trained neuroscientist in private practice audiology, Dr. Keith Darrow, Intermountain Audiology's director of audiology research.

"Our ability to treat more patients is in large part due to our association with Dr. Darrow, who has worked tirelessly to educate patients from coast-to-coast about the significant medical benefits of early treatment of hearing loss, including the reduced risk of cognitive decline and dementia and the next generation of auditory prosthesis."

When asked how a marketing guru ended up running one of the country's premier healthcare enterprises, Jared says the story begins back in his school days, where he grew up playing high school and college golf with a friend whose father was at every golf tournament.

"I always wondered what his father did for a living that allowed him to be at every kid event, at all the family activities, and to travel to our golf tournaments that were always in the middle of the day. What did he do that gave him so much flexibility?"

It turned out his friend's father, Mark, ran a hearing health care practice. So when Jared's grandmother needed a traditional hearing aid in May 2010, that's where he took her.

"Like most seniors, she walked into the clinic seeking help but not understanding the process or what her hearing loss might be, the options out there for treatment, all the way through paying for treatment and the investment required," Jared recalls. "I thought: Wait a second; we are failing a population in our country that deserves better."

Jared says he viewed the issues though a business and marketing perspective and believed the problem was on the business process side, which then relayed into the patient experience side. "I had always been one to focus on the finer things in life—how do we treat our fellow humans, how do we create a better patient experience. In business school you have examples of the Ritz Carlton and the Disney Institute, companies known for their customer service. All of that plus my MBA background played into my epiphany: Wait; we have to do something for these great generations before us."

While the clinic staff was very friendly and they ultimately bought a traditional hearing aid—as opposed to today's modern neurotechnology —Jared says, "I was surprised by the lack of education and follow-up care that I thought an eighty-year-old woman would need. Before leaving I asked the owner to contact me if he ever needed someone with a background in marketing and finance. I told him: *I just graduated business school; let me come in and help.* He ended up taking me up on that offer."

Jared started with part-time bookkeeping, researching to learn more about the financial side of the business, such as advertising and patient care costs, then was given a patient care coordinator role and learned about the practice itself from the ground up, answering the phones, cleaning hearing technology, washing windows, and greeting patients.

"The first twelve months, I thought I had made the biggest mistake of my life," he says. "Frustrated and working seven days per week with patients in the clinic and doing my administrative tasks on nights and weekends, working with me wasn't fun. I was stressed to the max, pushing my team beyond their comfort zone and wondering when I would finally start taking home a real paycheck that aligned with my MBA."

"After I transferred into a full-time messaging and marketing role, we really started to see the fundamental changes within the practice. I became serious about aggressively applying tested information-marketing principles to grow our patient reach and provide better education and care for our patients. I worked my way all the way up to director of business operations. And as I grew in the different roles, the practice also grew. We added more providers and audiologists so we could help even more people."

Four years into his time at the hearing clinic, which by then was enjoying significant growth, Jared was asked to present at the Oticon Marketing Bootcamp, a national conference for hearing healthcare providers. After speaking in front of about 1,300 professionals from across the country, he was approached by numerous people impressed with his marketing work that had grown the clinic and connected with more of the forty-two million people in need of treatment.

"A couple asked for my help, so that was the start of my consulting work," Jared says. "We started allowing doctors to visit our offices for a consulting fee to learn how we had massively implemented successful messaging campaigns to patients and prospects, business concepts, marketing strategies, and staff-training programs to grow our practice and earn this list of recognitions and awards."

Jared's approach was to put more emphasis on building lifelong patients, increasing the patient lifetime value, and beginning educational relationships with more new prospects. "Clinic owners around the country want more new faces walking in their door," he says. "They think it's easier to get a new prospect in the door, and sometimes it is. But getting that patient for the first time is the most expensive treatment opportunity. The hearing health care profession needs to change their messaging and marketing approach and focus on getting current patients to do three things: refer more of their friends and family in need, treat their hearing loss with proper technology, and maintain the proper treatment technology every four years—or more often if needed. We have forty-two-plus million fellow citizens in need of treatment, and we must do better."

While building his footprint in the profession, always top of Jared's mind was his personal mission to solve this problem of people in need. To that end in 2014, he founded the Sound of Life Foundation, a 501(c)3 nonprofit, to help people who lack the resources get the treatment they need, supporting the foundation by donating proceeds from his consulting work.

A year later he established AUDMA (audiology marketing authority), the profession's first automated—and worry-free—patient education and multiplier system. And coming from what he describes as an entrepreneurial family, it was probably inevitable that he bought out the practice where it all began with his grandmother, the cornerstone of what would become a still-expanding hearing healthcare empire. Every business move Jared makes is intended to advance his mission of reaching every American struggling with hearing loss.

"The main overarching problem is the sheer number of people in this country struggling with hearing loss—between forty-two and forty-eight million," Jared says.

And the problem isn't isolated among the aging or elderly. From baby boomers who frequented concerts and worked in factories around loud machinery to millennials who've grown up constantly connected to earbuds to soldiers who were exposed to the loud noises of war, hearing issues are a cross-cultural epidemic.

"Hearing loss is the third most chronic condition among seniors," Jared reports. "There is no other major medical condition out there that has forty million or more untreated people. Imagine if forty-two million diabetics weren't on insulin. Well, we have tens of millions of people suffering from a condition that is the number one most modifiable risk factor for the prevention of dementia. If it happened overnight, people would be screaming from the rooftops. If you woke up tomorrow and had a forty-five- or fifty-decibel hearing loss, you'd be freaked out. But because it happens gradually, we get used to the lack of stimulation, so it goes either undetected or untreated and has severe cognitive implications."

The relative lack of urgency over hearing loss also contributes to higher cost of treatment and less hearing research being completed. "Insurance companies are known to make their money by reducing the amount they pay out," Jared explains. "I would argue that if we could get insurance companies to cover treatment for those forty-two million people, the cost of treatment would decrease due to economies of scale."

But actually getting people in for treatment is the rub. Jared notes that in countries overseas where they have full coverage for the cost of hearing loss treatment, the adoption rate isn't much higher.

"We need a national *Got Milk?* campaign! We need a Smokey Bear *Only you can prevent forest fires* campaign. We need to get out there and show the overall medical impact of untreated hearing loss. But in my heart I'm a problem solver, so there's nothing that's going to stop me or get in my way from making a dent in that number. People often ask me: *Why is it that you have local hearing clinics, but you're also marketing for seventy-nine clinics around the country? Why are you consulting with and educating 1300 providers across the country?* The answer is because I can't treat forty-eight million people alone."

Jared says there was a time earlier in his career when his idea was to have a hundred clinics across the country that he would directly run. But on a management and scalability level, that would be impractical. And in doing the math, it wasn't enough. He realized that if he instead helped one hundred other audiology and hearing center owners around the country craft a message and market their practice, if he helped their staff treat more people, he could make a much bigger dent in the problem and advance his mission exponentially. Plus, he admits that in the clinics he does own, the daily nuts-and-bolts are not his strong suit; he's a big-picture leader.

"As far as hiring doctors and staff, administration, human resources—it's about building teams. I get in trouble a bit because I'm more the visionary. I'm not the day-to-day manager, the one who keeps my thumb on the button, the one to hold individual people accountable. But I motivate you from 30,000 feet above. So I'm out there leading the way and behind me are great teams in the clinics, a great team of doctors, and a great team of consultants and marketing specialists that help in all the different entities. And together, we're really making an impact each and every day."

A turning point in his business came in 2016. While presenting at

another audiology convention, Jared met
Dr. Keith Darrow, a Massachusetts
Institute of Technology and Harvard
Medical-trained neuroscientist and a licensed audiologist with a PhD in
speech and hearing bioscience and technology. Darrow was also the
founder of Hearing and Balance Centers of New England.

"He came up and hired me as a consultant after I spoke at that event.
As I got to know him I saw that he was the classic research doctor who
didn't have a marketing team behind him, and didn't understand how to
help more people by being the trusted authority in the industry."

Jared's marketing methods grew Dr. Darrow's practice 300 percent
year-over-year, helped him become an Amazon.com best-selling author
and an audiology influencer. "He became the face of this movement
because he had the medical science behind him. And I had the marketing,
the business savvy, and the way to help more people. So we were really a
match made in heaven. Today he's the director of audiology research at
Intermountain Audiology, the Hearing and Brain Centers of America, and
the Excellence in Audiology nationwide network. He brings me the
science and the human element of connecting people."

Dr. Darrow is equally enthusiastic. "I absolutely love what I get to do
every day for my patients, my students, and my private coaching clients. I
have the fortune of transforming lives and families every day. Treating
hearing loss is not magic; it's the perfect mix of science and experience
that allows us to use our skills every day to stimulate the brain, improve
cognitive function, and help patients remain independent. I'm honored to
be part of the revolution that is helping to advance the cause of private
hearing health care practices across the country."

Jared says the other integral person in his team is his administrator,
Rosie Barrick. "She's the one who is the day-to-day. She manages the HR,

the administration—she's more like the CEO. So when I've come up with a new idea or added a new clinic location, she's been the glue to hold it all together."

One of Jared's main approaches to the hearing loss epidemic is not to present it as a technology issue, meaning it's about more than getting a hearing aid and going on your merry way. Like asthma or arthritis, hearing loss is a progressive degenerative disorder.

"As your hearing and cognitive needs decrease, you're going to need different treatment," he says. "It's similar to diabetes; as your diabetes progresses you might need a different insulin dosage or other medication. So we're not selling a technology; we're selling a treatment plan for a medical condition. Our treatment plan calls for one, low monthly payment, instead of thousands upfront. And that subscription model—just like your gym membership or Netflix—is where we're getting the traction to help more people."

The subscribers come in every three months for checkups and cleanings, and to service their technology and stay ahead of their treatment. Then once a year the audiologist reassesses the patient's hearing and cognitive needs to see if the hearing loss has progressed and determines whether they need to make alterations to the prescription.

"And generally technology improves every three to four years so at that time we can really fine-tune a patient's prescription," Jared says. "So instead of being stuck with last year's technology, we're flexible with the treatment plan because it's subscription-base. This medical approach with regular visits keeps our patient-practitioner relationship strong and best serves the patient."

And he notes it has also made his clinics the highest-rated hearing healthcare clinics in the world. "The reason for that is we're changing consumer behavior, and we're changing the medical approach to hearing from that of a retail transaction to a relationship. Everything that we do from content education to direct response messaging and marketing to Dr. Darrow's proven process allows our team to focus on treatment decisions, not financial decisions.

"One of our core values is we treat every patient. Say I partner with a clinic in Los Angeles who uses our marketing and education; if they come across a patient that they can't treat because of financial concerns, we make sure the patient gets treated through the Sound of Life Foundation. There is no reason you should come to my clinic seeking treatment for hearing loss and leave without it because we have everything from subscription plans, to pay in full, to no cost treatments."

While his mission remains focused on reaching as many people as possible who need hearing healthcare, Jared has found that the work he does also benefits more than just the hearing impaired.

"As I've been able to travel the country and coach private practice owners, I know that bringing proven solutions to practices has allowed those owners to spend more time with their families and loved ones, more time traveling this beautiful earth, and more energy building the next generation of team members and leaders for their respective practices. I love that I can count on these practices to do exceptional patient care so I can continue to focus on developing additional marketing strategies to benefit our coaching clients and the patients they serve.

"Here's to treating more of the forty-two-plus million in need."

For more information about the Hearing and Brain Centers of America, please click here: www.HearingAndBrainCenters.com

The key to maintaining a sustainable business is to see opportunities that can help extend your company's reach to better serve more specific markets. It's a knack that has helped Leeward Business Advisors' CEO Michael Polzin take his company from start-up to the Inc 5000 in five short years.

Whether your company is an international conglomerate or a local small business, information technology provides tangible and intangible benefits that impacts the culture, operational efficiency, customer/client relationships, and security of the organization. While large companies have the deep pockets to have well-staffed, in-house IT departments and mid-range companies may prefer to contact IT support on a per case basis, small businesses are typically challenged to effectively manage their IT at an affordable cost, making it a widely under-served market. And considering there are more than thirty million small businesses in the United States, it was also a golden opportunity, one that prompted Michael Polzin to develop a service geared specifically for small business owners.

"One of the things we came to realize is that there was no consistency in the service being provided these small businesses," Michael explains. "They might have all kinds of different computer equipment, often older models using different software, different versions—just a lot of inconsistency in their environment. All that adds a lot of potential pain points. And trying to fix things after they break down or trying to Frankenstein back together an old PC, means higher support cost."

He realized that small businesses needed the same consistency, manageability, and support that Fortune 500 companies enjoy, done efficiently and to scale. The result was a new service line called Leeward Elite, which is essentially affordable one-stop IT shopping for small business owners that provides support and IT management for a flat fee per month.

"This is for small businesses with one to fifty employees," Michael says. "And unlike the other division of LeewardBA, it is a complete turn-key solution where a client gets a PC—desktop or laptop, whichever form factor is best for them—and all the support and security services that they would need bundled with that, including things like next business day on-site warranty. So if the part breaks, we have a certified technician at their door the next day with a replacement part. We're managing antivirus. We're managing unlimited backups for them. And they can get unlimited 24/7 phone support. So they can call our team here in Wisconsin and ask anything from: *How do I get this PowerPoint animation to work?* to *Oh, my goodness; my database is smoking. How do I make it stop, and how do I get that fixed?* Our team fields all of that and we do it for one flat price per PC, per month."

The Elite PC package that provides the new computer is less than $70 a month. The Elite Network that deals only with networking equipment like firewalls, etc., is under $150 a month. And similar to a cell phone plan, every third year when clients renew their subscription, LeewardBA provides a new computer, sets it up, then wipes the data off the old model and properly disposes of it.

"To really drive home the value we wrapped that with a virtual chief information officer that is there to not only address technical issues but serves as an IT strategist," Michael says. "So a business owner can call and spitball ideas. *Hey, we're thinking about acquiring another branch, and*

Michael Polzin

this accounting software isn't quite cutting it for us anymore. What's hot in the market that we should be looking at? We do not bill hourly for the consulting; that's provided as part of the package to help small businesses make the best possible decisions and investments in their technology. So instead of trying to go out and make their own hardware acquisitions or having to work with multiple vendors for support and software, with LeewardBA they get a concierge-type experience at a price point that just completely blows it out of the water compared to others. And that allows the business owners to concentrate on what they do best."

Humans are probably hard-wired to be suspicious when a deal seems almost too good to be true, and Michael admits that some clients have questioned why he would be so eager to help out small businesses. The short answer is, what's good for a small business client will eventually be good for LeewardBA.

"When people ask what's in it for me to lower their monthly bill, I explain that if I can make their technology less of a barrier and lower the money they spend to operate their business, my hope is that they are going to invest and grow from a five, ten, fifteen employee company to a one hundred or one thousand employee company because now we're the trusted advisor with a deep relationship, and we'll grow with them. It is so much easier to grow our business with current clients than it is to go out and snag new business. It's a much different sales cycle and marketing cycle. So why wouldn't we provide that type of comprehensive service and embed that chief information officer instead of nickel-and-dime? I don't want our customers to be strained for cash. I want our customers to be enabled for success. And then we all win and grow together."

It's a philosophy honed partly from Michael's years in IT consulting and partly from his own unique career path that proves you don't need to be a Wharton grad to succeed in business. You just need a strong work ethic, some opportunity, and a little faith. Michael grew up in Waukegan, Illinois, located on the shores of Lake Michigan about forty-five miles north of Chicago.

"Growing up in Waukegan, I didn't necessarily have the best launch into a career," he says with a laugh. "I had some difficulties in high school and ended up dropping out as a junior. I completed high school later through a little Sally Struthers correspondence school where you get your degree over the phone. I did that not too long after I dropped out so I'd have a diploma. But when hitting the job market, I had zero college experience."

He did, however, know a little something about computers, and his first jobs were entry-level positions at small IT companies. What opened the employment door further was passing a Microsoft certification test, which led to a job at Allstate.

"I didn't necessarily blow my salary out of the water the first year," Michael recalls. "But I certainly progressed at a very appreciable rate over the next several years."

While at Allstate, Michael enrolled in a continued education program and earned his associate's degree.

"It wasn't necessarily required, but as I was moving through the management and leadership track at Allstate, it occurred to me that if I was going to advance to a senior manager or vice president level, then at some point not having a degree would become a barrier, so that was a proactive move on my part. But then Microsoft came along so I stopped at the two-year degree and didn't pursue a four-year."

Working for Microsoft as a consultant took Michael all across the country troubleshooting.

"I would go in anywhere from a couple of weeks to my longest engagement was nine months at Wells Fargo. But all of them were based on the same concept: either teach a process improvement concept or come up with a roadmap of improvements to get their IT department operating more effectively and more efficiently."

Michael says he eventually left Microsoft because he was getting an entrepreneurial itch. Over the years he had dabbled in some small entrepreneurial ventures while also a salaried employee and ultimately decided he wanted to give being his own boss more of a full-time shot than just a fun side-hustle. He says he took a break from technology and started pursuing a passion project in completely different type of business.

"I guess you could say I'm a yachtsman. I like piloting big boats, so I pursued the purchase of a boat storage and service company where I would get to play with boats for the rest of my life. That did not pan out. So I was like: *Oh, crap; I've got to go back to work for a living again.*"

He took a one-year position with another IT company in Madison, Wisconsin, which he calls his light-bulb going off moment.

"Whereas Allstate was a large enterprise, and all my Microsoft customers were significantly-sized enterprises, that company serviced primarily the mid-market. And I was seeing the same patterns of problems here that I had seen at Microsoft, meaning the problems crossed industries, geography, and customer types. I had never actually thought about taking my existing domain of IT knowledge and creating an entrepreneurial role for it. Up to then I was always trying to doing something entrepreneurial off that beaten path. What the light bulb going off illuminated was: *There's a big blue ocean of mid-market companies and an even bigger ocean of small businesses that need IT solutions.* And that's really where the idea to build LeewardBA came from."

Michael set out to take his twenty-plus years' experience in IT operations and build a playbook. "Instead of going into a company and trying to get their IT department up to that level of maturity, what if I established my own IT department that could walk into any company with a playbook that delivered those services to a smaller mid-sized customer. And that's how it came together."

Once he had his *Eureka!* moment, Michael says it just seemed so obvious a path. "It's like the paperclip; why didn't everybody invent the paperclip because it now seems so obvious. But at the time it just hadn't clicked that although every mid-sized and small business can't afford the big-ticket prices that Microsoft will charge, but they still need these kinds of services."

But they needed them in a more structured way than simply getting periodic computer support. So Michael says he and two partners sat around his dining room table and hammered out a business plan.

"We took a step back and looked at what the opportunity was, assessed the risk a little bit but not too much. It's a fine line for entrepreneurs between being bold and being crazy. So we took the step forward. It was more of a leap of faith that it was a smooth transition, but it really came together quickly."

They named the company Leeward, which Michael explains is a nautical term for being on the protected side. "Our general concept is that we protect and shelter our customers from the complexity of technology so they can really stay focused on the mission of their business, and we take care of the rest."

From the beginning, the culture of LeewardBA has stressed relationships and communication, lessons Michael says he learned during his years consulting for Fortune 500 companies. "While positional leadership is great and all, more times than not it's really relational and service leadership that makes a difference. A company like Wells Fargo would hire me as a consultant, and even though their employees didn't report to me, I still had to make the changes happen and make the improvements take root in a very short amount of time. So to do that, I needed to really work for all the employees, meet them where they were at, understand their concerns and needs, get them aligned to support the changes and own it because I had to walk away and go onto the next engagement. I didn't get to stay there for five years and make it happen. I had to plant the seeds and get them to run with it. So servant leadership is definitely a consistent theme and tenet into what we do here at LeewardBA."

While setting up LeewardBA, Michael continued working at the consulting firm, which led to helping build the company's initial customer base.

"We were fortunate. When that light bulb moment occurred, the company was making some changes to their portfolio services. That resulted in me having contact with clients the company no longer had interest in servicing. So I had some conversations with these prospects and a handful of them started doing business with LeewardBA right away."

Another part of the LeewardBA culture is strong ties to the local community, which has turned into a business development channel.

"It happened serendipitously," Michael says. "Early on some folks at our company made a connection with a local charter school via a small business networking group. The school didn't have a lot of money to spend on technology, so there wasn't any business we could do with them. But they were very interested in creating experiences for their

students, like computer clubs and Hour of Code, which expands students coding opportunities. And we certainly have a passion for serving our community as well as in our industry."

A common challenge for any start-up can be finding staff with the needed skill sets.

"So this opportunity is standing in front of us now where not only can we immediately give back to the community as a small and growing business, but we could also start to prime the pump because as we grew we were going to need more and more staff. And the earlier we interact with students and get them onto a technology track and have a relationship, over time that can develop into potential employment opportunities."

LeewardBA now partners with a number of different schools in several cities, and Michael is on the executive committee for Building Our Future, an organization that focuses on uniting the community to improve education results. LeewardBA also helps sponsor an event called Harborfest where nonprofits set up exhibits to get more public exposure.

"There is no way small nonprofits have the budget to throw a big event every year, so we've helped created an event for all of them."

A side consequence of choosing to build partnerships instead of trying to "sell" is that LeewardBA has no sales force.

"We tried that once for about a year and saw zero results," Michael says. "So now we are just everywhere all the time, doing the best that we can with the resources we have to give back and be present in our community. And next thing you're at a board of directors meeting and somebody sitting across from you says: *Oh, you guys do IT services, don't you?* And that leads into a conversation that leads to an opportunity, and away we go. It's been a very profound way to grow. So the idea of corporate citizenship and community support and buy-in is a passion of ours. And it's special and unique that we can put it on our balance sheet as one of our primary sales channels. So we will keep investing in it, our staff and I will continue spending time in the community with these nonprofit and educational groups and get both the benefit of giving and receiving because it does have a direct business value tie in."

Michael stresses that the difference is one of involvement. Whereas many organizations' involvement ends with signing a check then writing the donation off at the end of the year, Michael and his LeewardBA team put in personal time with the community, communicating and building personal relationships.

"It's not a write off for us. It's an actual investment in our community and has benefit back to our business. It's a pretty powerful life-cycle."

While many tech entrepreneurs head for the coasts to establishing IT hubs, Michael hopes his success with LeewardBA will help convince other home-grown companies to stay in the area. He grew up in Illinois and has lived in Wisconsin most of his adult life, so leaving to headquarter LeewardBA elsewhere wasn't on the board.

"While location may be a challenge for LeewardBA's continued growth, I also see it as an opportunity for us," Michael says. "There is a large rate of brain drain in this Midwest area. Our competitors struggle to find employees. But at any point in time, we usually have two to three people on a waiting list that have done an internship or done some computer clubs with us. But through our school initiatives, like a cyber competition with all-girl groups in middle school, we're building our own organic pipeline that combats that brain drain, which is not only good for the local economy but is especially good for us because it allows us to keep pace with our business growth without fighting tooth-and-nail over everybody else's preexisting employees."

Nowhere is the adage that imitation is the sincerest form of flattery more true than in business. But in this case, Michael says he wishes more of his competition would embrace LeewardBA's community-centric model.

Michael Polzin at new office

"I beg them to do what we're doing because it's good for the community, and I still can't get them to come along," he says. "We created a pretty cool initiative called Start IT that we did in partnership with two other manufacturing companies: Modine Manufacturing and Twin Desk. The CIO from both of those organizations and I put our heads together to focus on helping disadvantaged youth who are significantly underemployed or not employed at all. We put together a partnership with Gateway Technical College and the local Workforce Development board. We've run two cohorts so far where we've taken folks living in poverty and in some cases homeless, sponsored them through a sixteen-week training boot camp, then secured them a six-month paid internship with a local company. A good percentage of them have gone on from that to have full-time employment."

The result was in just two years the initiative helped people go from poverty or homelessness to working a full-time role in an IT career pathway. But Michael says the biggest challenge to keeping the initiative alive is finding companies willing to participate and offer internships to those individuals who've gone through the IT boot camp.

"These companies are just not getting it," Michael says in frustration. "They're looking for college grads but the local college grads are looking to get the hell out of here. So we're trying to back that bus way up by finding people who need an opportunity and don't have the means to get out of here. More to the point, let's create a career opportunity for them so they don't have to get out of here, which solves multiple problems at once. So is our competition imitating us? No, and I wish they would. I really wish they would open their doors less discriminately than they are now and create these opportunities. Anything we can do to build that pipeline is good for everybody."

Another reason such opportunities are vital is that many companies won't look at a candidate unless they have a college degree. Michael notes that the days of a Microsoft certificate being enough to get a job are long gone.

"Right now in today's market, if I was to go and apply for a director or vice president position at any other company, they'd look at me and my lack of a four-year degree and say: *No thanks; we're not interested.* I wouldn't even make it through the résumé screening process, and that's despite the profound hands-on experience I have and all the things I did during my time at Microsoft and my time at Allstate. So that informs our culture here. We're not all about formal education. We certainly don't discredit the value of it but we also recognize that not everybody, myself included, takes the traditional path to success. We're very open and welcoming about that. We've been very well-served and supported by employees whose higher education path was just not for them. But they have learned the technical skills that are needed here at a fantastic pace, so we have zero regrets about making them part of our family."

As Michael points out, rarely do college graduates show up for a job ready to hit the ground running. There is still a training period and learning curve to go through that can take years.

"I think the whole world has gone mad. In what parallel universe does somebody think that a resource who has been trained to pass a test is then going to come into a real-world career path and be able to dynamically and with agility respond to the critical thinking challenges put before them?"

Michael has a theory on what has changed socially and culturally for many people—a lack of basic, foundational life skills.

"Not that long ago kids would have paper routes in grade school; they would get part-time jobs throughout high school that you had to interview for, where you had a boss, and learned how to balance a checkbook and manage money because either your parents taught you or your bank showed you. Then you went to college to add the theory on top of your life experience—and probably worked while going to college. Now more often than not, I encounter four-year college grads who have no work experience and lack basic skills."

Michael believes the opportunity for kids getting work experience in their formative years is almost completely gone because of the current state of the economy—or more specifically, the cost of living.

"The jobs that used to be available for high schoolers are gone because adults need them to pay the bills. And the education system has not caught on en mass to bring that real-world, project-based learning, critical thinking skills, hands-on problem-solving to students. Some schools do, but it's just not pervasive enough yet in our education system to make up for that change in the market. That's one reason why our initiatives have struck such a chord in the community. Students just eat this stuff alive and are so much more engaged when it's hands-on and when you present them a problem without the answer. And in some cases we present them a problem that we don't know the answer to so we've got to figure it out together and they learn troubleshooting and triage and critical thinking on the fly. It's been great to see that impact. Again the theory there is that becomes a pool of employees who will be available to us in the next couple of years here as we keep growing."

Despite its growth, LeewardBA still primarily operates out of its Kenosha office and there are no current plans to change that dynamic.

"As far as opening new offices and spreading out, yes, I have an interest to do that," Michael says. "I'd love to be like somewhere on the

Chesapeake with a boat, so maybe I'll find a way to get an office there at some point. But as it relates to our company's growth, it's not required that we do a satellite office. We do have a couple of our staff in the field, so that spreads us up into the Madison, Wisconsin area. We also have data centers in Chicago, Milwaukee, and Madison for our mid-market and larger customers that want us to host their servers—basically like a cloud service but regionally located. We don't have staff in those buildings; we're just on contract with people to operate those data centers and do remote for us."

LeewardBA Elite is a nationwide service offering, so the company has partnerships with a field operations team that has staff in all major metropolitan areas throughout the US.

"For example, we support all 750 retail locations for Batteries Plus Bulbs from Hawaii to Puerto Rico. One of the beauties of the industry that we're in is that very seldom do you need to physically be there to solve a problem. On the very few and rare occasions that we can't fix an issue over the phone by remoting in via the Internet, then we simply leverage that partnership contract and dispatch a certified technician based on whatever the scope of the issue is. They coordinate with our team here to be the boots on the ground and hands-on resource in the field."

While LeewardBA is currently a well-oiled machine, Michael knows the only constant for a successful entrepreneur is change.

"I don't think there's any such thing as stable ground for any business let alone the entrepreneurial small business space. The world around us is constantly changing, so we have no intention of just staying a great IT company. We will continue to be an excellent partner and service provider to our customers' needs and will continue to develop the solutions that meet those needs. So exactly where that takes us, whether it's three years or thirty years from now, I can't say for absolute certainty. But what I can say is that our model is based on being an adviser and a problem solver, which allows us to be agile at our core so that we can respond to those shifts in the markets very quickly. And that won't change."

Ribbon cutting at new office.

MCI

Here's a fun fact: The first switchboard operators were teenage boys prone to swearing and snarkiness, which explains why the early phone companies opted for unflappable female operators. Over the years manual phone exchanges have gone the way of blacksmiths and cobblers, and today's call centers are children of the Internet, cloud technology, and artificial intelligence, enabling a smorgasbord of features including automatic display of a caller's information, call routing, speech analytics, and interactive voice response. (*For billing, press 2...*)

It's one thing to have the technology, quite another to use it effectively and innovatively to meet the strategic needs of clients across multiple industries, something Anthony Marlowe has been doing consistently since he made the leap from college telemarketer to call center entrepreneur. In 2003 Anthony founded TM*one*, later renamed Mass Markets, which today under its multi-branch holding company MCI, provides inbound and outbound contact center services, telesales, digital services customer relationship management, and omnichannel customer services such as phone, text, chat, email, and social. Its growth has been prodigious, making the Inc. 5000 list of fastest-growing companies ten times, peaking at No. 452 nationwide, which was good enough to be the No. 1 fastest-growing company in its home state of Iowa.

"We've scaled from a humble, five-thousand-square-foot contact center with under fifty employees to more than 2,000 employees across nine contact center facilities," Anthony says.

Unlike the switchboards and PBXes of yesteryear, MCI does much more than simply connect businesses with their clients and customers. As the company website notes, "It enables business-to-business (B2B) and business-to-consumer (B2C) interactions across a wide range of industries, offering a unique combination of business process support and innovative technological frameworks" for enterprises large and small, from Fortune 100 corporations to emerging start-ups.

With twenty years of call center customer contact management, business process outsourcing, digital services, and telecommunications experience, Anthony is not exactly an overnight success. And while he didn't grow up with this particular career in mind, he is the poster child for recognizing an opportunity and going for it.

"I'm a guy from the suburbs of Chicago who wasn't the best student, preferring things like playing guitar and working on fast cars with my friends," he says, summing up his teen experience. "My mom asked me what I wanted to do when I graduated high school. I said: *I'm going to stick around here.* She said something along the lines of: *Pack your stuff now. I am getting you a U-Haul this weekend. You're going to go live with your brother and going to school at the University of Iowa. I'm not asking you; I'm telling you. You are not going to stay here and end up parking cars or something for the rest of your life.* It was some tough love, but she told me later she went upstairs afterward and cried because it meant I was leaving."

After a few months enjoying life in a college town, courtesy of the $200 a month his mom was sending him every month, she called and said: *You must get a job,* so Anthony took a job as a telemarketer at MCI Communications, at the time was in its pre-WorldCom days. At one point MCI Communications was the second-largest long-distance provider in the United States, back when people primarily relied on landlines. MCI was a renegade company that took on AT&T, claiming it

Anthony Marlowe

was a monopoly, which was later confirmed by the Supreme Court. Consumers had no choice over their phone service. In 1982 the courts eventually agreed, leading to the break-up of AT&T, then the world's biggest company and largest private telephone system that had provided local telephone service in the United States and Canada up to that point. Pick one. AT&T—also called *Ma Bell* because it was originally established by Alexander Graham Bell—was broken up into seven regional companies, the so-called Baby Bells. Along with the breakup of AT&T, consumers were given the right to choose their long-distance carrier, which started intense competition for customers.

"MCI wrote the book on telemarketing," Anthony says. "They had eighteen call centers of nine thousand agents in the mass markets division."

At that time a million people a day were switching back and forth between AT&T and MCI and then Sprint when it joined the telecommunications party. Each offered consumers various discounted deals for long distance—*Friends and Family*, five-cent (a minute) Sundays, ten-cent night calls—to entice people to switch their service.

"So I was trying to get people to sign up for MCI long distance, and for the first three weeks, I sucked at it," Anthony cheerfully admits. "Then I realized asking people to just give it a try could be a very simple equation. All I needed to do was get a couple of yesses, and almost overnight I began ranking not only number one in our call center but in the top tenth of a percent throughout MCI."

Anthony's epiphany was realizing there was power in keeping it simple. "It wasn't like in the *Matrix*; I didn't start seeing zeros and ones computing in my head. This wasn't computer coding. It was a matter of quickly capturing the person's attention by asking a couple of simple questions, which enabled me to make telemarketing something that was simple to do."

Anthony says the phone industry has changed since then. "The kind of marketing I did back then is only a tiny fraction of what is now known as the business process outsourcing (BPO) the industry currently does. Today it's about calling existing customers and upgrading and getting people to call you. But back then it went something like this: *Hi, Anthony Marlowe here from MCI. How are you doing today? What do you think of that $4.95 minimum fee AT&T is charging you whether you use their service or not? MCI doesn't have that minimum fee, and our rates are lower, so your bill will be less every month. All I need to get you started today is to verify your address. You're still at 123 Sample Blvd, right?*

Consumers proved hugely un-loyal to any particular long-distance service, so if it cost less, people would gladly switch, especially when there was an incentive or promotion involved. Anthony was offering people the opportunity to save money for something they were already using. His approach worked, and he quickly rose through the ranks.

By the time Anthony was twenty-two, he was overseeing more than two hundred telemarketers as an operations manager and became the youngest member of management to be inducted into the MCI Communications Hall of Fame. The company also presented Anthony with Best of the Best and MVP awards for his record work as a sales supervisor in the company's Arlington, Virginia, International Contact Center Services hub as he was rising through the ranks.

But WorldCom was teetering. In 1997 MCI had agreed to merge with WorldCom, run by flamboyant CEO Bernie Ebbers, to form MCI

WorldCom. Ebbers had turned WorldCom into the nation's second-largest long-distance telecommunications company through a series of rapid acquisitions that also left it heavily in debt. In 2002 MCI WorldCom filed for bankruptcy after admitting to improperly reporting $3.8 billion in expenses. The Justice Department opened a criminal investigation into its business practices while the Securities Exchange Commission focused on $400 million that WorldCom personally loaned Ebbers. The company's stock price tumbled from $64 per share to a little over $1. (Three years later a jury convicted Ebbers of securities fraud and other crimes, and he was sentenced to twenty-five years in a minimum-security Louisiana prison.)

Anthony saw the writing on the wall, and after four years at MCI, knew it was time to get out of Dodge and start his own company. In 2003 he co-founded TMone, a business process outsourcing (BPO) company, and served as its CEO. In 2007 *Inc. Magazine* recognized Anthony as one of the twenty-five youngest CEOs in America. By 2013 TMone had ranked on the Inc.5000 list of America's fastest-growing companies for eight consecutive years.

In 2013 he and his partner sold the company to Enhanced Recovery Company. Anthony provides the *Reader's Digest* version of why. "The first reason is that somebody was willing to pay us a boatload of money. The second is there was pending legislation during the Obama Administration that would hamper our business in terms of healthcare costs and other anti-business regulations, which we saw as something that could potentially collapse our margins. We ultimately decided that we wanted to pull most of our chips off the table, so to speak."

Two years later Anthony bought TMone back, this time as a sole proprietor under his wholly-owned holding company, Marlowe Companies, Inc., and renamed the company Mass Markets, another homage to his tenure as a young telemarketer in the MCI call center. (*Mass markets* was the business unit that handled MCI Communications' sales and customer service.) But the new branding was part of a larger strategy, not simply a marketing exercise: Mass Markets would operate a network of domestic call center and managed information services locations.

In the years since he founded TMone, the company has evolved into a more full-service enterprise services provider. In addition to providing database and infrastructure services, especially relating to cloud computing, Mass Markets provided and managed more software, particularly in the customer experience, digital experience space.

"We developed and integrated a pretty substantial suite of software that we started to provide to the market, with or without staff support," Anthony says. His plan for Mass Markets also included developing more software internally and acquiring other companies with those capabilities.

In a 2015 article Anthony noted, "This is maybe where people are confused locally who think I'm just trying to put a spin on a call center. It wouldn't be the first time I was underestimated. But we will also leverage the Mass Markets platform to grow and support our own software as a service and applications business, which includes software that we have already developed in-house, and software apps we were acquiring.

"I'm launching Mass Markets to help companies reduce the costs of doing business by participating in the combined management of information services and the modernization of telecommunications. No one can aggregate, develop, procure, and manage this type of platform in the United States as efficiently as we can, so we're optimistic the company will have continued growth."

And it has. Today he notes, "From the time I bought back my company, it has gone from literally a couple hundred people to 2000 people. It's gone from $15 million in revenue to what we're projecting will be more than $100 million in 2020 or 2021."

Anthony's portfolio has also grown accordingly. Self-described serial entrepreneur, he's founded several companies that have distinct synergy. In addition to Marlowe Companies, Inc., Anthony owns MBM Developments, a commercial real estate firm that owns some of MCI's locations; software company Gravis Apps, bought in 2016 to bolster Mass Markets' technological capabilities; and Iowa City Capital Partners (ICCP), his private office, which was the sole sponsor to launch the MCI roll-up strategy.

"For a period of time, ICCP made minority investments in other businesses, but I quickly learned I wasn't a big fan of that because of how people would forego my advice based on someone's social media footprint or because they spent time in Silicon Valley," Anthony says. "I said: *Enough with focusing on other investments; I'm going to use ICCP to invest in companies that Anthony Marlowe runs and controls.* As a result, ICCP is MCI's largest shareholder."

Today MCI owns and controls five operating companies GravisApps, the Sydney Call Centre, OnBrand24, Valor Intelligent Processing, and Mass Markets, with plans to acquire a few more in the near future.

"Making the top five hundred of the Inc. 5000 in an amazing feat. It's been a tremendous ride; I can't thank my team enough," Anthony says, and he calls running MCI and its holdings his main job, which takes approximately seventy-five hours a week. "The companies all have things going on—multiple acquisitions at different stages, multiple business developments, new client opportunities at different stages, multiple internal initiatives—so I have to deal with what are the most pressing issues that day. I've never

had the same day. Sure, there might be the same conference call every morning with the same key executives, but not one day has ever been the same as another. Never. But I find life kind of has a way of self-prioritizing."

Which in Anthony's case boils down to two main categories.

"If I'm not sleeping, I'm working," he laughs. "Today I did spend time with Julia, my wife. She understands what we are all working toward, and moments like saving the call center in Sydney, Nova Scotia, make it all worth it." But he acknowledges, "Massive ambition is tough on non-work life, time for health, friends, etc., but she's very supportive and amazingly understanding of how ambitious I am and believes in my passions."

One of which is Anthony's commitment to his employees. "I am deeply passionate about teaching people how to succeed as BPO, DXP, sales, software, operations, IT, call center, and customer service professionals. When you are part of the MCI team, you are part of a legacy of hardworking, creative, and fun people who come together every day with the drive to make an impact on themselves, their teammates, and the growing organization."

A large percentage of workers that work at MCI either move up within MCI or further their careers outside of MCI, a major stepping stone. And that includes himself. As such Anthony says his fiduciary responsibility and primary job as CEO is to always look at what's the most upside for MCI shareholders as well as his employees.

"So, sure, my day is consumed partially by what's on fire this month, this week, this day, this hour. But my number one goal is driving as much value as possible. That was true when I made my first telemarketing sale in March of 1998 to now creating wealth and increased opportunities for thousands of people. We've got going on two thousand employees. Add to the average family size is three or four people, and that's a lot of people. So it's a big responsibility, but the ambition drives us."

As Anthony points out, success requires a lot of work and quality workers. "Our ambition is highly demanding, especially on the key contributors. We maintain a small core people who have the weight of the world on their shoulders and their sacrifices go beyond eight- to ten-hour days. The people that are best in their jobs tend to be the ones that others in the organization lean on because they're dependable, reliable, fast, and get stuff done. The way we generate revenue is via services, so without employees working hard, making and taking phone calls, and having high-quality interactions with our clients, customers, and prospects, there is no revenue."

Anthony says that while he's not involved with hiring on a frontline level, he is when it comes to management. "Especially senior management, I'm involved. There's something in call centers that's very unique from other businesses. You can be from any background, any level of education, with previous experience or not, and find your way in the call center business. Some of the most successful operators, executives, and managers found their way in this environment. Let's face it; it's not Morgan-Stanley. But it's a business where people can find their confidence and work their way up. A lot of people find tremendous careers in this space— regardless of who they are or what they look like—because they're good at it. Further, call centers aren't just a huge industry in the United States; business process outsourcing is probably approaching a trillion globally."

Technology has fueled a lot of that growth. Anthony believes that interactive voice response was the first truly transcendent moment in the industry. The second was e-commerce.

"Sure, bots and AI are increasing, but the real revolution is that so many companies that used to be brick and mortar and wholesale-driven are now going direct to consumer (D2C). Because of the D2C revolution, we have clients you wouldn't have heard of with online stores selling $50 million dollars of goods. Because they have to field thousands of calls every day, they spend a million or  two a year on contact center services, such as an IVR, a bot for simple questions, and a live agent for more complex issues. We also handle their chat, email, credit authorization, inbound sales, and returns. You'd be shocked at the amount of business processing opportunities coming out of mid-tier e-commerce companies."

Anthony admits it's been a challenge educating their clients about all the technological services MCI now offers. "Some would seek other vendors for that and spend a lot more money than necessary. I'd call and ask them: *What are you doing? What you spent a $100,000 on, we could have provided for a tenth of the cost.* But for all the technology, there's still going to be agents behind the AI. You might not need two hundred people to do your customer service anymore; you might only need one hundred now. However, those one hundred people are still sitting behind your bot to finish the interaction should it be unable to provide the answer."

While advancing technology will help all call centers become ever more efficient, the most successful companies will continue to have the best management, strategy, and culture regardless of market trends or smart systems.

"In our industry there's a lot of consolidation," Anthony notes. "All these companies tend to buy competitors then like to slash and burn the brand that they've acquired. I take a different approach. The brands of the companies I buy have been successful. They have their own culture. They have their own customer base. And they have different verticals they service and different products and services they perform. So where some in our industry are just business process outsourcing companies that focus on call centers, MCI is a multi-faceted, tech-enabled, business process outsourcing company that is also a customer experience provider and a digital experience provider. So we have software, we have call centers, we have tools, and we have managed services making us a one-stop shop for any company's diverse needs. We were very late to the nearshore/offshore call center trend, but we're not skipping the trend in digital transcending automation and modernization. Our software offering puts us at an advantage ahead of that curve."

Anthony says MCI also rejected the industry trend of competing for temporary project work, preferring to partner with companies that need help starting or maintaining ongoing programs, which are longer-term and more stable.

"As a result we typically don't charge for setup or implementation costs, making it up over time in the form of inclusive pricing. You see these other companies focused too much on vertical concentration, and they get in trouble. We have different companies that specialize in different verticals, and that enables us to have customer and vertical diversity, dependability, and sustainability."

While Anthony has found professional strength in diversity, on a personal level he finds fulfillment in mentoring, with both strangers and employees.

"I mentor my staff, particularly spending a lot of bandwidth on the operations management roles. I've thought that once I get to the point in time where perhaps I'm thinking about retiring or not playing as active of a role—in five years, twenty years—who knows?—I would absolutely plan on mentoring. It's a very cool experience.

"I was twenty-three when I started my first company, and I quickly got a taste of real life. The government regulations, policies, and administrative red tape was a little bit shocking—the triennial review order, the telemarketing sales rule—we had to figure these things out quickly. I pride myself on never having any kind of violation or inquiry in almost twenty years, we play, and always will play, by the book."

Anthony also tells entrepreneurs to carefully consider any potential business partners.

"A lot of people want to have a partner or partners, but they're not easy. Just like half of marriages fail, half of business partnerships go sideways too. To offload risk they go into a partnership saying: *You do this; I'll do that.* Early on, especially in younger companies, I think that's helpful, but when things really take off, it can sometimes become difficult because people grow in different directions. Making it more problematic is that the partner you've been in the trenches with is often a family member or close friend. If you're not on the same page, how do you contemplate making a fiduciary decision that will aggravate your best friend? Companies really need to predefine a plan of what happens when things take off, who oversees the decision to stay organic or add non-organic growth to the mix. If there's a 50-50 partnership and it's never decided early on where the buck stops, a lot of value could be left on the table, with too much time spent on partner relations. Every company needs a clear chief executive officer, someone has to have the final say."

Lastly, Anthony believes a lot of success is a matter of finding the right position that best fits your personality and life experience. "I was the youngest of three siblings, and my brothers were much older than me. They were of college age before I was in high school, so I always got dragged to adult situations. And we are of Greek heritage, which is where I'm sure I inherited my work ethic and skill for making a business. I know my mom and her Uncle Alec (Papastavrou) Papastavros, really had an influence me in terms of my work ethic, perseverance, and ambition."

He also played hockey and found there was something empowering about playing a contact sport with equipment.

"If you have a helmet and facemask on and someone punches you in the face and you don't feel it, all of a sudden you're not so scared walking down the street. So interacting with adults, being able to take a lick and realizing that I'm going to live, and having just enough ADHD, ended up being the formula for me to be successful when I stumbled into the call center where I was trained in sales."

Anthony notes that he's been selling telecommunications service directly or indirectly for the last twenty years, taking the opportunity and turning a part-time job he originally took for beer money while pretending to be in college into a $100 million-plus company.

"Having been on the phones and having done just about every role in this business means I'm able to speak from experience. Also, when you have an understanding of what it's like on the ground in the trenches, that goes a long way in my interactions with employees, clients, and just about any department, internally or externally. But in the end, success just has to do with energy, urgency, and not being afraid to try things, do things, or ask for things. In order to have a business, you have to have revenue, in order to have revenue someone needs to sell something. Some people make sales,

and some make excuses. If you're too scared to pick up the phone and pitch your product or service or too scared to leverage your network to get a meeting with a buyer or investor, forget about it. I don't know why so many people are so timid in life. One day the magnetic field could be weak, and the sun could sneeze and turn us into Mars overnight, so pick up the phone already, get that meeting, handle that objection. In business *no* means try harder or a different way the next time."

The best entrepreneurs have a knack for looking around social, technological, and cultural corners to identify coming trends or opportunities. And one of today's biggest bullseyes is the green rush brought about by individual states' rapid legalization of cannabis. By 2020 it is expected that fifteen states plus the District of Columbia will have legalized recreational adult use. Thirty-three states, plus DC, already have legalized cannabis for medical use.

Research firm ArcView Group reports that legal marijuana is the fastest-growing industry in the United States. And IMARC reports that the North America legal cannabis market was worth more than $10 billion in 2018, and was expected to reach $43.19 billion by 2024.

That's a lot of smoke.

No emerging industry is an island. As it grows, so do adjacent businesses. In the case of cannabis that includes a broad spectrum of career options such as specialized legal firms, new medical research, planting products such as environmentally-friendly greenhouses, hydroponics trade schools, cannabis-inspired restaurants, and cannabis-infused drinks.

One of the more integral needs for both cannabis distributors and consumers has been effective packaging that kept the cannabis fresh, was Earth-friendly, and passed the smell test, as it were. Founded by Scott Martin on 2013, N2 Packaging Systems' patented process of packaging legal cannabis involves hermetically sealing lined, food-grade, containers after they have been flushed with liquid nitrogen to create an air-tight and completely odorless package. N2's containers come in various materials: metal, plastic, and reclaimed paper from recycling centers. While the nitrogen process does not alter the product, it does eliminate the two main enemies of freshness: light and oxygen.

Scott notes, "Our goal is to ensure that the time and money invested in the cultivation process is preserved so that a quality product is delivered to the end consumer. The time, effort, and money it takes from seed-to-sale are all wasted if the end product is delivered to the customer damaged or destroyed. So we feel that packaging is one of the most important steps in the process. If you put perfectly cured product in our can, you can expect a perfectly cured product when you crack the seal."

N2's patent-pending, child-resistant lid, which has been certified by an independent testing lab, also enables the can to hold multiple doses or servings and remain child safe.

"We also care deeply about child safety, compliance issues, and the environmental impact of packaging, so our product delivers on all those fronts," Scott says.

In the entrepreneurial world people find any number of unique ways to get their business off the ground. Pitching their idea to investors, maxing out their credit cards and home lines of equity, or tapping family members for loans are all tried and true avenues. Semi-stalking a celebrity ... not so much. But taking a page from the desperate-times-call-for-desperate-measures handbook was the unique approach Scott used to get his product noticed by someone uniquely positioned to promote it—Willie Nelson.

#

Prior to starting N2, Scott was a money guy. After selling his mortgage company in 2013, he did private financing, which was when his career took an unexpected turn.

"I was approached about a $65,000 loan by an inventor who had

Scott Martin

previously patented a system for packaging of ammunition in a hermetically sealed container with a modified atmosphere," Scott says. "He had duplicated that patented system and tied it to packaging federally controlled substances, such as cannabis. I knew nothing about the cannabis world or packaging, so I started researching and found that one of the main problems in the cannabis space is that it's a rapidly degrading product, which is why the modified atmosphere packaging had the potential to be a huge solution for the industry. I also saw that it was a very environmentally-conscious group."

Scott says that after reviewing the application, he didn't feel like it would be a good loan. But he was intrigued by the potential of the inventors' sought-after new patent.

"So I made an agreement to give him the $65,000 with the following terms: if we received the patent, we were partners; if we didn't receive the patent, then he didn't have to pay me back anything."

With Scott essentially Godfathering the inventor by making an offer he couldn't refuse, the deal was sealed. Scott says he took about five minutes to come up with the name N2 Packaging, then he established an LLC, transferred the patent application, and gave the inventor the funds. In 2014 they were issued the original patent. And that's how Scott, a self-described fairly conservative person, found himself the owner of a cannabis packaging company—and a bit out of his element.

First, the legal cannabis industry conducted in states—cannabis is still considered illegal by the federal government—is awash with regulations. "When I was in the mortgage industry, I operated my company through the Great Recession that started in 2007 and led to a host of new laws," Scott recalls. "In one year we had more than two hundred rule changes, making compliance and managing the intricacies of those changes incredibly demanding. So I figured if I could do that, then this was going to be very simple. Well, this has truly been one of the most difficult things I've ever encountered."

Then there was the struggle to get potential clients to consider his product. "My background was in finance. I literally thought: *If I can come to the industry and eliminate shelf life as one of their major issues and bring an environmentally friendly package, this is going to be a cakewalk.* I very quickly figured out that it absolutely was not," he says with a laugh. "When I first started making phone calls, there was such a negative response. I'd say: *We can eliminate your shelf-life concerns, and you can better manage your margins*, and the basic response for six months was: *Dude, I'm not gonna put my weed in your fucking cat food can.* I was so shocked. This solution was just not on their radar."

In retrospect, Scott thinks there were a number of reasons for the headwind. N2 started out in Oregon and Washington, where there was an abundance of supply, so the price had dropped. Also, many consumers still wanted to see the product.

"I think when we came to market, we were just a little early."

What Scott needed was an advocate/spokesperson/ to help the fledgling company get some traction. But who? He came across some articles about Willie's Reserve, a line of Willie Nelson branded marijuana products that, according to the ad copy, celebrate Willie's love of cannabis and the culture surrounding it.

"I'm from rural Idaho and a huge Willie Nelson fan," Scott says. "He's an icon in our area. So when I read that the Willie's Reserve brand was going to be available in multiple states in 2015, I thought: *What better way to promote our product than through someone like that?* Our packaging was perfect for product that would be shipped to multiple states because you could guarantee that your consumer is always going to have the same experience every time. You wouldn't have to worry about something being on a shelf somewhere drying out."

Imagining this would be a bit of a no-brainer, Scott confidently reached out. He sent several emails explaining the virtues of N2 and attached sample product pictures, even mocking-up a can with Willie's Reserve logo on it (complete with a *Sample* watermark).

"Basically, I was kind of stalking him," Scott says. "Ultimately, I ended up receiving what was basically a cease and desist letter, informing me: *Mr. Nelson has no interest. Do not try to contact Mr. Nelson. And do not use his likeness.* And basically let me know I'd be sued if I used his likeness to promote N2."

Legal threats notwithstanding, Scott wasn't ready to give up. "When I heard that Willie Nelson was coming to Nampa, Idaho, I bought a ticket, had some sample cans made up that said Willie's *Preserves* instead of *Reserves*, and snuck them into the concert."

In the package he added a note that said: *Mr. Nelson, I understand that I am not supposed to continue giving this to you, but I believe this is the best packaging medium for your brand.* Then Scott managed to get the package delivered backstage. Then he waited.

"I was hoping it didn't backfire on me. But then about two weeks later, I got a call from Willie's granddaughter. They loved the can—and had no idea I had been trying to get the sample cans to them. They connected us with the group that ran Willie's Reserve up in Washington. Someone from there called me, and after talking for about a half-hour, she said: *Next time you're in Seattle, bring up some samples.* I said: *I'm going to be there next week.* She said: *Well, don't make a special trip because it's not something we're going change direction on.* I said: *Oh, no; I'm going to be there.*"

Scott had some samples prepared and took them to the meeting, which was held in the top floor of an office building in downtown Seattle.

"We showed up with actual cans of cannabis. After we sat down with people from Willie's group, who were just staring at these cans."

Scott explains that if you package cannabis in a regular metal can, the moisture in the buds will fill the available area and condense on the walls. But nitrogen does not allow for the transfer of moisture, keeping the cannabis inside fresh, which is the biggest value proposition of the process. The packed can is also positively pressured.

"So we were sitting in that office and when they cracked open this can, one of their purchasers jerked as if hit in the face and exclaimed: *What the fuck was that?* He went out, brought everybody else in, and cracked open another can to show them. I had prepared a very basic presentation, but the purchaser said: *Here's the deal; we're going to bring in our other managers to meet you. But you need to do a real presentation.*"

Scott went back to Idaho, put together a proper presentation, then returned to Seattle and made their case to a roomful of managers. And Willie's Reserve integrated N2 into their line of packaging. But it was a random TV moment that may have helped N2 get over the hump. In 2016 Nelson was performing at a Farm Aid festival in Virginia, whose governor at the time was very anti-cannabis. As a news outlet observed:

Governor McAuliffe swung through to check it out, posing for a picture on the country icon's tour bus. There's a pretty well-understood if unspoken rule of common sense that if you get on Willie Nelson's tour bus, you're going to be around some weed. Somehow Virginia Governor Terry McAuliffe missed the memo.... What he failed to notice was the canister of Nelson's own brand of marijuana, Willie's Reserve, sitting right there on the table. Local ABC affiliate WRIC reached out to the governor's office for a comment and was told that McAuliffe was unaware of the drug's presence in the picture.

Willie Nelson and former Virginia governor, Terry McAuliffe. (N2 can circled)

More specifically, it was Willie's Reserve in N2 packaging. "He also posted a picture of his handwritten travel schedule that had one of the cans in it. It just seemed like those kinds of exposure were the big change for our company. Almost overnight people accepted our packaging. We went from nobody talking to us and struggling to get out there, to all of a sudden getting contacted from places all over the country. So Willie Nelson became a major part in the initial launching of our company. All from stalking him."

That didn't mean it was clear sailing and being able to kick back. Demand presented a new set of challenges.

"The reality is we hadn't built out our back end. So the equipment we started with was very poor. I still have our original piece of equipment, which was an old canning machine from the 1950s; we call it Shrek." Scott explains the business model is a supply agreement. "N2 doesn't do the packaging; we don't touch any product. What we do is set up a system in their facility, then they buy the cans from us."

The inventor did not have an active role in the company, so originally it was just Scott. Then in 2016 Mike Stanley became a partner in N2.

"He was one of the most valuable assets we brought in," Scott says. "I manage the sales, and he worked on designing and developing all of our equipment. It was just the two of us, so when we first started out, Mike and I were on the road with my truck and a trailer full of equipment, driving around and setting up all of our original customers with a guy we hired to do the actual installation. We had a lot of windshield time. Mike's son had a plane so we started flying. We were traveling every week in that little plane, bouncing around the West and meeting with customers."

Once they started to gain a foothold and acceptance into the industry, maintaining the ability to fulfill was another challenge because of the association with cannabis.

"I was always very straightforward to people about what we do," Scott says. "I didn't want to waste the time of setting something up and then hearing: *Hey, you're in cannabis.* It was a problem getting can manufacturers to work with us. We'd initially get the okay, but then within a very short period of time, we'd be eliminated."

There was also pushback at Scott personally. "I live in Idaho, and starting a cannabis company there was not super. I was at my son's basketball game in a nearby town. The auditorium was full. At half-time the assistant coach of my son's team came over, and in front of me, my wife, my wife's parents, and everybody else says: *Hey, I'm having a little trouble. How do I tell my son you're not a drug dealer?* It was very negative here."

So much so that Scott and his wife considered moving their family away from the area. In the end he stayed and kept plugging away, and eventually he found companies that would sell to N2, enabling the company to move forward. The next hurdle was defining the most effective business model. Scott says that originally they were supplying the equipment based on the clients' production volumes. But that didn't work on a couple of levels.

"We couldn't get any money as far as financing because we're in the cannabis space, and so we were funding these things ourselves. And the original seamers were so expensive; our cost was about $40,000. Then it was $20,000 for the doser. It just piled on. So every time we set up a system, we'd go backward about $60,000, and our goal was to make it up over time. But it really restricted our growth, so we started working with an equipment company called GTI. They supplied the equipment, and we paid them a monthly fee for every system out there."

N2 grew to where it had nearly thirty systems in place, paying that monthly fee for each. But the production numbers from its customers were so low that it wasn't offsetting the cost. So Scott says he forced the sale of GTI to N2 in October 2017.

"It was one of those tough things," he admits. "But the financials weren't penciling. After purchasing GTI we started selling the equipment to our clients. And from that point forward, things changed for us. We've been able to develop better equipment, we've been able to bring in other manufacturers and become distribution points for them. We've been able to offer better options to our customers who purchase the equipment. But the only reason our company is even in business today is that we continue to watch the regulated market. If we had just sat back and relied on that original patent, we'd be out of business."

One of the issues that came up right away after they made the deal with Willie's Reserve related to compliance. For them to integrate the can in Colorado, N2 needed a child-resistant lid. Scott assumed it would be a simple matter of going online and finding a supplier that would have one. He assumed wrong.

"I started searching all over and quickly realized: *Oh, shit; there's no such thing.* Of course there wasn't. Cans are for food. Nobody's ever needed to put anything in one that needed a child-resistant lid. So we started developing one."

Over the next ten months, they went through multiple designs for a child-resistant lid, developing several different styles before settling on the one they currently use. The lid went through the federal certification, which Scott says was an ordeal. The testing was done by a company in Salt Lake City that would take the can to a daycare and give a range of children five minutes to open it.

"They can literally do anything they want to remove the cap," Scott says. "They bite it, they stomp on it, they pull on it, throw it. If they can't remove it in five minutes, the testers then show the children how to remove it. At that point you need at least 80 percent of the kids to still be unable to open it."

Once the child-resistant portion is acceptable, then the cans are tested to see if they pass the senior-friendly test. For that part of the certification, they go to a retirement center and give the participating residents five minutes to open the can with no instruction.

"During the testing of a previous model, this lady rolled up on a little motorized cart and asked what we were doing. The tester handed her a can, and she started pulling up on it and ripped her thumbnail. It was horrible, and the tester announced: *Stop. We've got a bleeder.* So, they shut that down. Obviously, we had to go back and make some changes, but we eventually got our certifications. It was incredibly stressful, but our business depended on it, so we had to do it. Ultimately, every state will require child-resistant packaging. That's where everything will be as soon as the US Consumer Product Safety Commission starts overseeing the industry. Currently, not every state complies, but long-term that will be the case. We filed the patent once we got our lid operating, and by far it is our most valuable asset because that child-resistant lid has nothing to do with cannabis or controlled substances at all. It is simply a child-resistant lid for a seam-rolled can, that can be used by many other industries. For example, we've been contacted by people outside of the industry from beverage companies to an ammunition manufacturer looking for a child-resistant can. We've already sold millions of those lids."

Scott says N2's strategy has been to identify the direction they think the industry is going as they've continued to develop different applications and patents that expand the company's original patents.

"I'm thankful that we recognized early on we needed to push toward innovating, creating different styles of packaging, and branding out that intellectual property because that's what's sustained our company."

Perhaps the most ongoing issue for any business grouped under the cannabis umbrella is the inability to have a bank account. When US Bank found out that N2 provided packaging for cannabis—even though the company itself never bought, sold, or handled cannabis in any way—they shut down N2's banking accounts.

"They also shut down my other business's banking accounts and my personal accounts," Scott says. "They shut down my savings accounts for my kids. They shut down all of it and basically said: *We'll have a cashier's check for you*. And there was a delay between when they shut me down to when they actually gave me the check, so it was a difficult time. But we've continued to manage, and now we do have a very good banking relationship."

The same can't be said for many of N2's clients, who are still prohibited from having a business bank account because banks are governed by federal laws, and the federal government still considers all cannabis illegal.

"Managing their cash deposits is very difficult, so we are continuing to develop solutions on how to deal with the cash," Scott says. "Our thing is, when we receive cash, we deposit the full amount, however much it is. If it's a large deposit, that raises a red flag leading to a suspicious activity report. That's what triggers them to review who our customers are. And that's what led to us getting shut down. Luckily we've been able to kind of get some pretty good relationships put together, but it's still very difficult to operate in this industry."

Scott does believe that the banking loggerhead will ease sooner rather than later as more influential companies and large industries start to enter some aspect of the cannabis space. "Larger companies, who until recently have been waiting on the sideline, bring a lot of political clout. You know things are changing when [former GOP Speaker of the House] John Boehner is now running a cannabis company. With these kinds of people getting in, you'll start to see some action."

Many in the industry, including Scott, believe the government's stance—based on politics more than science—is not just socially and culturally out of step, it is also irresponsibly dangerous.

"What they've done is put people in jeopardy. Cannabis companies are forced to deal with significant amounts of cash at their facilities, making them prime targets for robbers, which put employees at risk, all because they can't open a bank account. Yet, the US government requires and accepts federal taxes from all of these licensed state companies. So it's okay to take their money, but they won't clear up the issue with the banks? It would be very simple for them to provide safe harbor to any bank working with legal, state-licensed cannabis companies."

Most people might not realize that the prohibition against cannabis is a relatively modern phenomenon. Cannabis has been grown in the US since colonial times and was sold in liquid form and as hashish. It was also a common ingredient in numerous medicines. Hemp, the fiber of the cannabis plant extracted from the stem, was also a popular—and extremely environmentally friendly—industrial material. But political agendas and social perceptions changed in the early twentieth century. After the Mexican Revolution started in 1920, there was a surge of immigrants flooding into states like Texas and Louisiana. As always, immigrants bring elements of their culture; for the Mexicans that included cannabis, which they called *marijuana*, as a medicine and relaxant.

Anti-immigrant politicians and members of the press spread xenophobic rhetoric about Mexicans, using their marijuana use as proof of their danger to our society. The irony being more Americans than not had products in their medicine cabinet with marijuana in it. After El Paso, Texas, outlawed marijuana, giving authorities cause to search, detain, and deport Mexican immigrants for breaking the law, it quickly became a national strategy for controlling immigrants and other minorities. In the 1930s "experts" claimed marijuana caused men of color to become violent and sexually aggressive toward white women. That frightened the public and paved the way for more laws targeting cannabis.

One of the most notorious, anti-marijuana crusaders was Harry J. Anslinger, a former assistant commissioner of the Prohibition Bureau who headed the US Treasury Department's Narcotics Bureau from 1930 to 1962. Playing on the public's fears, he pressed for uniform anti-narcotics legislation in all the then-forty-eight states.

When testifying before Congress, Anslinger presented a litany of murders and rapes allegedly committed by people high on marijuana. In an article he wrote titled "Marijuana, Assassin of Youth," he stated: "How many murders, suicides, robberies, criminal assaults, holdups, burglaries, and deeds of maniacal insanity it causes each year can only be conjectured."

Anslinger lobbied for the Marijuana Tax Act of 1937, which effectively banned the use and sale of cannabis, and worked to discredit any research that contradicted his views on the danger of cannabis or disputed the effectiveness of prohibition (even though the alcohol prohibition had been a dismal failure). When the New York Academy of Medicine prepared a report in 1944 that concluded marijuana was only a mild intoxicant, Anslinger lobbied the *American Journal of Psychiatry* to publish an article refuting the claims. He also tried to prevent publication of a joint American Bar Association-American Medical Association study that argued penalties for cannabis possession were too harsh. Anslinger's perspective was that heroin, cocaine, and marijuana were all equally addictive and dangerous.

The cultural revolution of the mid-1960s brought cannabis to a new generation who wanted to turn on, tune in, drop out. For most youth, smoking pot was harmless fun, and the legal penalties for cannabis came under scrutiny. It was one thing to lock up minorities and immigrants, but the American public wasn't eager to lock up a generation of college students for what now seemed like a victimless crime. Major publications and newspapers questioned why it remained illegal.

But the government resisted. After the Marijuana Tax Act of 1937 was eventually ruled unconstitutional decades later, Congress passed the Controlled Substances Act in the 1970s, which established schedules for ranking substances by their dangerousness and potential for addiction. Cannabis was placed in the most restrictive category, Schedule I, again alongside heroin. It was supposed to be temporary until a commission could determine where it belonged.

President Nixon's Schafer Commission declared that marijuana should not be in Schedule I and questioned designating it an illicit substance at all, pointing out the plant had been used safely by humans for around five thousand years. However, Nixon rejected the commission's recommendations. And as of 2019, the FDA continued to classify cannabis a Schedule I substance.

While the federal government clung to its outdated policies, progressive state voters have defied federal law and passed state initiatives legalizing cannabis for medical use, which has proven an economic, humanitarian, and wellness success. Now recreational use is quickly gaining traction.

As Scott observes, "I think the industry has evolved too much. With cannabis legal in some form in three-fourths of the fifty states, it's passed the tipping point. The states that don't allow even medicinal are in the significant minority. I'm not a cannabis user myself, but if you look at the statistics of what has happened since this was rolled out, and you look at the lack of harm to people, you look at the difference between alcohol, which I am a consumer of, and cannabis, it's clearly much safer for people to utilize cannabis."

Perhaps the most interesting statistic is who exactly is using cannabis. Worries that legalization would turn all young people into stoned zombies, the biggest group using cannabis and CBD oil products are the fifty-plus AARP crowd because it is—at least anecdotally—effective at managing pain.

"It's a much better option, especially considering the opioid crisis in this country. Transitioning people away from something that is truly addictive and harmful to something that's not should be a priority in our country," Scott says. "And I can't believe that we are still having this discussion."

While some cannabis companies make educating the public at large a priority, Scott says he'll leave that to others because he doesn't feel the need to explain himself anymore.

I know who I am. I know who we are as a company. We have great, dedicated people who work here. And I understand the value that we provide. So I don't care what people say. After I started N2 a lot of people I thought were close friends distanced themselves from us because of the negativity surrounding what we're doing. But through that I found out who my very true friends are, which is a great thing. And there are a lot of great, extremely intelligent people in this industry, so as it and N2 grows over the next three to five years, you're going to see the evolution of something that'll be very well respected."

From the time humans evolved socially enough to be fashion-conscious, men and women have been battling hair loss. Treatments for hair loss are as old as civilization itself. An early formula in China was made from safflower oil, herbs such as rosemary, and mashed animal testes that was rubbed into the scalp. In India yogis recommended standing on your head, believing the additional blood flow would stimulate hair growth. And according to a medical text dating back to 1550 BC, the ancient Egyptians used a variety of treatments, including ointments made from porcupine hair and hippopotamus fat.

The Romans were particularly follicle-conscious. According to historic lore Julius Caesar revived the Greek tradition of wearing laurel leaf crowns to conceal his male pattern baldness. He also wore toupees, which by then had already been around for three thousand years. Romans were also known to paint their bald heads to look like they had locks of hair. A couple of millennia later, options for those suffering hair loss weren't all that much better. The 1800s saw a parade of snake oil salesmen peddling magic tonics to cure hair loss. The mid-1900s introduced technological "breakthroughs" such as a head cap that used heat and light to supposedly revive hair follicles or the suction cup that promised to stimulate hair growth. Late-night commercials of the '70s and '80s touted aerosol dye sprays to cover bald spots.

The hair restoration industry needed fewer hucksters and more real innovators. Enter Amnon Zakay, who founded Raz International and has operated it since 1982. While he performs all methods of non-surgical, non-invasive hair restoration and hair loss treatments, it's Amnon's flagship restoration method—integrated thread hairlines (ITHL)—that attracts clients from all over the country. The procedure sews hair into the client's existing tresses, very close to the scalp, using a special thread instead of uncomfortable glues, chemicals, or painful surgery. Rather than shaving or trimming, he blends in more hair to enhance what's there. And there is no damage to the natural hair.

In 2016 Amnon received his accreditation as a master hair replacement specialist from the American Hair Loss Council, a nonprofit organization. A licensed California barber, Amnon is now a sought after guest speaker at industry conferences, where he also demonstrates his groundbreaking ITHL method and shares his expertise on other hair loss topics. But most of the time you will find him at the Raz Hair studio in San Diego working with clients, and business has never been more brisk.

According to a 2019 report, North America is currently the largest hair restoration market, with more than 130,000 individuals undergoing treatment annually and an anticipated CAGR of 20 percent by 2024. The report notes: "Growing celebrity and media influences, increasing awareness regarding one's appearance, peer pressure, societal pressure, growing urbanization, high income, and growing word of mouth are the potential drivers for the North American hair restoration services market growth." The industry is also seeing worldwide growth, especially in Asia.

While an expanding market is good news, it's not top of mind for Amnon. "Our goal is not to conduct massive sales," he says. "We are looking to build a lasting relationship with our clients."

To that end Amnon still conducts every consultation personally so he can assess the client's unique hair situation and provide them with a highly personalized treatment recommendation. That one-on-one, consumer-

Amnon Zakay

centric philosophy, commitment to quality, and the proprietary ITHL method, are the foundation of Raz Hair and Amnon's niche market success. But his foray into the hair restoration industry was less a calling in the beginning and much more a serendipitous—an unexpected—opportunity.

Amnon grew up in Israel, where military service is compulsory for all eighteen-year-olds. In the 1970s that basic enlistment lasted three years for men, two years for women. So after high school

he joined the Israeli Army where he became a professional officer. Eight years into his service, when he was twenty-five, Amnon started losing hair on the crown of his head, and his older brother referred him to a hair replacement specialist in Tel Aviv who Amnon says was known as a magician when it came to hair loss solutions.

"His method was very revolutionary back then," Amnon says. "But I did it to fix my hair, and I became a client. Nine months later when I came for another treatment, the older gentleman who owned the company told me he was going to retire and that he wanted me to take over his business. Even though I was doing something completely different in my life, he said: *I love my clients; I've know them for years, and I want somebody like you to take of them and this business. I think you're the right one who will do a great job.*"

The offer came out of left field, and Amnon was taken aback almost to the point of insult. He said he would think about it, but the proprietor kept the pressure on, saying he needed an answer within two days.

"He told me he had another candidate, but since he'd rather sell his business to me, he agreed to first give me the opportunity to make a decision yes or no. I thought about his offer the entire drive back to the base, which was about five hours. It was unbelievable timing."

The truth was, Amnon had already been thinking of leaving the Army. After eight years of service, he realized he didn't want to keep pursuing a military career and was ready to change direction in life. His plan was to go back to school and eventually own his own business although he hadn't decided exactly what kind of business or precisely when he would leave the military.

"Being an entrepreneur was my goal, but my plan was not to immediately jump into a business but to move forward with my studies and eventually get into some kind of business. I was drawn to the idea of owning a business and creating something, improving something, building something. I knew that would be a good thing for me."

Even though hair restoration had not remotely been on his list—or radar—here was an opportunity being handed him as if by fate, but he only had forty-eight hours to decide. He couldn't even discuss the offer with his parents, who were traveling at the time in the United States. And being before the days of cell phones, they were unreachable.

Amnon admits he was skeptical at first about the business because it was so different from his current profession of soldier. "If someone had told me the day before this was going to happen, I would have laughed. This was not something on my list at all. I thought: *What do I have to do with hair?* But then I thought I shouldn't reject it straight out because I was planning to leave the army anyway. I should think about it. So I spent the following two days collecting information about what exactly it would mean to own a hair restoration business, what I would have to do."

"In the end, I decided to give it a chance. After hours of debating with myself, I said: *You know what? This has happened for a reason, so I'm going to use this as an excuse to quit the army right away, and I will take over this business.* His offer just meant I became an entrepreneur faster than planned, but it was where I had already decided I wanted to be."

Amnon accepted the proprietor's offer. Six months later he quit the Army and took over the business, which he knew was healthy and sustainable. "He was considered a big shot who did great things and people used to come visit him from all over the country. I was sure I could make a living off the business; whether I'd like the work or not, I didn't know. I'd have to wait and see. But I figured the worst-case scenario was I could always sell it and change directions again. So for the next year and a half, I worked with the previous owner at the salon, took all the required classes, and got the training I needed. Then my mentor left, and I was on my own."

Over time Amnon was surprised that the more he did it, the more he loved what he was doing. It was more than his occupation; it became his vocation, feeding his artisanal soul.

"First of all I am an artist," he says. "I sculpt and paint and back then was doing music as a hobby. And I consider myself a compassionate people-person. You need both in hair restoration. In this business my work is always related to art and creativity. And every individual who comes here, men and women alike, I can make them laugh and comfortable. And when I bring them back to look as they did five, ten, or sometimes even twenty years earlier, it makes them so happy."

Just as often, Amnon says he helps someone with hair loss simply look their actual age rather than fifteen years older. He not only helped their physical appearance, but the treatments also improved their self-confidence and emotional outlook.

"Hair loss is a sensitive issue," Amnon says. "It's an honor to serve my clients and to be compassionate with them. Because of those things I found myself really happy with what I was doing. It was fun for me and also a bit like therapy. So all those earlier thoughts, of how this would be a temporary business and how I would just sell it and move on, faded away. The work I was doing gave me such a great feeling in so many ways; I soon knew I was going to keep doing it, and ever since then I have been in the hair restoration business."

His commitment to the business long-term gave him an entrepreneurial shot in the arm, and he instinctively knew he could not simply rely on the status quo. He traveled the world searching for the best sources of human hair and continuously looked for ways to advance his procedure.

"Moving forward meant I always had to be creative," he says, "improving existing methods while trying to come up with new ones."

Because he had started as a client, Amnon viewed the business from a different perspective than his predecessor. He made a point of talking to clients and getting their feedback, making constant adjustments and improvements. He still does.

"I'm thirty-six years in this business, and I'm still working on improving things all the time," he says with a quiet laugh. "It's an unending story because the more technology is advancing around us, the more things you can improve."

That constant drive to get better is what eventually led to ITHL, which Amnon describes as complex and unique. "Even though there are people using a similar system to ITHL, every individual has different ways of doing it. I developed my method over many years. I'm not saying mine is necessarily better than others, but it's for sure different. For me, whether or not its good depends on the feedback I'm getting from my clients, and the most of it has been very positive."

While he was successful and professionally secure, after twenty years into it, Amnon got personally restless. By then he was in his mid-forties and married with three sons. He seemed to have it all but needed something new.

"I was looking for a big change in my life," he says of his mid-life crisis.

Amnon and his wife had visited the United States several times to visit relatives he had in California and other places. He had never considered moving there full-time because he loves Israel—until it was time for a reboot.

"In August 2001 after two years of thought and discussions with myself, I decided to move to San Diego and open a branch of my business there. It wasn't the best location to open such a business," he says. "I can tell you had I if moved to Miami Beach, New York, or Los Angeles, business-wise I would have done much better, much quicker. But I was okay with it because I was looking for a place that I was comfortable to live in and raise my kids, who were sixteen, fourteen, and seven back then."

Amnon moved his family to California in June 2002 but kept the Tel Aviv salon open. He still owns the business—which is managed by his sister, nephew, niece, and several employees—and says, "We continue to serve people from all over, including some who have been our clients for decades."

While his business in Israel continued without a hitch after he moved, setting up a salon in San Diego would prove more challenging than he anticipated although initially, Amnon was more interested in acclimating to his new surroundings than worried about building a start-up.

Certification

"The first year I had no rush to open the business," he explains. "I wanted to enjoy time with my kids. So we traveled and visited many places exploring and learning our new country."

When Amnon ultimately turned his attention to Raz 2.0, the challenges were considerable. He spoke English but nowhere near fluently. Technology was more advanced. The San Diego market was a mystery to him and happened to be competitive. Also American culture in general—and Southern California culture specifically—was so different from the culture he came from.

"I had to learn the mentality of the people, their body language because you need to read clients. When you're consulting with or treating people, they don't always say what they feel. In this business you really have to be kind of a shrink. You have to talk to them and make them comfortable. It's a mutual process—a collaboration—about what exactly their expectations are. How they want to see themselves after the treatment to make sure you're on the same page with the client's desires."

The culture disparity worked both ways. "This type of business is mainly about trust," Amnon notes and says being an immigrant put some potential clients off. "People needing hair restoration are searching for a very personal connection, and some are not always comfortable when your accent is not American." On a more practical level, being a start-up also worked against Amnon, even though he had twenty years' experience. "Especially in this field, which is very personal and sensitive, many people want to work with companies that are existing, that have a local track record., that are stable. They want to have confidence in the company and be sure the hair restorationist can provide them with service whenever they need it. And at first many didn't see that in our company because it was new, at least in San Diego."

But his biggest challenge occurred in 2004. While traveling in Israel, Amnon suffered paralysis from the waist down. The symptoms started abruptly, while he was driving. Within minutes he couldn't move his foot from the gas pedal to the brake; he had to manually lift his leg. He was

Before   After
treatment   treatment

rushed to the hospital where doctors eventually discovered some swollen blood vessels had caused edema that had impacted the spinal cord and corrected the problem.

Noting that his job requires standing for much of the day, Amnon says, "I very grateful God wanted me to stay here not in a wheelchair but on my legs."

Although the paralysis was temporary, doctors told him it would take a year to fully recover from the nerve damage and get back to normal. "I am a very strong, but it was a big struggle," Amnon admits.

If that wasn't enough of a challenge, a couple of months later when some acquaintances offered him the chance to jump into a new business opportunity that marketed medical devices, Amnon accepted. "My hair restoration business requires lots of standing, so I couldn't fully promote Raz for a year. At that point my clientele was still very small, and I decided it was a good time to take their offer."

Amnon ended up working for the medical device business for four years, letting Raz go into a holding pattern. He stopped promoting his hair business during that time although he continued getting some clients by word of mouth and referrals. In the end, the medical devices opportunity turned into a bust and yet another challenge to overcome.

"I ended up losing the acquaintances and money with that adventure," Amnon says. "I think at that point most people would give up and return to their home country. Just like I could have gone back to my own business in Israel, which I fortunately kept."

But giving up is not in Amnon's nature. Although his right foot never returned to 100 percent, physically he was healthy and strong, so in

January 2009 he fully devoted himself to methodically building his client base in San Diego. Today business is strong and growing, and Amnon has earned a great reputation in Southern California as a premier hair restorationist. He says he has clients all over Southern California, many who drive up to four hours one-way to see him.

"I also have clients who fly in from Vegas, Arizona, and even Mexico City. And once you start the treatment, have to maintain it every six weeks on average. It's a big commitment. And they keep coming back, some for more than fifteen years."

Amnon credits much of his success and repeat business on two key factors, both of which he believes are unique in his industry. The first is his integrated thread hairline method. One of ITHL's biggest selling points is that it doesn't require any chemicals or glues, which many clients, especially women, don't like the idea of.

"It melts down underneath and blends with the sweat and the oils that the skull produces," he explains. "Glue's not a nice thing, but many women use that method because they don't know there's an alternative until they hear about ITHL. People love the idea of not using any chemicals, which is why they come from all over the place coming to see me. With our method, we blend and mix real human hair that matches their own hair. They're freely able to wash it, brush it, swim with it, blow dry it, color it—all the things they can do with their own hair."

The second key is his personalized approach. "Most, if not all, of the other companies are owned by men and women who are not hair professionals. They own the company but hire others to do the actual restorations. I approach every client as a new artistic creation. When I have a woman sitting in front of me, I approach her treatment the same way I do a sculpture or a painting. I am focused on bringing her the best natural appearance."

Amnon has three stylists that assist him, but he performs the most important stage of the process. "The fact that I both own the company and am also an expert who does the treatment makes a huge difference for clients. If there is any concern, it's resolved right away because I'm the owner and the expert in one. If a longtime client falls on some hard times financially, I'll do my best to help. If I have a client who is sick, we go to their home for a treatment. These things can happen, so you need to be sensitive and compassionate because clients become a kind of family. Honestly, it's not just words; that's how my wife, who works with me, and I really feel."

There might have been a time when most of that clientele family were men, but over the years Amnon says that's changing. "When I started the business thirty-six years ago, I had 98 percent men and 2 percent women. Years later I realized so many more women than I thought suffer from hair loss and thinning hair."

According to the American Hair Loss Association, there are up to thirty million women in the United States who suffer from thinning hair, mostly women over forty or fifty years old. Unlike men who get pattern baldness, women's hair thins out, so they are looking to add to and enhance the hair to fill it out.

"So I started promoting the business to women and aiming my services at women. Today at my San Diego salon, our clientele is about 80 percent women and 20 percent men."

Because of his one-on-one approach, Amnon has judiciously controlled Raz Hair's growth, opting to focus on one salon rather than seeking to open additional locations. "It's not a franchise business, and it's not a chain. I'm not going to train another assistant in two days just so they can start producing money. The standard of treatment I'm using is so high that it usually takes months before I get comfortable with employees to do certain things. So I'm not out to grow as big as we can because I want to keep the quality consistent."

Which means remaining as hands-on as he's always been. "Back when I made the decision to jump into hair restoration, I could not have predicted how much I would enjoy what I'm doing. It was really an accident, but a very happy accident."

And he has no plans on leaving the profession or Raz Hair anytime soon. "I have no thoughts of retiring," Amnon says. "That's my therapy place. As long as there are people willing to pay me, I'm happy to keep serving them. If I didn't have them, I'd have to find people and pay them to be able to keep doing what I'm doing."

For much of human civilization, if you needed an item, you traded for it or paid some sort of currency for it, then you owned it. But in the mid-twentieth century, some enterprising entrepreneurs came up with a new service model—why buy when you could just temporarily rent? The rental industry traces its roots to post-World War II Southern California, where mom-and-pop rental shops sprang up that rented anything from catering supplies to construction equipment. By the late 1950s the handful of rental shops in California had grown to more than five thousand rental businesses throughout the United States. The appeal of rentals was largely attributed to an increase in homeownership and the growing popularity of DIY handiwork. projects. During the Eisenhower years, American workers spent less than forty hours a week on the job, so there was more me time for home projects.

Today the US rental industry is valued at more than $35 billion and encompasses just about any product or service. There are party rentals, car rentals, vacation home rentals, farm equipment rentals, clothes rentals, and clown rentals. You can rent-a-wreck, rent-a-Santa, or rent-a-cop. And now thanks to Larry Sutton's innovative RNR Tire Express, you can even lease tires to own and custom wheels for your vehicles.

Since its founding in 2000, RNR has established more than one hundred and thirty franchise stores in twenty-five states, its growth spurred by the company's convenient, consumer-friendly payment options designed to fit any budget, enabling clients to pay off name brand tires and wheels on an affordable weekly or monthly plan. Its unique business model earned RNR the top category ranking for tires and wheels in Entrepreneur Magazine's 2017 Franchise 500 list and in 2019 was one of the top two hundred of all franchises in the country, number seven in Florida.

"If somebody would have told me when I started this company that we were going to grow into the seventeenth-largest tire dealer in the United States, there is no way I would have envisioned that," Larry says, adding that when it comes to dreams, "he doesn't like to put limits on things. It's a journey, and you have to keep doing the right things."

Larry's professional journey began in Tampa, Florida, while still a high school teenager. Raised by a single mom in a one-bedroom duplex along with two siblings, Larry helped out by working at his uncle's appliance and television retail store.

"That's where I learned to sell on commission," he says. "My senior year I sold every teacher I had a television or an appliance."

That same industriousness led Larry to later become a business partner in Champion TV and Appliance Rentals, which he says "became one of the most admired rent-to-own businesses in the Southeast."

To help other rent-to-own dealers become successful, Larry would travel around the country to give seminars. "I must have sounded like a preacher spreading the gospel," he says with a laugh, "because I became known as the reverend of rent to own."

In 1997 Larry sold his share in the company and retired while still in his forties. Up to then, he had always loved golf.

"I played golf for about a year until I got so bored, I couldn't stand it anymore. Loved it before retirement, hated it after. I missed the camaraderie and sense of purpose you find going to work and interacting with associates."

Feeling restless and maybe a little adrift, Larry decided to spread his

Larry Sutton

entrepreneurial wings and try his hand at some new business opportunities. It didn't go as planned. Deciding life was literally too short, a check cashing venture lost its appeal after one of his stores was held up at gunpoint. Larry also bought tropical smoothie franchises, which he calls a humbling experience.

"When I found myself dressed in a banana costume out on the street giving away free smoothies, I thought: *What am I doing here?* I needed to find something I loved and was excited about. A while later I was visiting a friend of mine in Atlanta. He told me about some guys out in Texas who were renting-to-own tires. That intrigued me. So I got on an airplane and spent a couple of weeks out there. I was basically just looking for a really good product that fit the business model I was familiar with."

Larry says he liked the idea, but also saw a lot of things he didn't like. So he came back and did some research.

"At the time, it was really just about custom wheels. I had never bought a set of wheels in my life. I'm thinking: *A wheel comes with the car; why would anyone ever want a different one?*" he laughs. "But I discovered the industry was growing fast and the demographics of who was getting—and who wanted to get—custom wheels seemed to be exploding, so it became attractive."

Larry came back to Florida, put his own spin on the concept, and created a company called Rent-N-Roll Custom Wheel & Tires, a play on rock 'n roll.

"Entrepreneurs are all a little cocky," he acknowledges. "They see something and always think they can do something a little different or a little better. And I was no exception. Rent-N-Roll was about getting custom wheels to a whole bunch of folks who didn't have the cash to go and spend a big dollars for them all at once. We only provided tires to go on the custom wheels."

The first Rent-N-Roll store opened in September 2000. And despite having to learn the ins and out of a new product, business was better than Larry could have hoped, exceeding his most aggressive models. A few years later, one of Larry's acquaintances from the rent-to-own industry, Mike Kent, wanted to open a business using the same model.

"Mike had a tremendously long history in the rent-to-own industry," Larry says. "He also loved automotive and came down to spend a couple of days to see what we were doing. He said: *I want to do this.* I said: *I'll help you out any way I can. I'll give you all of our paperwork, and you can just go get her done.*"

Kent was adamant that the arrangement be more formal, where Larry received a percentage of sales. Larry called his attorney and made Kent a licensee. Not too long after, another acquaintance wanted to open up a store in North Carolina.

"I called my attorney again and told him I had another guy wanting to do this. He said: *You're going to have to be a franchise.* I said: *I don't want to be a franchise.* He asked why. I said because I didn't want to tell people how to run their business. I wanted to run my business and let them run theirs. He said: *Well, you have no choice. You have to be a franchisor because that's what you're doing. And I'm not going to let you get sued for not being official.*"

Larry jokes it was basically peer pressure that led him to become a franchisor in 2003, which had previously not been on his radar.

"I could barely spell franchise, much less have a clue what we were doing. We just did everything we could to give those guys as much service as possible—helped them train, went there when they were having problems, and just learned to be a franchisor."

One of the things a franchisor has to do is protect the brand. That means sometimes holding people accountable.

"When my attorney informed me I had no choice but be a franchisor, he said a funny thing. *You're going to be a franchisor, but I know you well enough that you're not going to be a good one.* I said: *What do you mean I'm not going to be a good one?* He said: *Larry, you don't know how to tell people no.* And it turns out that he was right. What I learned about franchising is that not everybody is going to work as hard as you. Not everybody is going to follow the plan. So now you have to protect your brand and protect your business model."

Rent-N-Roll's focus on lease-to-own custom wheels began to shift around 2006 when Larry started looking at the passenger tire industry.

"It was a huge business, much larger than the custom wheel business," he says. "And we saw a gap in the marketplace. Nobody knows when they're going to end up needing new tires. In 2000 you could buy a decent set of tires to last three or four years for under $400. By 2010 it was double that or more. A lot of families just don't have that extra cash lying around, or it's not a good time for their budget. We felt we literally had the perfect solution and saw that our model would work very well with tires."

The key was actually getting passenger tire customers into their stores. Simply changing the name of the company to RNR Tire Express (RNR in homage to *Rent-N-Roll*) wasn't enough to attract their new target market.

"The passenger tire folks were not visualizing us as a tire company because we were a wheel company, which was obvious by our showroom and the way we positioned our business. Up to that point we had been a wheel company that had tires. We knew that if we were going to penetrate the $22 billion passenger tire industry, we had to become something different. We realized that as much as we wanted to be a tire dealer, we didn't look like a tire dealer; we looked like a wheel store. It just didn't fit. So around 2010 we started going through another transition that included remodeling stores, new signage, and relocating stores—just a metamorphosis to a whole different concept. We also we had to create a new model."

Larry explains that with RNR's lease-to-own model, the customer doesn't have to apply for credit. The choice is theirs.

"What we did with the wheels was set up a lease-to-own model, but on our passenger tires we added a six months same as cash option. If they get it paid off in six months, they never pay anything more than the original cash price."

RNR's model is similar to the layaway plans that used to be commonly offered by retailers like Sears, except in this model, the customer gets the product upfront. The appeal to consumers is that no interest is charged, as there would be if using a credit card or store charge account, as is the case in traditional tire retail stores.

"We looked at it from a different perspective. More than a million Americans don't have any savings. So they're not prepared for an emergency expense like a set of tires. And even if they have a credit card, the interest rate is probably at least 21 percent. So if they are like most consumers and make only the minimum payment, they'll end up paying as much as three times the price of the tire by the time they get their credit card paid off."

While some credit cards will offer no interest on purchases for a certain number of months, if the consumer doesn't pay it off within that window of time, then they're hit with a big retroactive interest charge.

"We rebranded once again, to RNR Tire Express, came up with our six months same as cash model, and it just blew up. Our stores—and revenue—just started doubling in size. It was an amazing turnaround. From 2014 to 2019 we grew 20 percent across the board every year since bringing this model into play."

One particular appeal of the model is that it is designed to be consumer-centric—as customers can turn their products in with no penalty.

"Which is huge," Larry says. "But more than that, if they come back later because their circumstances have changed, then we reinstate them and apply the money they previously paid. That's unlike any other industry in the world, which is why I believe the pay-as-you-go model will continue to grow in popularity—just as our franchises have. It's been a fun, exciting, and challenging learning experience."

Larry says that they have an ambitious franchise growth plan and are on track to develop four hundred more stores over the next six to eight years. He suspects many of those will be family affairs because currently, more than half of RNR's franchisees are father-son/daughter business partnerships, and Larry would like to see even more.

"When we started, because I had a well-known reputation in the rent-to-own industry and was a board member of the Association of Progressive Rental Organizations, we got a lot of attention from those guys. Now it's come full circle. We just completed a thirty-store deal with a brain surgeon as well as a Pennsylvania deal that's a father and son. We have another father and son team in Kansas who have just opened their third store."

It's not surprising Larry has a soft spot for father-son enterprises since his son Adam is part of RNR. When the company was starting, Larry says Adam worked as an unpaid board member. His eldest daughter, Ashley, is a franchisee in Indiana.

"Adam was here at the very beginning when we opened up. He formed his own creative agency, and I relied on him a lot for design, video production, and marketing materials. Adam had an opportunity to merge his company with a top agency that did experiential marketing. Adam spent most of his career building that business. His clients were people like Microsoft, Disney, and Under Armour. I needed some help, and I needed a serious player, so I wanted him to come on board here. I knew some large companies were trying to recruit him, so I took him to lunch, and we worked out a deal."

It was an offer Adam says he couldn't refuse. "It was a God moment. Working with my father—my mentor—was a childhood dream. We've always had a unique relationship. Even before I was working with him, people would say: *You're more than father and son; you're friends.* We certainly don't agree on everything," Adam says. "But neither of us have the type of ego to let it interfere in our relationship. The great thing about my father is

Adam B. Sutton

he cares about people; it's his entrepreneurial spirit to want people to succeed."

The move to RNR also meant being able to spend more time with his wife and three children. So it was a win-win—just like focusing on tires was a boost to the RNR's original business.

"The fascinating thing is we sell 70 percent of new product just in tires," Adam says. "But our wheel penetration not only didn't go down, but it's either stayed the same or gone up. So we're selling just as many wheels as we always did, but now we're spending the majority of our efforts on tires, helping a cash-strapped, underserved demographic. A large portion of our society are buying used tires over and over. They're spending $50 every time they get a used tire, which in most cases are not held to safety or quality standards. They've been sitting in a warehouse dry rotting, or they barely have any tread. So instead of getting tires that don't last, they can put $20 down with RNR and drive away with four brand new tires."

Larry also notes that tires are essentially a recession-proof product. He says that in a stretched financial market, RNR's potential customer base grows immensely.

"If there is such a thing as an economy-proof business, we're probably the closest thing to it. We do pretty well in a good economy, and we do pretty well in a tough one. Either way we've always been about serving our customers and not just providing a service. Now we have these beautiful RNR Tires Express stores that provide the underserved but hardest working people in America with a world-class experience. Customers are being treated better than they are anywhere else with payments on their schedule and based on their budget."

While RNR focuses on the payment options as a business model, Larry says the company does a lot of retail as well.

"As part of the name change and our evolution over the years, we attract everybody. We have professional athletes come into our store and buy thousands of dollars worth of wheels or tires. Sometimes people will tell us they would have normally paid in full but take advantage of our payment options so they can get tires and keep a little more money in their pocket. People like to have options, and I like giving it to them."

Adam says one of his dad's strengths is his inherent love of people, whether they are customers or employees.

"He's always had the philosophy of the upside-down pyramid leadership style. The ultimate goal is to lift up and serve our team members, and after that they will serve our customer. You can't do that with a bad-looking store or mediocre service. We've evolved into something that's designed to please all people and elevate the experience for customers who are not used to it as well as meet or exceed the expectations of those who expect it."

As the company has evolved, so has Larry's approach to franchising. He admits it was a steep learning curve.

"We've learned a lot and are still learning. It's funny; looking back, when the franchising first started, we sold them. Now we award them because we figured out that not everybody should have one because our franchise doesn't fit them, or they don't fit us. We had to undo a bunch of stuff we did wrong and renegotiate, and we had to get some people out who should have never been in."

Larry says they are bullish on training. Again, a lesson learned from experience.

"Now we have field trainers that help franchise owners get their store open, and every new franchisee comes here and spends a lot of time with our key people learning the business. And we mandate that the owner/operator is involved in the training because early on we had owners who would send an employee down instead. When they went back and tried to tell the owner what they learned, the owner would say: *Well, we're going to do it my way.* Because they didn't go through the training, they didn't understand why we do things the way we do. They would change things up, and it led them to not to be as successful. Now we tell owners they have to be a part of training to understand our brand, so it's working a lot better these days."

Which is not to say that Larry believes in micromanaging. He encourages franchisees to make suggestions that will improve customer service and improve a system.

"If you're dealing with a bunch of entrepreneurs, they're going to have some ideas. Why would you want to shut those down? Even if somebody comes up with something we've already tried, we've been open to it because what if we didn't implement it the correct way the first time.

Just don't mess with the brand. Don't try to change the things we know are essential to our success. But if you want to try something new that is right for the customer, we're pretty open-minded about it."

Adam says that over the years they've found the proper sweet spot between protecting the brand and encouraging innovation. "We're not McDonald's; we're not going to tell you where to order the straws from. But we are going to be strong-footed where we need to be and open-minded where we should be. I attribute a lot of our success to finding that balance. We're going to come in and hold your hand as much as you need it without being overbearing. Just enough to help you be successful."

One of the areas that the RNR brain trust keeps a close eye on is growth. "There's just so much room for the concept," Larry says. "But you don't want to get crazy with growth, either. We sit down with every new franchisee and help them plan their growth strategy, holding them accountable to an opening schedule that makes sense and won't get them in trouble either financially or people wise. We know what makes sense from an employee standpoint and with financials. So we watch that pretty closely. But in terms of over-penetration, we'd have to open a hundred stores a year to even get close to where we need to be. As of now we're at more than 130 stores. We are targeted to have 350-plus stores by 2025, covering thirty to forty states."

If there's a secret to all his entrepreneurial success, Larry says it's doing something you love. "If you don't love it, if you don't love the customers, your team members, if you don't love the process, then being successful will be much tougher. Secondly, we believe beyond a shadow of a doubt that culture is the single most important thing that we have to watch over and maintain. Our main tenets are founded on good principles and values. It starts with our mission."

RNR's mission statement is deceptively simple: to be the best tire and wheel concept in America.

"Some people might think it sounds weak," Larry says. "But in reality it's very deep because every single person in every single position in our company can measure their daily activity against it. They can determine if they're performing to the level of someone at the best tire and wheel concept in America. Everything you do with a customer, everything you do with an install, everything you do with an employee, everything you do is measured against that statement. We do that by constantly —almost to an annoying point—talking about *serving the customer* instead of *providing service* because there is such a huge difference between the two. When you deal with customers with a servant attitude, it's a completely different way to do business than just providing customer service. We are insistent that everyone adopt that concept."

Larry says by trying to be the best, RNR is able to change lives. "It starts with the employees and customers; we are the leading supplier of tires to single moms in the United States. Last year we were so proud as a group to give more than $1 million to charitable organizations. We actually gave away three brand-new cars to single moms on Mother's Day last year, and we want to grow that going forward. We want to get franchise participation to a point where every single RNR store in the country gives away a car to a single mom on Mother's Day. We're always thinking of more ways to change people's lives."

Adam adds, "One of the reasons we've had success is because he cares for the employees and franchisees. It's always been a family environment. It's always about empowering our people to rise."

RNR store in Tampa, Florida

For the average consumer there's a truism about technology that reflects the *love it, can't live without it, don't really understand it* relationship people have with the Fourth Industrial Revolution's rise of the intelligent machines. Case in point: the Internet of things (IoT), which is the connection of chips or sensors embedded in everyday items that can send and receive data to and from each other via the Internet. All these smart devices—from watches and TVs to garage doors and refrigerators—make up the IoT.

Anyone who has ever used a smartphone to text, send photos, or engage their home security system, knows *what* the IoT enables devices and their users to do. But the number of people who fully understand *how* it works is exponentially lower. Two of those few are Schwarm Technologies founders Ben Ibata and Stefan Jaegers.

"We're dedicated to giving companies of all sizes the power to create value by leveraging IoT," says Stefan. "Our vision is to be the leading IoT open-source platform and to accelerate IoT industry adoption."

Open-source refers to software that is made available free of charge to other users who can then modify and distribute their own versions of the program. There are many benefits to open-source. For example, on a consumer level it enables people to use a variety of devices from different vendors. (In contrast, certain smartwatches can only be paired with that company's smartphones—we're looking at you, Apple.) Likewise, many vendors of IoT devices want to increase the number of technology ecosystems their devices can be integrated into.

Open-source provides scale, speed of innovation, and flexibility that enables developers to support a broad range of devices without having to develop vendor-specific code. In Schwarm's case Stefan and his team have developed an open-source connected-device platform for the energy and utilities market.

"Our product simply connects and integrates data from a variety of hardware sensors and allows energy providers to better monitor key metrics and drive critical provisioning decisions," he explains. "That allows us to integrate new devices and encrypt the data transport more effectively, securely, and quickly than competing vendors."

Schwarm's primary business model is software-as-a-service, but the company also offers the platform to on-premises customers and monetizes by licensing proprietary platform extensions.

"At present," Stefan says, "we have completed the platform prototype and are in discussions with solar installation prospects to launch market pilots."

Schwarm has also provided IoT software to Biogents, a German company that studies insect behavior, such as mosquitos' sense of smell, which led to the development of an innovative trapping technology to count and recognize mosquito species. Despite the young company's accomplishments and the potential of its open-source technology, Schwarm has largely stayed under the radar as it built its customer base of client's interested in using their software.

"We've just started," Stefan says. "So at the moment we are still a small company. We are finding customers through our network and already have so many that we can't work with more. At some point we will have a big public launch and invite everyone to use our software for free."

Prior to founding Schwarm Stefan had enjoyed a successful IT career

Stefan Jaegers

in his native Germany and says his interest in all things computers dates back to when he was a teenager in school, more than forty years ago.

"I started developing software when I was sixteen, though I was a hardware freak at first," he says. Stefan attended RWTH Aachen University, where he studied electrotechnics, the science of practical and industrial applications of electricity. "In general I've always wanted to know how complex machines work but especially computers."

When he was twenty-seven, Stefan started a software company, which "is a whole other story, and I would need a day to explain," he says with a laugh. Starting in the early 1990s, I was hired by a number of well-established companies as a software developer or software engineer."

The two terms are not totally interchangeable. A software developer is the creative mind behind computer programs. They determine what the program users will need and then develop and create programs that will meet those needs. A software engineer is involved in the complete process of creating software programs; a process that includes the design, development, and maintenance of software as well as analyzing existing software and modifying it to meet current application needs.

"But after being a chief technology officer, I was ready for something different," Stefan says. "So I thought it was time to be a consultant, showing companies how converting their systems could benefit their companies."

He also set up a business where he developed software for several companies. Stefan's interest in the energy industry began in 2012 after he and a colleague got into a conversation about renewable energies

"We agreed that renewable energies in Germany had a problem: the software used to all the small power engines in the field. We had lost many big power plants and now have grids for many small power engines in the fields. It's too complicated for people to handle; it needed to be served by software."

So Stefan and his colleague set up a small company called Gridsystronic, which developed an artificial intelligence (AI) software for virtual powerplants. Software that is capable of intelligent behavior can simulate a number of capabilities, including reasoning, learning, problem-solving, perception, and knowledge representation.

"Virtual powerplants need highly intelligent software that implements artificial intelligence to analyze the data—what the weather is going to be the next hour, day, week; how the solar panels or windmill machines are producing, and how much energy people are consuming," Stefan explains. "Bringing everything together required a very complex system that would have to be built as a monolith with standard technologies like the big companies do. We saw that our software could also work with other devices in the industry, which had the same problems that were then being managed out of the cloud."

But Stefan says they could not find investors in Germany willing to fund their start-up, which led to the decision to start over in Silicon Valley. "In Germany nobody really understood what we were trying to do. We moved to California, the one place in the world where investors understood what software companies needed to grow. So we settled in San Francisco and in 2017 started Schwarm as a small company."

Not only did Stefan experience the culture shock that accompanies moving to a new country with different customs, language, and social norms; he says they also experienced a technological culture clash as to how software programming worked.

"We thought we had a very cool software and very cool

programming, but then we saw that Silicon Valley was two or three years ahead of us," Stefan recalls. "We realized we needed to take our powerplant software, break it down, and rebuild it from scratch."

Stefan says the same team that worked on the virtual powerplant 1.0 in 2012 was now working on the 2.0 platform. "All of us had to rethink our approach. For one thing the market in the United States was totally different. Working locally in Germany we were in a small segment of energy market. Now we were in the big market of all the machineries in the world. There were many platforms out there, but they didn't have our latest version."

They called the 2.0 version of their software Volery (from the Old English word for *flock of birds*) and determined they needed to develop it as open-source to foster growth and acceptance by a wide swath of users. "We implemented a universal design pattern for IoT in our software, and

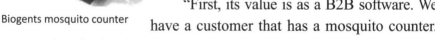

small and big customers alike can handle this software."

No matter how innovative the code, what makes or breaks a software is what it does to improve its customers' lives or businesses, both as a consumer product and as a B2B solution.

"First, its value is as a B2B software. We have a customer that has a mosquito counter.

Biogents mosquito counter

There are hundreds of these counters in Florida that track the mosquito populations in various cities. Using our software you can analyze the data in the cloud to predict how the population ebbs and flows."

The consumer will only see the impact of Schwarm's software in a B2C context when the environmental department reports a warning that a mosquito swarm is coming. Stefan describes Volery as an enabling system like Linux, which is an operating system that manages the communication between the software and hardware on your desktop or laptop.

"No consumer sees Linux under the hood of their computer," he notes. "They only work on systems with Linux. We want Volery to be the Linux of IoT. Just like Linux, our software is so easy for our B2B customers to use that they don't develop such a platform again. They use our software and make their application on it."

One of Schwarm's customers uses Volery for an agriculture sensor to measure fungal spores that can cause diseases in agricultural systems. Another develops intelligent mattresses that can accurately measure the weight of a person lying in the bed within one gram (.035 ounces). Stefan says the smart mattress can also move "in a thousand different directions so you don't lie too hard in the bed, such as for an older person who can't easily move in bed by themselves anymore. Our artificial intelligence software is what analyzes the data of how people are lying in the bed and how to best move them. The smart mattress company uses our software to transport their data from the bed into the cloud, to show all the data in the clouds, and to analyze the data to make the appropriate movements."

Stefan estimates he has been developing software for more than fifty years but says despite all the advanced technology, it's always a challenge.

"It's definitely cooler because we make open-source, so everyone will get this software for free, but it is not easier than when I started developing as a teenager. We analyzed thousands of software under the hood to develop Volery. Think of how many software products were written over the last thirty years—hundreds of thousands. And we use that software to build Volery on top. That's the only way to make a software better and cooler and easier to implement than we could ever do before," Stefan says. "Part of our goal is to bring our software to the open-source community and make it better for them and easier for them to implement their business on our system."

Schwarm's open-source business model is simple and straightforward: they give away the software for free—no license—and then receive a consultant fee to help the client implement Volery, and they also have software as a service.

Ben Ibata

"This platform is very complicated to handle in production systems, so we tell customers: *We can help you to bring the software to life and make your business on it.*" Customers can also sign up for a maintenance subscription with Schwarm. "We guarantee that the software is working and running properly. It's similar to Red Hat's business model," Stefan says.

Growing any start-up is an all-consuming endeavor. The challenge goes up exponentially when you're also running another business across an ocean. Stefan says he splits his time between San Francisco and Germany and has managers in both locations who run things when he's not there. Stefan says having such a peripatetic, frequent-flyer-hoarding work life is made possible by having a strong partner.

"It wouldn't work without the strong co-founder I have found in Ben."

It also doesn't hurt that Stefan has a supportive wife and their grown children are out of the nest and away at college. "We have four children, three boys and a girl," he says. "All of them are at university except the oldest one who already finished. None of them live at home anymore. My wife has work that she can do from any place in the world, so this was my great chance to do something really cool. Seizing the opportunity to move then to San Francisco was no problem, so I said: *Let's do it.* And my wife said: *Why not?*"

Stefan laughingly adds that having three children in college at the same time and moving five thousand miles away was only possible because in Germany citizens do not have to pay for education. (That sound you hear are American parents everywhere gnashing their teeth.) He also admits he was completely naïve and unprepared for the realities of starting a tech business in Silicon Valley.

"I showed up in America and said: *I'm here!*" he says of joining the thousands of other technological savants who flock to the San Francisco area hoping to achieve tech glory. But Stefan says establishing himself wasn't just about know-how and expertise.

"I'm fortunate to be a skilled networker and quickly started making contacts. I went to events and to every kind of meeting and conference I could, looking for people to meet. Then I started to hire some people, seeing if they worked well and fit in, so my network grew and grew. After about a year I finally felt like I was really starting in Silicon Valley. And now I've also started friendships with some people in the Valley."

Not that he has a lot of time for socializing. Stefan is gearing up for a major launch event of Volery in mid-2020 that will be global in scope, occurring in six locations to maximize B2B awareness.

"We want to start in the software community with Volery so developers help us develop it more and more. We want to start in San Francisco, we want to have one in New York, and we want to make it into Europe—Paris, Munich, or Berlin. We are also talking about a launch in Asia."

But Stefan is quick to note than a splashy launch is not enough to generate the awareness necessary to kickstart fast-growth. He plans to attend all the major consumer and software industry trade shows and conferences. Of course, Stefan jokes, the most important task is to actually finish the software.

"I'm the CTO, so I have to get the software ready. That's what I will focus on," he says. "For the rest, Ben, who is CEO, will hire the professionals to make that happen."

The pressure of a looming launch notwithstanding, Stefan says he is still enthralled with developing software after all these years. "It's cool stuff. I love to think about ideas and how we can implement them. Most of the time Ben says I have too many ideas. But to work on such a project gives me more energy than it takes because it's so fulfilling when I see our customers working so easily and successfully with the software. And they have real opportunities to grow with the software. That's the spirit behind developing that kind of open-source software."

Stefan says he has to remind himself that as CTO, it's not just about ideas; the software won't program itself. "But to see your ideas developed on a daily basis, and to see the software run, and perform the way you envisioned is so amazing."

Especially after having to navigate through the unavoidable setbacks and obstacles that come with developing innovative software. "I have experienced every problem you can have on the way to develop software, sometimes to the point where you have to smash everything down and start all over at the beginning. Writing software is like book writing because you are inspired by what you want to do. Every day that you work on the book moves it closer to fruition. It is both inspiring and exhausting to bring ideas to life. If you don't work your hardest every day, you can't finish it."

Once the software is finished, Stefan's plan is to put it into a foundation, which will be set up prior to the launch and which will continue to develop new iterations of Volery for the next twenty years, much the same way Microsoft continually releases new versions of its Office suite of programs.

"This foundation will develop this platform. And Schwarm will develop for customers a business model based on this platform. Schwarm will also develop its own software based on this platform. We have also ideas to bring our own business models into the market based on this platform."

His vision for Volery is reflected in the company name. In German *schwarm* means *swarm*. Both Stefan and Ben are from Germany, and they thought using a word that was as identifiable for Americans as for Germans was fitting. It also stands for *swarm intelligence*, an emerging field of biologically-inspired artificial intelligence based on the behavioral model of birds and social insects such as ants and bees.

"That's what we're doing with the cloud," Stefan says. "That's the idea of the Internet of Things."

So much has changed in computer science over the last forty years; the world is such a dramatically different place technologically that few if any people could have imagined how their daily lives would change. But we take for granted that today's lowest-tech smartphones pack far more computer power than the Apollo 11 spacecraft that first took men to the moon, while to people in 1969 it would have seemed otherworldly—true science fiction. Now IoT is changing the world by providing an avenue for intelligent connectivity between machinery through AI.

"No one had the idea for this kind of software," he says. "When we started out in 2012, we were the first to start with such software; the concept of an *Internet of things* did not yet exist. It wasn't until 2015 or so that someone came up with the term. So we started a software that was the right idea at the right time. When you think the idea through to the end, our platform is like Linux spread over the world. People don't talk about using Linux because it is under the hood. Similarly, their cloud software is running on our Volery."

Looking forward, Stefan believes the software he and his team are developing will help usher in more seismic technological shifts that we can only begin to imagine. Whatever direction the technology of the future goes, Stefan believes his software will be in the middle of the innovations.

"For more than twenty-five years now, I have been developing software and hardware in a leading position. I love to develop great products, and you do that by looking beyond one's own nose. Everyone talks about having their own data, that the currency of the future will be data. Volery can also work with other Volerys and together to create business models that companies can have in the future. When they have the same platform, they can share the data with other companies. We want to implement Volery over cryptocurrency, where every machine is paid for its service. Where every machine that gives its customer data is paid. That will enable business models that can't be implemented because there's no platform for it that you can monetize—yet. Blockchain will be part of this next evolution, but bitcoin will not; it will be another as yet developed cryptocurrency. But monetizing the data will be the next leap. And you need an IoT platform that has most of the market. And we intend that to be our Volery."

SECURE *medical*®

It's a mainstay of many science fiction television series: medicine of the future will heal what ails you with the wave of a high-tech device, invasive surgeries are a relic of the past, and doctors are more technologists than hands-on physicians, aided by machines capable of instant diagnoses.

Whether or not we'll ever develop artificial intelligence that blends Dr. House with Yoda remains to be seen, but digital technology is creating telecommunication opportunities for healthcare providers to transform how they interact with patients. These new platforms are designed to both improve health and remove some current barriers to seeking treatment, from time constraints and transportation difficulties to anxiety or embarrassment going to a doctor's office.

One of the leaders into this brave new interactive world is Secure Medical, a Tempe, Arizona, company that provides advanced telemedicine products and services and was one of the first telemedicine companies to specialize in marketing and technology. Founder Kyle Rao says the birth of the Internet provided the opportunity to improve the delivery of healthcare from clinics and pharmacies through telecommunications.

"Right around the time I graduated high school in 1997 is when this whole operation took off," he says. "With an investment from my father and help from my friends, we knew we had something that would work."

Kyle founded his first start-up, Viamedic, in 1999 while attending Arizona State University then later launched eDrugstore to provide so-called lifestyle medications that were available by prescription only. In

October 2001 he established Secure Medical as the central, overseeing company for his growing network of telemedicine start-ups such as Edrugstore.com

"The primary objective in founding Secure Medical," he says, "was to promote telemedicine and drive remote patient care by designing the technology necessary for patients, pharmacies, and physicians to more easily communicate with each other," he says.

When a patient agrees to be treated remotely for an illness on one of Secure Medical's approved partner web sites, they are assigned a licensed US physician. In lieu of a physical exam, the patient completes a detailed, secure online questionnaire, which is then reviewed by the doctor. The final step is a HIPPA compliant "face-to-face" video or audio consultation via Secure Medical's telecommunications technology. After the consult the physician may then issue a prescription to address the patient's condition. Once approved, a licensed pharmacy fills the prescription, which is delivered to the patient within a day or two. As an added safety measure, patients who have not had a physical exam within the previous twenty-four months may not be approved for prescribed medication.

"Although online consultations will never take the place of traditional medicine," Kyle acknowledges, "they do provide a means for patients to receive treatment for minor conditions that may not require an immediate physical exam."

Telemedicine is not a new breakthrough. Throughout the twentieth century physicians utilized radio, television, and microwave technology to reach patients and share medical information such as X-rays. However, the rapid advancements in digital technology over the past few decades have turned telemedicine into a much more personal, integrated service. And with the vast majority of Americans familiar with video teleconferencing using FaceTime, Skype, Facebook's Portal, and other devices, using the

Kyle Rao

technology to communicate with physicians is a logical evolution.

Kyle notes that telemedicine not only saves time and resources by enabling people to see a doctor for minor but urgent conditions from the comfort of their home or workplace, it also provides hospitals and medical centers access to specialists located anywhere in the world. And from a business perspective, telemedicine is a strategy that can give medical centers a competitive edge in an economic environment that makes it difficult to remain independent or sustain profitability.

Telemedicine is part of a growing trend of people using technology to become more involved and proactive with their health and wellness. There are now mobile health apps to keep tabs on sleep and diet; affordable consumer medical devices can take blood pressure and body temperature readings or conduct upper respiratory recordings and throat scans; and at-home tests for conditions like Lyme Disease or colon cancer, enable people to collect medical information a physician needs for a diagnosis without requiring a visit to the doctor's office. As people have increasingly embraced the use of technology to monitor their health, they have also become more open to alternative methods of receiving care.

Secure Medical is Exhibit A of that trend. The company has struck a nerve with consumers through platforms where people can consult online with a physician (OurDoctor.com), fill prescriptions online (HealthyMale.com), and interact with other patients through a social media site (WhoIsED.com.), a public forum where patients can openly discuss their conditions and treatment options. Secure Medical is also currently working on a new platform called BidRx—referred to in-house as the eBay of pharmacy pricing—which is designed to bring low cost prescription medication to the masses by letting customers bid online in an auction type setting for the lowest medication prices available, including pet medications, specialty drugs, and large wholesale lots. The participants will get an offer in minutes and shipping is included.

"These are platforms that helped eliminate the stigma surrounding telemedicine, created an environment where people feel comfortable to order the products they need from the safety of their homes, and increased the availability of treatment options for many patients," Kyle says.

The platforms have also propelled the company onto the 2019 Inc 5000, with a three-year growth rate of 62 percent and revenues of $29 million. But Kyle says Secure Medical's fast growth doesn't just reflect the user-friendliness and value of telemedicine; it's also an indictment of the current medical system.

"The truth is, the medical industry in the United States is heavily flawed," he says. "Take a snapshot of any point in the chain from coming down with let's say a rash, to the prescribing process, to the treatment, and it's clear the entire system is very obtuse. Dancing around insurance premiums and finding the time to get seen by a doctor is becoming increasingly more difficult for many people. That was the inspiration behind Secure Medical. We wanted to create a convenient way that patients could receive the care they needed without having to adhere to the nightmare that the conventional medical path takes."

Kyle believes access to real-time, 24/7/365 support is absolutely key to the future of the medical industry, a reality that has become increasingly clear as technology has advanced. And for as far as the company has already come, it's only started to scratch the telemedicine potential.

To promote Secure Medicine's telemedicine services, Kyle has adopted a retail marketing approach. "Statistically speaking, customers who browse the isles of retail clothing stores purchase more products and are more likely to spend more money overall than ones who come in, grab what they need, and leave immediately," he explains. "We wanted to apply this thinking to our online platforms. And these efforts have had a profound effect on overall customer satisfaction, which means not only are we listening to our customers, but we're giving them what they want."

And what Kyle believes they want most is more immediate access to physicians that doesn't require waiting a week to get an appointment. And actually getting to speak to a doctor. Some HMOs now make plan holders speak to a nurse rather than a doctor because their condition isn't deemed serious enough for a physician's time. Promoting an easier path to connect with a physician was always at the core of Kyle's purpose.

"Instead of the old-fashioned method of going to an office for an ailment, now you can simply turn on your camera phone or computer video for communication right now. Granted, seeing a doctor via phone or video might not work for cancer patients, but for conditions such as hair loss, acne, high blood pressure, eczema, being overweight, it's just not necessary to see a doctor in person for some ailments."

Over the years Kyle's vision has evolved and expanded along with each technological advance. Secure Medical made its first connection with consumers through erectile dysfunction medication dispensed over the phone. "When Viagra was introduced into the market in 1998, it seemed made for telemedicine. First, it's a conversation many men would find embarrassing to have with their physician in person; being in your own surroundings provides a level of emotional safety. Second, erectile dysfunction wasn't something a doctor was going to diagnose for you. So we set up a telephonic doctor-patient relationship, and working with the physician, we developed a medical form designed for that ailment."

The service caught on so Secure Medical moved onto a another condition, targeting clients for Vaniqa, a cream for women approved in 2000 that removed unwanted facial hair. That too proved to be a popular early telemedicine product. Soon Kyle was envisioning the wide-ranging possibilities of their service and the needs it could fill.

"We had an idea for a kiosk that we'd send to Third-World countries and place it in a pharmacy so people could jump into this booth, quickly communicate with a doctor, then fill their medication right there. That was around the time when I had a flip phone and a pager," Kyle says with a laugh. "But then cell phones became smarter and featured cameras so you could video chat in real-time via Skype, and the kiosk idea never took off. It was too bulky of a unit to ship, and phones made more sense. Just like in the early days of computers, a server took up an entire room; now you have tablets that fit in your bag and phones with more computing power than the Apollo 11 space capsule that landed on the moon."

After shelving the kiosk idea, Kyle took Secure Medical in a different direction and eventually developed the OurDoctor.com platform, which provides individuals who don't have health insurance a practical solution for common ailments such as allergies, upper-respiratory infections, digestive or intestinal complications, STDs, skin and eye conditions, and much more. Kyle notes that the platform doesn't just benefit individual patients. Businesses and schools can use that platform in lieu of paying high insurance to save on healthcare costs.

"The increasing costs of covering employees can force many business owners to forgo healthcare coverage altogether," Kyle says. "Luckily, we have created new options for the fledgling business owners out there looking to provide healthcare options to their employees. And we really just give it away to small mom-and-pop businesses as a trial. Typically an employee would cost around $3100 a year to insure, so for a company of 350 people, that would be more than a million dollars a year.

But that company would only spend $500 per month for our platform, or $6,000 a year. Not only does it greatly save the company money, it's more convenient. Normally if someone on your team gets ill, they'd have to go to the doctor or urgent care to get an antibiotic or cough medicine. But with Secure Medical, they can consult with the doctor from the comfort of their cell phone in your office."

Kyle observes that just the economics of modern healthcare alone has forced businesses to reevaluate their options. "I've seen a big change over the last few years in attitudes toward the telemedicine marketplace. The desire to modernize their business practices are weighing heavily on organizations that have been around for years. There is no doubt society is evolving rapidly, and what may have worked for us in the past is no more, so companies that fail to ascend these obstacles and evolve are doomed to antiquity."

Kyle says he and his team see Secure Medical as an advocate against the insurance industry, which is tops on his soon-to-be-dinosaurs list. "The huge premiums they charge and the reimbursement hoops they make you jump you through—healthcare shouldn't have to be that hard. But it's all just a big business to them."

He speaks from experience. Kyle had a back surgery that was approved by his insurance company. Months later he started receiving unexpected bills for charges the insurance company had previously agreed to pay. "I wrote letters telling them don't approve me upfront and then all of sudden change your mind. It's just a very lucrative business, and patients are the pawns."

The public's overall dissatisfaction with industry practices is one reason Kyle believes insurance platforms, as we currently know them, will be a thing of the past.

"Insurance is big business, and those companies want to hold tight onto their niche. But healthcare is changing. People are going to find alternatives. Young doctors are setting up technology-based practices at home and building a clientele without having a storefront office. Granted there will still be the need for specialized physicians for serious illness, surgeons, and for procedures like Lasik that need to be done in an office. But for regular checkup and those minor illnesses and conditions that occur, telemedicine is the way of the future."

Doctors aren't immune from the same bill-consumers-early-and-often business model mindset, which furthers telemedicine's appeal. Say you have a chronic condition like allergies. Kyle notes how doctors will require you to come back for an office visit to get a refill on medication you are taking long term. It's not that they give you an exam; it's simply to charge you for an office visit to write a new prescription.

Again, Kyle shares his personal experience. "I take a gout medication, and my doctor tells me I need to take it for the rest of my life. But he also wants me to come into the office every few months. I said: *Well, I can just do the bloodwork and send the results.* But no, I have to go in to talk in person. There's no need for patients to do that when there's telemedicine."

While the technology is making life easier for patients, Kyle admits recent rules and regulations Secure Medical and other telemedicine platforms suddenly had to navigate was almost overwhelming. Since telemedicine is a relatively new technology that is a blend of medicine and IT, in the beginning regulatory management was minimal—until it wasn't.

"Our entire company was hit hard when the state regulations abruptly changed. We went from servicing all fifty states to just thirteen literally overnight. We were scrambling and considered liquidating all of our assets, but we obviously persevered. My crew came up with ways to remain marginally profitable during the period of adjustment, and we eventually got back on our feet and obtained the certifications and documentation we needed to comply with state and federal law."

Many of the changes related to mail-order pharmaceuticals. For example, a new rule required doctors being licensed in the state certain prescriptions were shipped to. So if a patient in Michigan needed some prescription, even though the consultation was over the phone, that practitioner would have to be licensed in Michigan. Another new telemedicine rule is that patients who consult with a physician need to be able to contact that specific doctor if they have any follow-up question or have a reaction to a medication. Despite the challenges Secure Medical faced ensuring they were compliant, Kyle says these and other changes were for the better because the regulations make patients safer by, among other things, preventing unscrupulous companies from shipping counterfeit drugs.

"Online pharmacies operated in a grey area for a long time and are only just now being regulated," Kyle explains. "We are a vocal advocate against companies that sell counterfeit products or illegally ship products to the United States from overseas that aren't regulated and don't have lot numbers. We warn patients to never ingest something that could be harmful to their health. It's not worth the risk because you have no idea what you're taking. It could be something benign like a pill made from plaster, or you could be consuming something deadly. All they really care about is making the pill look real; they couldn't care less what's in it."

Kyle points out that this is where big pharma comes in.

"Sure, on one hand they don't want people getting sick from medicine bought overseas, but their profitability still comes first. For example, Viagra costs about $90 per tablet at your local pharmacy here, so you could see why someone suffering from ED would want to go overseas to get it for $10. Medicine costs are sky-high, which forces many people to give these unscrupulous online pharmacies a shot. It's a vicious cycle."

Kyle says as far as regulations go, Secure Medical learned from its past experiences and now takes a proactive strategy to the regulatory aspect of the industry. Part of that approach was to create a regulatory management team that helps the company preemptively take measures to ensure Secure Medical is always in compliance with ever-changing state and federal laws and regulations. Secure Medical will also continue to make improvements to its platforms and services so more people will get the care they need, especially preventative care.

"Suppose your trucking business has our platform, and one of your drivers turns fifty years old. We know that's an age when they need to get some testing done," Kyle says. "But the reality is a lot of people are either too busy, too adverse to the doctor's office, or just too lazy to stay on top of such testing. So we would automatically send them the test kits they need, such as for at-home blood testing and collecting a stool sample for colon cancer screening. They can use the kits in the privacy of their home and then just mail the samples back to our physician to get their results."

Certain professions, such as pilots, have regulations that require annual testing for everything from diabetes to high blood pressure. Noncompliance could get a pilot's license revoked.

"We just see what the customers needs are, we find a solution for them, then we can implement the software and make tweaks to it and then let it run on its own. My team works very well with customers. We can make changes on the fly, and we are always accessible. A customer can immediately get directly to a technical department; they don't have to go through a robo-operator making them press a half dozen buttons to funnel them to the right person who can answer your question. There are too many companies that forward calls to voicemail or don't promptly respond to an email. I just can't believe how much of that is out there because it makes it hard to get work done."

Kyle suggests that the automated voice response/call center style of customer management is largely an American epidemic. "I'll tell you, when I look for solutions in other countries like in Japan or even Canada, it's unbelievable how great the contact is. And that's what we take pride in as well. At Secure Medical we want to talk to you and work together. To that end we have partnered with organizations to create and maintain mutually beneficial relationships fostered by genuine customer service. We are always striving to provide a platform where people feel they can develop a relationship with us."

Keeping customer service top of mind is one of the management golden rules he stresses to up and coming entrepreneurs. He also advises them to avoid aggressive management.

"There's just no need for that. I was talking to a friend of mine the other day, and he has a boss who comes into a meeting and just starts yelling. Some employees get scared, others just decide they need to get another job. Yelling is all negative; it's bullying; it's never a solution. It causes stress and weighs heavily on your team's mind. You don't ever want to be that kind of leader. Just calm down. Be thoughtful. Don't accuse; ask questions. Open up the lines of communication. Listen to other's opinions and suggestions. When people see that, they'll work better for you. They'll work harder for you."

Kyle says the lesson he's learned is that people with a strong work ethic and a desire to succeed are the key to a strong company. Having the mindset to be your best, being coachable, working well as part of a team is more important than a college degree.

"Those are the values that matter most. Things like appearance and mobility are not important to me. And employees who cannot take criticism because they think they are perfect due to their great education, outstanding work history, or expert-level experience, are undesirable. Everyone can learn something new or a better way of doing things. We hire a lot of veterans, and they seem to have a very good understanding of what our goals are as well as a good grasp about our customers' needs. Those qualities aren't exclusive to military vets; we find that anyone with a mission and a goal they set for themselves is the ideal employee."

Every employee who joins Secure Medical is educated via a goal-oriented training style on how quickly technology is changing the telemedicine industry and how the company is poised to impact the future of medical care and insurance.

"We are a laid back organization that believes working smarter and not necessarily longer is key to employee satisfaction," Kyle says. "We have built an environment that affords employees recreational time, flexible scheduling, mentoring, coaching, and management skill development. We believe that a company where employees are fielded in the best possible position leads to a more robust organization as a whole. We hear our customers wants and needs then build the solutions to market to other entities. Once you establish the necessary framework, the system will thrive and evolve on its own. We live by the motto: *Build it right the first time, and you'll never have to build it again.*"

Kyle credits an organization-wide restructuring with helping improve company and employee performance. Traditionally, the go-to structure for organizations has been a top-down hierarchical system with distinct divisions. The intended advantages is an obvious chain of command intended to establish clearly defined responsibilities and specialized departments to improve efficiency. But there are also some distinct disadvantages, most notable is that such a structure does not always foster communication and collaboration throughout the company.

"The top-down managing style worked for a time at Secure Medical, but over the years we have adopted a more fluid managing dynamic," Kyle says. "While we still maintain the structural hierarchy of management, we encourage fledgling employees and trainees to present ideas and showcase skills unique to them to help better the company. We also have created an environment where our staff comes to work prepared to excel. The vast majority of improvements over the last two years can be attributed to employees feeling empowered to make suggestions. This is more than just company-wide surveys; this is genuine listening and real-time implementation of ideas."

Such as when a customer service representative shared his idea on how to reduce the wait time for having a doctor contact a patient. They implemented the process within two months and since then overall sales have shown a 7 percent increase.

"The beauty of this approach," Kyle adds, "is that collaboration and communication has become part of our culture. A company is a reflection of its people. We all work for each other at Secure Medical, and that mentality is the driving force behind our success. We all lift together."

Secure Medical telemedicine kiosk

Skyline· | **TRADETEC**

The concept of artisans, traders, and merchants displaying their wares to would-be customers in a public setting may be as old as civilization. The ancient Chinese and Egyptians touted fabrics and spices; every Greek town and city had an agora (open-air market); the Forum, historic Rome's civic center, began as a marketplace; and in North Africa visitors and traders wandered through vast souqs, maze-like bazaars with hundreds of merchants. These early businessmen and women used artful displays and verbal showmanship to attract potential customers and convince them their offerings were the best to buy or trade for.

For millennia this type of exhibition was the most efficient way to sell goods. Then in medieval Europe, farmers and craftsmen would attend open-market trade fairs held far and wide to display and sell their goods. During the eighteenth century this type of exhibition became commonplace in North America. Eventually brick-and-mortar specialty shops became the preferred way to sell goods and services to the public. But the spirit of those vibrant, ancient marketplaces and medieval trade fairs would live on in a decidedly modern platform—the trade show. Whether they come in the form of a weekly street fair in Small Town, USA, a multi-million dollar exhibition in a huge convention hall, or a virtual show online, trade shows remain an integral key to facilitating the exchange of goods and services.

By definition a trade show, or trade fair, is a "regular trade event at which a large number of manufacturers from a particular industry present their products and show their capabilities to distributors, wholesalers, retailers, and end-users." Perhaps the best-known trade show in recent years has been the Consumer Electronics Show (CES), but nearly every industry you can think of, large or small, domestic or international, holds a trade show where they present their wares. And in most of those shows, today's booth displays would make the most elaborate of the famed bazaars of the Middle East look like roadside lemonade stands.

Exhibiting is a dynamic industry that is continually evolving, driven by technological innovations and ever-increasing demand for goods from all parts of the global economy. And just as in the ancient marketplaces, merchants and their brands are looking for the competitive edge an eye-catching exhibit booth can provide.

And that is where Ken "Bucky" Buckman's TradeTec earns its keep. Founded in 1999 and headquartered in Chicago, TradeTec is a full-service exhibit, event, and environments studio that produces innovative, modular, and custom portable trade show exhibits.

But as the company website notes: "More than a trade show exhibit company, we are your brand marketing partner with a commitment to execution that delivers predictive performance and dramatic results. TradeTec creates memorable connections between your brand and your customers."

A four-time Inc 5000 honoree as one of the fastest-growing companies in the United States, most recently in 2019, TradeTec currently has six locations across five states, generating more than $30 million in annual revenue. The company has also been named one of the best places to work in Illinois four times by the *Daily Herald Business Ledger*.

And in his spare time Ken has founded two additional successful businesses—Rainy Investments, a real estate investment company with a $60 million-plus portfolio of industrial and residential Chicago-area

Ken Buckman

properties and a two-time Inc 5000 honoree, and Rainy Solar , which built Illinois' first multi-million dollar commercial community solar array—and also advises and invests in several small businesses.

To the casual observer it seems obvious that Ken was born with the entrepreneurial gene, so it's ironic to discover that if it weren't for one of the sales staff calling in sick at a local bike shop, he might have ended up Dr. Buckman.

"My father is a cancer specialist," he explains. "And from a very young age, I was groomed to be a doctor."

But working at a local Schwinn store while in high school store provided two epiphanies. The first: "I needed to sell something."

Originally Ken was hired as a bike mechanic. "I was only allowed in the back, but one day the salesclerk didn't show up, and there was a crowd of customers in the showroom, so the owner said: *Bucky I've got no choice; come on out and at least talk to these people and I'll try to get you out of there as soon as I can.*"

That day he sold a couple two bikes for themselves and another their child, and just like that, Ken's future professional path took a hard left. "I swear I've never done cocaine, but I'm pretty sure if I did, it would be the feeling I had that day," he laughs. "That night I sat my father down, apologized in advance for disappointing him, then told him I wasn't going to be a doctor. Selling is what I had to do."

The second light bulb that went off was: "I was creative."

Ken believes that 90 percent of being an entrepreneur is selling, and he had a knack for coming up with ideas that gave customers a better experience, which led to increased sales. One of his first marketing ideas at the bike shop was to post two articles; the first reported that wearing a helmet reduced the chances of traumatic brain injuries in bicycle accidents by more than 50 percent. The other was about the high incident of bicycle thefts. The articles were posted near a helmet display and a selection of bike locks Ken had set up. He convinced the owner to pay him a 10 percent commission on accessories in addition to his minimum wage hourly wage.

"Nine times out of ten, the customer would buy both a helmet and a lock not just for themselves but for their entire families," Ken says. "So I'd sell a $200 bike and $350 worth of accessories and make an extra $35 in the days of $3.35 minimum wage. And that was my birth into entrepreneurship. Even though I didn't know that's what it was because they didn't use the word *entrepreneur* much in the 1980s. But I really loved coming up with creative solutions that were so obvious to me but that nobody else thought to do."

And as serendipity would have it, the general manager of that bike shop was the person who sent Ken down the path to the trade show business.

"He became engaged to a woman whose uncle was a trade show industry legend. I went to the wedding, and my manager's new wife's uncle came up to him and announced: *You've got to get out of this Schwinn bicycle job. You've got to get in our industry. I have a spot for you.*"

Soon after, the GM was hired away from the bike store by the uncle-in-law's company, and Ken was made general manager.

"Then five years later when I graduated from college and couldn't find any other job, I was hired by the my old GM's company, Skyline, for a sales job, and that's how I got into the trade show industry right out of college."

Irony number two. After graduating from the University of Iowa,

Ken says he wanted nothing more than to be a medical equipment sales rep, which would have kept him in the vicinity of the medical profession and provided a lucrative income.

"Those were the days when medical sales reps drove fancy corporate cars and were given huge expense accounts, and I wanted to do all that. But the year I graduated college, 1992, was when the US government cracked down on incentives given to doctors by sales reps so they would use certain drugs or equipment. So overnight all the fun stuff disappeared."

As did his desire to be a medical sales rep. Instead, through his former manager at Schwinn, he went to work in the trade show business, at a job that was 100 percent commission. Ken says he was given a commission draw of $1000 a month.

"My friends were all getting jobs as lawyers and investment bankers and stockbrokers, and here I was selling booths. And they were like: *Did you say boobs?* They had no idea what a trade booth was. I was completely embarrassed to tell anybody what I was doing because it didn't seem like a respectable job."

But his perspective changed as his sales mojo kicked in. Within three years Ken was one of the top five sales reps in the world for Skyline out of about 850 reps—but he was bored. He credits his boss with stepping up as a mentor.

"The owner of that Skyline company knew I was bored and pulled me aside. He said: *If you're willing to continue selling at the level that you're selling, I'm willing to teach you how to run the business.* I would wait till the end of the day when everybody was gone then went down to his office each day to learn all aspects of what he did and why he did it. It was a path I was totally enthralled with."

The mentoring ultimately led to Ken creating a company within his boss's company. He started hiring people on his own dime, only getting paid back when he hit new, higher sales quotas and says, "I was a punk twenty-five-year-old kid making a ridiculous income. And my boss was making a lot off of me, but I was dead loyal to him and enjoyed making money for him. The only reason that six-year career didn't turn into a thirty-year career is he sold the company."

The company was bought by a newly-minted millionaire who had earned his windfall as one of the first employees at US Robotics, best known for bringing the computer modem to the masses. He sold his stock and set out to buy his own company.

"Whereas the trade show world was 100 percent relationship-based, this guy grew up in the tech world where they don't give a shit about people," Ken says. "There it's all about developing a product as fast as possible then looking to get bought out so you can cash out and start developing the next product."

Ken sensed the new management was not going to be a match made in tradeshow heaven, and his pessimism was richly rewarded. The very first day the new owner took over the company, he told Ken that as the top sales rep, he had to fire everyone working for him under those special deals Ken had with his old boss.

"He said it was high time I learned I was no better than anybody else. I quit on the spot, with no job prospects. And oh, by the way, I was two weeks away from getting married. So I had to go home and tell my fiancée that her supposedly successful sales rep husband-to-be was now unemployed."

But not for long. That same month, October 1997, he became an equity minority partner in an exhibit distributor and manufacturer with six locations. Ken's understanding of the job was to launch an Orlando location from scratch, which sounded like an exciting opportunity, until the reality of the situation sunk in.

"The majority owner gave me 25 percent equity in the company. I didn't really know what that meant at the time; I later learned that meant you were basically an employee and had no rights, which is why I'll never do that again."

Being a minority partner would be the least of his problems. Ken started the Orlando job as soon as he returned from his honeymoon and went to Florida with the anticipation the owner would teach him everything I needed to know like how to lease a building, how to start a local bank relationship, how to hire the employees that he needed for my warehouse, etc.

"I had never done any of that. Although I'd sold and had people working for me, I'd never handled any of the backend stuff. But not only did he not help me at all, he left me on a complete island."

In addition to figuring out the Orlando operation, Ken was also quickly charged by the majority owner with flying to the other six locations to troubleshoot their problems. "I was having to work way too many eighteen to twenty hour days, six to seven days a week. Thank goodness my new wife was in international flight attendant. She'd go away up to a week at a time, so she didn't realize I was working a ridiculous amount of time."

But Ken was a quick learner, and week by week he got the operations up and running and making money. Then shortly before his one-year contract with the company was up, some financial irregularities came to light, as in employees' paychecks started to bounce, and vendors weren't getting paid. It was time to move on. "I knew the company was going to implode, and that's what happened."

Despite all the negatives, the big positive was that the experience was the kind of hands-on learning that no MBA program can truly teach and laid the foundation for Ken to start his own business. The wheels to that entrepreneurial move began turning when he relocated back to Illinois after his year from minority owner hell in Florida when a friend offered him a position at a custom exhibit house.

"When I was at Skyline for those six years after college, I sold modular booths made from pre-manufactured parts and pieces that come together to make a structure. It was like playing with really expensive Legos. I did the much smaller booths that were generally off in the fringes. I wasn't the big, exciting booths that everybody came to see. Those booths were custom made, which is basically like building a house. You start with nothing and create a structure that can cost between six and seven figures."

In 1998 a friend of Ken's, who was running a successful custom exhibits business, Superior Exhibits, was commissioned to build the worldwide Apple computer accounts. Back then Apple Stores were only a gleam in Steve Jobs's eye; trade shows were the prime avenue to expose Apple products both B2B and B2C.

"Instead Apple established their own global roadshow circuit that consisted of about fifty custom booths," Ken says, "as well as about two thousand of the small booths that I had built my career on."

The friend made Ken an offer he couldn't refuse: *Come work for me and teach me everything about modular booths, and in return I'll teach you everything about the high-end custom booth world.* Ken accepted. The gig only lasted about a year and a half, but for Ken it was a huge win.

"I learned a ton, so when Skyline called and offered me the

opportunity to be an authorized dealer of their products in Chicago if I opened my own company, I was ready. Ironically, the company I had previously worked for out of college was still there, but Skyline basically wanted me to put it out of business because the tech millionaire owner had grown out of favor with Skyline. So it was going to be like a World Wrestling Federation cage match; we'd be fighting, scratching, and clawing for every single deal."

It would take several years, but eventually TradeTec scored the knockout punch, and the other company changed its name and switched product lines.

Trade Tec opened in November 1999, just as the Internet was elbowing its way into changing the world. "I partnered with another sales rep I had worked with at the first Skyline office. We became fifty-fifty partners and opened up our company with everything that we had both learned about the much higher-end custom world. But we decided our company was going to be unique. Instead of selling, we were going to only rent the modular equipment. But we hired a super high-end designer who usually created multimillion-dollar booths and had her design $50,000 to $75,000 booths that looked like a million dollars."

Ken targeted the dotcom market, which was creating an investment tsunami.

"That was when it seemed like anyone could write .com on a napkin and get $10 million in venture capital. They didn't give a crap if they made any money; they just wanted to go public as fast as possible, and companies were changing names every three months."

Ken's pitch was simple: *We are here to provide you dotcomers with a high-level design and rent it to you because it's stupid for you to buy something when you're not going to be the same company in six months. So just rent it and give it back to us at the end of the show, then we'll do a new one the next time you come back.* In TradeTec's first year, the company did about $2.5 million in revenue, with 95 percent coming from dotcom companies.

But in dealing with the first wave of dotcom companies, Ken said he realized few of their business models had a prayer of succeeding or actually making money. "So we pivoted and took those great designs and deliberately targeted only traditional companies, ones that actually wanted to make a profit and planned to stick around for a while. And lucky for us we did because on March 21, 2001, the dotcom bubble burst. Sixty-eight of the dotcom companies we worked with during our first year went bankrupt. Thankfully, we weren't exposed to a single one of them. We still rent almost half of our products, but it was that pivot and completely changing how we went to market that set us up for where we are today. Since then we've been adding layers and layers of services around the sale or rental of the exhibit, such as audiovisual, flooring, furniture, storing the booths, shipping them, sending out traveling ambassadors that provide personalized treatment, and other ancillary services."

Ken says that the trade show industry has evolved and since 2008 exhibits have largely become blended custom and modular. "There's very little distinction between the two sides anymore; it's a combination, if I built you a booth tomorrow, it would mostly be made out of stretched fabric and aluminum, but you would have a really cool reception counter or kiosk that's custom made."

With his various businesses humming along, Ken is spending more time toward mentoring others to pay forward how much his mentors helped him.

"I think just about every legit entrepreneur I know that is decades into this, has a similar story about mentors. When I went to college twenty-five years ago, if you said the word entrepreneur people would look at you like:

So you can't get a job? There was a negative connotation to the word. We didn't have the luxury of having classes available that taught us how to think like an entrepreneur, how to act like an entrepreneur, how to understand finance and cash flow so you don't go bankrupt in two weeks by mismanaging your cash. Thank goodness nowadays any college worth their salt has entrepreneurship programs and that I had mentors to help me. So about three years ago, I started putting myself out there as a mentor and speaking at university entrepreneur classes at places like Northwestern and the University of Chicago about a variety of topics, with the idea of helping them learn how to think like an entrepreneur. Not textbook stuff, but things I had to learn the hard way."

There are several key points Ken stresses in his talks. First, he says everyone is so focused on becoming the next Facebook or Google or Amazon that they think they have to come up with a revolutionary idea.

"That thinking is so dangerously wrong and needs to be recalibrated," he says. "Just about everything on the planet has already been invented. The key is improving on what's already here. With the helmet and lock display at the bike store, I didn't invent anything new. Then later I didn't invent booths, but the way I packaged them and presented them to the clients was unique. If you look at it statistically, inventors almost never make money. They're usually the ones that go broke. The ones that get rich are the ones who repackage an idea and present to the masses in a useful way. That is the key. I want kids to recognize that their ideas are going to come from life experiences, not from them sitting in a corner with a whiteboard thinking they've got to be the next high-tech company and make billions of dollars. That's not how it works."

Ken also warns his mentees that if they want to be an entrepreneur for the money, they may as well go get a salaried job. "Eighty percent of entrepreneurs make less than $50,000 a year. If you got an idea or a concept that you're passionate enough about to fight through the inevitable years of things going wrong, legal situations, and product problems, if you're willing to fight through all that and make less than your friends who have jobs then you might actually end up on the other side of the coin. But if you're doing this for money on the front end, you are sadly mistaken."

Another lesson learned: company dictatorships are not as productive as a more democratic leadership approach. "I used to rule by a monarchy, and my view was the only view that mattered. There certainly were a lot of friends and great stories behind the scenes, but it was a pretty rough environment because I didn't share leadership as I should have. The core change happened when I finally recognized the need to have a deep leadership team running the company. I needed to take a big step backward and push the others forward and encourage them to fail and support them when they did. Today I would argue we have one of the strongest management teams in the industry. Our culture is phenomenal, and the last four years in a row we were named one of the best places to work in the state of Illinois. That and the four times on the Inc. 5000 hasn't happened by accident."

According to Ken, another integral secret to his success has been the singular support of his wife, Heide.

"Entrepreneurs spouses are rarely highlighted publicly, yet they are the very foundation that allows people like me do what we do. TradeTec simply wouldn't have happened without her," he says with emotion. "From the very beginning, she encouraged me to go for it, even while sitting in a brand-new, mortgaged-to-the hilt house we would have surely lost within a year had I failed. Heide has always been my rock-solid cheerleader through many dark days, assuring me: It's no big deal; you'll figure it out. She is the real CEO and success story. Without her there is no me."

Ken is emphatic that he feels a moral obligation to mentor and help as many entrepreneurial people as possible who come to him because "there's no chance in hell I would be where I am if dozens hadn't helped me. And the earlier, the better. If I can help them race through a bunch of failures that could hurt them and instead race them toward more likely success using what I've learned the hard way, that's exciting to me. That's my payday. So going forward I see myself doing a lot more volunteer time in high schools, universities, working with students in incubator initiatives, and spending one-on-one time whenever I get a chance. When someone reaches out to me, I love spending that time. And I suspect doing some form of that is going to be my retirement."

Ken also pointed out that as someone with learning disabilities—he has ADHD—he's particularly excited to help other aspiring entrepreneurs with similar conditions. To that end he has done Internet webinars and has been featured in a book about recognizing ADHD as an asset, not a liability.

When the time comes and he does leave TradeTec, Ken says what he'll take with him are the many creative, passionate entrepreneurs he's gotten to know.

"To me, probably one of the coolest things ever about working in the trade show business, especially having kind of a crazy mind like mine, is that I get to meet entrepreneurs. I tell them: *If you expect me to do my job correctly, you need to tell me your story*. I work with some big companies that are way removed from the their origins, but the bulk of the thousands of clients that I've worked with over the years were the founders of the company. So during my whole career, I got the gift of having entrepreneurship bleed into me all day, every day—and I got paid for it. How's that for a great job?"

As American Entrepreneur went to print, Ken announced that private equity firm Gemspring Capital had acquired TradeTec, just months after the twentieth anniversary of him founding it.

While surveying may not be the world's oldest profession, it's probably in the top ten. Defined as the science and art of determining the relative positions of points on Earth, surveying was used by ancient Egyptians to accurately divide land into plots for the purpose of taxation and to restore boundaries after the Nile overflowed its banks. Since then every civilization has used some form of surveying to allot land, set ownership boundaries, determine distance, collect data for maps, and aid in engineering everything from bridges to buildings.

Since founded by Mathew Barr in 2009, SurvWest has been one of the fastest-growing surveying and mapping companies in the United States, making the Inc. 5000 three times by offering top-tier customer service, state-of-the-art technology, and innovative solutions to clients in the transportation, railroad, oil and gas, real estate development, communication, and construction industries. Based in Denver with an office in Fort Worth, Texas, SurvWest has expertise across the surveying spectrum.

"Inside the surveying world you have a multitude of different disciplines," Mathew explains. "First is mapping the existing conditions, everything you see. In order to design something, you have to know specifically what's there. So say before a railroad could lay down new tracks, they'd need to know the vegetation, the grade breaks, the terrain, the underground utilities, etc. So we map all. Sometimes this is called topography surveys, but I just call it mapping because we really do a vast number of things beyond topography."

Then there is boundary surveying to define existing rights, another important service for railroads, one that often requires Mathew to act as an expert witness in legal proceedings. "I'm often hired by BNSF and Union Pacific to protect and defend their title basically across the entire country from people who adversely attempt to take title from them."

There is utility surveying, which is part of subsurface utility engineering (SUE), a process that combines civil engineering, surveying, and geophysics to accurately map underground utilities such as pipelines and cable lines so that new projects can adjust their routes to avoid the existing infrastructure. It can also help determine the condition of the below-ground utilities.

Lastly there is aerial photogrammetry, which uses photographs for mapmaking and surveying. A fixed-wing airplane is fitted with a mounted camera pointed vertically toward the ground to take overlapping images, which are used to create two- or three- dimensional models. Generally speaking, aerial photogrammetry is used to create topographical maps so that geographical areas can be analyzed. This type of surveying can be used for architecture and land development, watershed or deforestation research, city planning, and even film production.

It is estimated there are more than 25,000 surveying companies in the United States. Mathew says what sets SurvWest apart from the competition is a combination of his team's expertise and his personality-based approach to building business relationships.

"My primary competition comes from large engineering firms, which are typically very conservative. They're run by hired CEOs who are absolutely not going to take a lot of risks because they're not entrepreneurs. I'm the opposite of that. It's my company; I can take those risks. After that it comes down to marketing. I'm much louder in the room;

Mathew Barr

I'm a bigger personality than most people in my industry. My personality type is very flamboyant. Engineers and surveyors are technical people; they're not professionally built for public speaking engagements. They don't seek out opportunities to literally rile up their co-workers."

Mathew, on the other hand, loves the bully pulpit to preach company culture and end goals and get employees and other stakeholders to believe his vision for SurvWest.

"I'm more of a motivator, which is another trackable skill set an entrepreneur needs to have. My competition are much more purely technical. They believe in selling technical things. Just as I started my business by selling myself, now I believe in selling my people and our company culture."

While it may seem that Mathew was born with surveying in his blood, he admits that he ended up in the industry completely by happy accident. After attending Northwest Kansas Technical College to study technical drafting, Mathew went to work for a Kansas City civil engineering company, JBM, which is now TranSystems Corporation.

"They had a flood of survey and mapping work and said: *Why don't you go try that?* I was twenty years old and said sure. Up to then I didn't know anything about it. It was purely accidental, the company trying to fit me into a place I liked. I started out as a survey helper, working in the field operations side. Went out into the field every day, traveling all over."

Rather than move on looking for other job opportunities that utilized drafting such as a CAD technician or in architectural design, Mathew discovered he had a knack for surveying and worked his way up to senior surveyor.

"I started doing that in May of 1995, and by the following May I realized I was just naturally talented at it. So merely based on that I made the decision to stay. There's no better way to progress than when things are easy. If you find your job hard, you generally don't move up the ladder, or at least it certainly takes a lot more effort to get there."

In 1998 the company moved Mathew into the office because they were short on CAD technicians with a survey background.

"I came into the office as a CAD technician to learn the software that they had, even though I knew nothing about it because I'd been working for three-and-a-half years in the field."

A quick study, Mathew had a rapid learning curve, and by 1999 he was a senior CAD technician, making presentations of the software at national conventions and teaching others how to use it.

"In 2000 the company relocated me from Kansas City, Missouri, to Fort Worth, Texas, to market and drive the business down there," he says. "I rapidly progressed to what they called the team leader, and over the next four years developed a lot of relationships and helped build the survey practice."

Mathew left the company for a job at Carter & Burgess in Denver, Colorado, a full-service, engineering, architecture, and planning firm headquartered in Fort Worth that had more than thirty US offices before being acquired by another company. He stayed there two years then went to work for a New Mexico-based consulting firm specializing in engineering, spatial data, and advanced technologies that had him establish an office in Denver.

"By 2009, I finally thought: *Well, what the hell am I doing? I should just do this for myself.* It was obvious I could put together an office and build businesses offices, so I just decided to start my own company. I would like to say that I spent years planning and strategizing, but that's not the honest truth. I literally decided, then got up, went into my boss's office, and said: *I think I'm going to start my own business.* He told me to take thirty days to make my decision. My wife said: *I think you have to plan it out, create a business plan.* I'm like: *Oh, I don't think you need any of that crap. None of that makes any sense to me.*"

In thirty days Mathew walked back into his boss's office and told him he was going to leave.

"He told me I had to be out of there in a month because I'd be essentially competing against him. I said: *Okay, I'm going to do that.* After I left his office, I literally walked back to my desk and made numerous phone calls to my clients. I said: *Hey, I'm going to start my own business.* And they were like: *Great! Where do we send the contracts?* I knew I was going to get those clients. After that I went and found office space, hired some people, and then opened my company."

While Mathew says he really didn't overtly think about starting his own company until that day of epiphany, at the very least he had prepared for such an occurrence by declining to sign a non-compete contract when joining the firm.

"When I took that job, they had multiple locations, and the owner of that company said: *Matt, we're going to need you to sign a non-compete.* I said: *Not a problem. Just let me estimate the damages that would incur for me over the next five years. Then you can write me a check for that amount, which I'll absolutely sign.* He just gave me a funny look."

Mathew went home, did the math, then went to see the owner and gave him a number. "I said: *If you write me a check for that amount, I'll take five years off whenever I leave here. But I am absolutely not going to hinder my ability to make a living by starting my own company. Totally up to you.* I believe in always giving a choice. Well, thank God he didn't actually write that check because I severely sold myself short with that dollar-figure estimate," he says with a laugh. "That's how I pitched it. In the end I didn't have a non-compete because they really needed me. I worked there during the Great Recession and brought in a ton of revenue and clients' money because the rail business and all the market segments I could get work from were still booming and provided plenty of work. So I propped them up. If they had forced the issue, I probably would have turned down the job and would have just gone and started my own business at that point."

While most employees assume they have no choice but to sign non-competes, Mathew believes it's a strategy that can stand on shaky legal ground.

"Attorneys talk businesspeople into coming up with these ridiculous contracts against people that limit their ability to make money, which almost never stand up in court by the way. You can't impede somebody's ability to make money. Now, if they had said: *Hey, sign this non-compete, and I'll give you $300,000 dollars*, that would be a different story because then that's an exchange of services. Luckily they didn't."

So Mathew was free to establish his business within a month of making the decision. He named the company SurvTech Solutions and started with $38,000 in cash and no real plan, just faith in his skills.

"I knew I was really good at vision and understanding that I could get somewhere. I'm extremely competent in my technical background and with my relationships. Among my first clients was BNSF Railway. I worked in twenty-three states the first year and did all their surveying. And at the end of that first year, we did almost $2 million in revenue."

The following year SurvTech added Union Pacific Railway and a couple million more in revenue, and from there quickly progressed up to $6 million and then $12 million in revenue.

The first real obstacle in the business occurred three years in when they discovered a small Florida-based survey firm had filed a trademark on the name Survtech Solutions, meaning they could no longer use that name for the company. "It was a set-back, but within a month we changed our name to

SUE vactruck

SurvWest, created a new website, logo, and email addresses—basically everything," Mathew says. "The hardest part was working through all of the confusion with our clients on why we re-branded; it was my first lesson in scaling a business."

Back on branding track, Mathew began doing survey mapping, but it was always his intention to become more full service and expand the business. He opened a second office in Fort Worth in 2016 and a third in Portland, Oregon, in 2020.

"I've ramped it up fairly quickly," he acknowledges. "We have sixty-plus people. And everything I did in the beginning has changed. Now that I'm CEO, I'm no longer out in the field. I always tell my people I don't work in the business; I work on the business."

But getting to that point wasn't easy. Before he could delegate, Mathew had to find people to delegate to.

"Working on a business is difficult to do when you're a fast-growing start-up," he says. "You need to find great people, you have to train them, then you have to put everybody in place and diversify your work. Which I did. So now my goal every day is to work on the business; otherwise, our growth will severely shrink, and then we'll just be like any other firm that went up to a point and just stopped."

Mathew admits that transition from founder to CEO wasn't the easiest. "I was awful at it because I was an entrepreneur. I want to do everything because that's how entrepreneurs are built. To start a business you have to do legal services, business services, contracts, marketing—a master of all, right? Delegation is not something you ever do naturally. So I was awful at it. I understood I had to do it, but I fought myself the entire time."

Until the universe stepped in. Mathew says he was diagnosed with cancer, which forced his hand. "Then I had no choice but to delegate. Now, in a quick nine weeks, I was able to kick cancer's butt. Before my diagnosis we had really good growth but not explosive growth. But in that nine weeks when I was forced to delegate, the business grew tenfold over what I was doing before. I realized I had become the constrictor of it because I was not delegating and not empowering the people around me. So I made a 180-degree flip, and now I run the business like a CEO and not so much as an entrepreneur."

That said, Mathew finds his entrepreneurial itch scratched through establishing new verticals and when opening new offices, which he says has all the same elements as starting a new company.

"Creating diversifications and the process of opening new offices absolutely feeds my vice of being an entrepreneur. When I went from Denver and opened an office in Dallas, it was a brand-new landscape both vertically and geographically, where nobody knew us. So you have to do all the same things you did before when you first started."

Picking locations for new offices seems a mixture of analytics—population growth, demographics, labor pool, big tax base—and looking into a crystal ball.

"For Dallas, Texas is steadfast with one of the fastest-growing populaces. Austin is slowly becoming the next Mecca of millennials and the tech industry. That creates a lot of opportunity for me and provides all those things that feed my company. Same with Portland. Seattle's already had its little boom; to me it doesn't have a lot of room for further growth. But with Portland being literally a stone's throw away from Seattle, millennials are moving to Portland because Seattle became too expensive. That overflow creates a lot of work for me because Portland is having a growth boom, but its infrastructure wasn't built for that many people. I always believed that you should follow both the labor and the money."

Despite the opportunities, Mathew isn't worried about an influx of competitors trying to go mano a mano with SurvWest, mostly because of the steep investment needed for the state-of-the-art technology that's integral to the services the company offers.

"The capital expenditure side, especially for the survey and the SUE side of the industry, stops a lot of people from entering it. Just to equip one office will probably cost you $1.5 million, and that's not counting labor. Even large firms consider that capital a big risk." But Mathew sees it as a necessary cost of doing the kind of business he provides. "Not making that investment would severely hamper my ability to progressively move my company forward."

And it's not a case of the equipment having a long shelf life. Mathew compares it to laptops. "You buy a new laptop and then three years later it essentially has little value because technologically it's become antiquated. The same is true for most of the equipment I use. It's disposable equipment that costs a lot."

To ease the financial hit, Mathew sells his old equipment to individuals or companies that can't afford to buy the latest machinery—the *one man's trash is another man's treasure* school of capital recoup.

"I call those the sub-tier markets. You can sell to them and get a decent return. We can use the top-end equipment for about two years, then turn around and sell it for about half the original cost. Not everybody does it, but that's what I do."

While the mathematical foundation of surveying hasn't changed, the techniques and technology used to measure have evolved exponentially, which has significantly increased the accuracy of surveying results. Hundreds of years ago land surveyors would use levels, tape measures, and hand-held compasses to measure distance and horizontal angles. As time has gone by, land surveying tools and techniques advanced, expanding the role of land surveyors. But of all the various technologies used in surveying, Mathew says perhaps none were as game-changing as GPS. Not only did it enable much better accuracy, it also streamlined the process.

"Once upon a time you needed four people on a survey crew," Mathew says; "Today, you just need one person supplied with the equipment and you have an instant survey crew. So GPS along with other technology not only advanced the profession, it also made the profession more scalable, which in turn made it possible to be much more profitable."

When considering SurvWest's future growth, Mathew says he is always looking at least five years out.

"I should always be five years ahead of where I am right now in my thinking process. There are a lot of factors to consider, so you have to be a master at reading market trends and making some guesstimates as conditions change. The political climate can affect our economic climate, so there could be shifts there. I'm always looking. Even when I'm focusing on a new office, I have other ones in my peripheral vision that I'm already potentially targeting. It will come down to where they are in their life cycle. Every city or region has a life cycle. I live by that. I look at Portland and see a ten-year life cycle operating at top margins before its growth slows, before housing slows. There's no market that just perpetually goes. People make the mistake of plopping in an area and thinking their opportunity there is going to last forever. That's not really true."

Mathew believes that each new generation of young adults coming out of college wants to settle in a different area, so there is a natural ebb and flow.

"Simply look at Austin, Texas, and the way it was ten years ago; that wasn't the Austin it is now. And ten year from now, it's not going to be the Austin it is today. California was a hot market for a long time, but it's cooled, and there's an exodus of people from there to Texas. There's always a gradual shift because every location has a shelf life. Millennials are attracted to Portland and Austin but the next generation likely will not do the same thing and become migratory again."

By that he doesn't mean an area will turn into a modern-day ghost town or that it won't generate money. He's referring to windows of when you can facilitate maximum growth and maximum profit.

"As a business you want to get in and maximize that. For Portland, I see that as a ten-year opportunity where you can make a bunch of money, grow your business up, stabilize it, and then it's going to level off. It's going to become static. And that's okay because from a business perspective, the more you have of those markets, then you can focus on the next markets entering the high-growth phase of its life cycle."

Mathew says too many would-be entrepreneurs make the mistake of starting a business without taking the time to thoroughly understand whatever market they are targeting,

"It doesn't matter what business segment they want to be in; they need to ask themselves what will it look like ten years from now and how big will my business be? What's the scalability? Are you creating a lifestyle business or trying for a high-growth business? Do you plan on selling the business? Those are the questions you need to have an answer for before you start. If you can't answer them, then you really don't understand the market. Sometimes people's goals of what they think is going to happen versus what they're actually setting out to do don't match up. At the end of the day, it doesn't matter what you're creating. You can make a good living out of a lifestyle business, but you need to match up the other end of the scale for that."

Mathew notes that there is a generation change every ten years, so anytime you're creating a business, you have to build it for both the generation that you're currently targeting as well as the generation to follow because the only constant is that it will shift again.

"Looking ahead and anticipating those shifts and the opportunities that come with them has served us well, and I expect it will continue to do so going forward."

TAKTIK
LOGISTICS GROUP

At its most basic, logistics is the process of moving something from point A to point B. In today's business parlance it refers to managing how resources are acquired, stored, and transported to their final destination, which includes inbound and outbound transportation management, fleet management, warehousing, materials handling, order fulfillment, logistics network design, inventory management, supply and demand planning, third-party logistics management, and other support services—in short, logistics services are involved at all levels in the planning and execution of the movement of goods, from the food we buy in the grocery store to freshly-minted automobiles.

As an industry, logistics transportation offers many opportunities, which is why competition is intensely fierce. So when a company like TAKTIK Logistics Group breaks out, people take notice. Founded by Tyson Lawrence in 2015, the Pleasanton, California, company has become one of the United States' fastest-growing transportation and logistics enterprises. Tyson's vision for his company was to create a logistics company that provided the highest level of customer service by implementing state-of-the-art technology to give customers 24/7/365 access to their freight.

"Logistics was one of the last places technology came into, which for years I never understood," Tyson notes. "It's something we started integrating years ago."

Through the development of a proprietary, web-based platform and partnerships with like-minded transportation management technology companies, TAKTIK customers enjoy greater visibility of their accounts and better control of their freight costs.

While Tyson's rise in the industry may seem like a smooth, fast ride to the casual observer, it took years of learning the business and a devastating company closure before TAKTIK rose from the entrepreneurial ashes to become one of the leading logistics companies in the country.

#

After graduating from college Tyson says he had no concrete career plans. He could have gone into some tech field but didn't. Instead he got a job at the Bay Area office for CH Robinson, a huge, national third-party logistics provider. His thought was to work there for maybe a year then go back to school for a law degree. But one year turned into three, and the education he received was in logistics, much of it by osmosis.

"I was in truckload, but I was always interested in the other parts of the business. I became good friends with my coworkers and would spend a lot of time over beers asking my friends what they worked on and just listening. From that I got an idea of how the entire process operated."

While he liked logistics, he wasn't a white-collar kind of guy. "I didn't like the corporate environment. Plus my personal trajectory at CH Robinson really seemed limited because I realized that if I really wanted to advance at that company, I would end up having to move to Minnesota where their corporate headquarters is. Otherwise I'd end up managing an office, but I wouldn't be able to choose which office. The one in San Francisco was being headed by somebody who was pretty much going to stay there for a long time, and I didn't want to be the manager of Winnemucca, Nevada. I wanted to choose where the next stage of my career was going."

Tyson says one of the advantages of working for CH Robinson was

Tyson Lawrence

other logistics companies were constantly trying to poach employees.

"People were always asking if you were interested in this or that opportunity. And it would usually be an offer to work for a smaller brokerage or whatnot. After a couple of years working there, I was getting bored because I wanted more. I wanted to do more. I wanted to grow faster than I was currently was able to within CH Robinson' corporate environment. And there were people nibbling at me: *Hey; we love your pedigree, that you're at CH Robinson—does this position interest you?*"

Eventually Tyson accepted an offer to work in drayage, which is the process of transporting containers over short distances locally as part of the supply chain process, such as to or from ports or from a port to a rail yard to be loaded onto a train.

"I got a lot of experience in the drayage aspect of the industry, which also gave me an insight into the trucking company's perspective as opposed to the third-party broker in the middle, which is what CH Robinson is."

From there Tyson went to work for a produce transportation group, West Coast Distributing, which introduced him to the refrigerated aspect of trucking. But the restlessness soon came back.

"I wasn't liking my trajectory at that point. I felt like I was leveling off, even though I'd only been in the business about four or five years overall—two years at CH Robinson, a little over a year at the drayage company, and almost two years at West Coast. I didn't know where my next step was. But I still wasn't really envisioning starting my own business; that still felt like too big of a move."

That is until his superiors at West Coast Distribution had him start working from home so he wouldn't have to commute to and from Monterey.

"It was a beautiful drive and a nice place to work, but it was taking a physical toll," Tyson says. "My girlfriend, who is now my wife, worked in the Bay Area, and I didn't want to move to Monterey. So the company allowed me to work from home on a regular basis, and I saw very clearly that I could probably do that on my own. I was getting restless again and thought maybe I should book some freight during the day and go to law school at night. I didn't know if I wanted to be a lawyer. I just wanted to add that skill-set to the toolbox."

Tyson negotiated his way out of his day job, and in 2005 started his first company, PacWest Distributing. His first client came courtesy of his former company.

"My biggest client from the old job said they'd book a few loads with me on the side, and that's what I did. Once I did that, I saw my career trajectory just open up. They were bringing speakers into class, talking about how they were making six figures after being attorneys for five years. But they were working eighty hours a week. And I'm sitting there thinking: *I'm making that working part-time with my business right now. What could I do with it full time?*"

Tyson said his time at CH Robinson and the other companies had provided him a solid education in the logistics industry as had working with various mentors along the way at each company.

"I felt like I could replicate that with people who worked for me, and then I could grow the business better that way rather than getting a law degree."

The only thing holding him back was himself. Tyson admits that it was hard to get past his upbringing, which had instilled traditional work values: you go to college, you get a job, you stay at that job thirty or forty years, you get a gold watch, then you collect a pension at the end.

"Our parents didn't know that the world was going to change the way it has, where now people move from job to job and staying at the same company for decades as an employee is almost unheard of. Once I was able to get that thinking out of my mind, I realized I really could own my own company." Tyson says he had that epiphany while out walking his English bulldog, Rocco. "I felt like I could take this as big as I wanted to and was wasting my time in law school," he says with a laugh. "So I dropped out after my first year, and from that point it just caught momentum."

There was also a little good fortune involved. Freight brokering is a capital-intense business, and Tyson didn't have much cash to start out with. "If your customer doesn't pay you in time, you can't pay your truck. If you don't pay your truck soon enough, they are not going to take your freight. I was lucky enough that one of my customers paid me in fifteen days, and I didn't have to pay my trucks until thirty days. So I was able to build up two weeks of cash flow, which helped immensely. I was able to start allocating funds and build a war chest, getting ready to set up an office and start hiring people."

PacWest quickly took off, and by 2009 had reached $5 million in sales. Tyson says, "Everything I touched turned to gold."

Until it didn't. Even though the company was doing ever more business, growth stalled, and his profits decreased. Tyson had hit a bump he couldn't seem to get over. He eventually realized the business had become too reliant on its biggest client, and it was stifling PacWest's growth.

"The retail grocery company I started my company with supplied the money to help me get started. Then they continued to give me more and more business until it grew to a $3 million account. Well, as we kept growing they did too. I was always trying to diversify away from them, get some other clients to avoid wholly relying on them."

Tyson says the awareness that he needed more clients would keep him up at night. So he started hiring people to kill two birds: to increase the business with current customers and to free him up to bring in new business. And he did but still couldn't really break away from the main client.

"It was easy business," he admits. "Any time they had a new project, they'd come to us because we did such a good job for him. When someone hands you business, you take it."

Then the client company was bought by a private equity group, which made many changes in terms and in tone. For example, if there were damaged goods—even if the damage wasn't PacWest's fault—Tyson had to eat the cost. The company started paying less for jobs and was not timely with payments. If Tyson wanted payments processed more promptly, he'd have to pay a 2 percent fee.

"They were also more by the book," he says. "I had a lot of handshake deals with the company because the transportation industry is market-driven. Prices can go up during one time of the year and down during others. So I would take losses at certain times and then make up those losses when it would come back around in my favor. That's how we worked. When the private equity group came in, they wouldn't give me the chance to make up the money I had previously lost as part of the cycle by eliminating the deal."

The move cut PacWest off from about half a million dollars of funds needed to keep the business going. Attempts to negotiate failed.

"It was a David and Goliath situation to begin with. We were a small company with eight employees, and they were a multimillion-dollar behemoth. And what they said won. Basically if we pissed off one part of it, we were going to lose all of it."

It was a fraught time. Not only did Tyson and his wife have two young children and live in one of the most expensive areas in the country, he had employees he considered family members. Their reality was figuring out survival. Tyson says he gathered his most trusted friends, mentors, and advisors together in his office and laid out three options. 1) Bankrupt PacWest and walk away to another profession or job. 2) Try to negotiate rate concessions, which he knew was a non-starter. Or 3) fight it out with them and start working on a new, different enterprise and see what happens. Tyson says he and his crew decided on option number three.

"We to renege on our contract by turning down freight, starting a war of lawyers. I knew I was going to have to take PacWest into bankruptcy and start completely over. "And I needed to start the new company right away because I only had about $15,000 in my personal savings."

So while Tyson was finishing out PacWest, he built the foundation for his new company, TAKTIK Logistics Group, the name reflecting his intention to be more tactical and strategic the second time around. But there were casualties as he only took his top five people from the PacWest staff to start over with the new enterprise, which Tyson says was founded with a completely new mindset.

"I had the benefit of having ten years' experience learning practical solutions for running a company and all the good and bad that comes along with that."

TAKTIK also had to build a new client base as well.

"I started out really niche, but even before the end of the first company, my efforts to diversify into other modes of transportation beyond refrigerated freight was just starting to get a foothold. So I had a running start the second time around

because we had a few customers. It definitely was not enough to pay the bills, but I had always been a patient person, and I wanted to exude patience on this. Obviously I wanted to get back to supporting my family and all that, but I believed in the long game of developing relationships individually with these customers. And then being along for the ride as they grow."

Tyson credits his team for trusting his vision even in a time of uncertainty.

"I think it was refreshing for them not having to deal with the pressure of working for a bigger company, walking on eggs shells worrying about making them mad."

Having learned the value of diversity the hard way, Tyson wanted his clients and his new company to be as diverse as possible across all modes, including less than truckload (LTL), full truckload, intermodal, flatbed, international air cargo—whatever.

"And I wanted clients across all industries as long as they fit with our culture. I was more interested in the values of the company and the people running it because I wanted to have those relationships at top."

Tyson was also happy to grow with start-ups that might not have much sophistication when it came to logistics.

"Transportation is an integral part of a lot of different businesses. But when people first start making their product, they often don't think about having to move that product from where they're manufacturing it to their customer. So there's a learning curve there, and we like to help with that to help build trust and the relationship up from that perspective. Unlike before, now we're in more of an advisory role where are clients want our input and listen to us. We're able to work together as a collaboration."

While start-ups and smaller companies might not have the volume a large national client would, in Tyson's experience they tend to have a more personal approach to business relationships.

"I could always go chasing large companies that ship thousands of loads a day and whatnot, but you just become a commodity to them," he says. "And they start telling you how to run your company."

Been there, done that. This time Tyson has positioned the company so they can choose who they work with.

"We don't take everybody, and that's given us a sense of power. We know the customer, they're going to pay their bills, they have a longer-term vision, and they're not going to cut us off and leave us hanging like we were before with PacWest."

Tyson says that even though the implosion of PacWest and the resulting bankruptcy was a terrible experience personally, going through it and building the new company that is so much more solid was the best experience. "In fact, I didn't call myself an entrepreneur until I came out the other side of the situation because I didn't feel like I'd really earned it. Those first five years, I never really had any adversity, and I feel part of being an entrepreneur is overcoming adversity no matter how big or small it is. It's getting punched in the face and coming back. And I was clearly punched in the face with PacWest. But I will take the experiences from it and make this company better for it."

So far, so good. In 2019 TAKTIK was named to the Inc. 5000 list of fastest-growing private companies, with a three-year growth rate of 193 percent and annual revenue of $ 7.3 million. What makes the achievement especially significant is that it was done in such a highly competitive industry.

"This is a really interesting time in the industry that I'm glad to be here for, but there are a lot of people out there that do what we do. We have a lot of competition small, medium, and large. Logistics is about an $850 billion industry, but there's a lot of fragmentation, which gives us an advantage over other industries. CH Robinson is the largest company but just has an 8 percent market share. And just recently Amazon has come into the space as has Uber. But even with big players like that, they're not going to suck up the remaining 90 percent of the market share and put anybody else out of business. So there's still a lot of space despite the competition. It really just comes down to identifying where our comfort level is, knowing where our customers are coming from and putting ourselves in their shoes to understand what they need in order to be successful. I don't think a lot of companies do that in this space. They just try to move the freight from point A to point B to make money. We try to get into our customers' heads and understand what they're thinking and what's important to them. And those are the things that have differentiated us from a lot of the others."

Tyson says many of his customers get constantly inundated by cold calls every day, especially when they reach the $50 to $100 million in sales, from transportation brokerages all over the country trying to get their business.

"Fortunately we've already established a strong, sturdy business relationship with them, so it would be a lot harder for them to get out of that and put their whole supply chain at risk to take on somebody who just happened to call that day. Yeah, it cuts both ways, but we've really developed a process where we focus on building a relationship."

To get where he is today, Tyson literally had to blow up everything he'd created to rebuild a business that was stronger, smarter, and more secure. The experience also left him wiser, with a unique perspective on running a business and achieving success—an approach he calls the four Ps.

"These are principles for whatever you're pursuing. The first is you must maintain a positive, can-do attitude even during the hard times. You need to be persistent when working through the daily challenges that are never going to stop as long as you run a business, something that every entrepreneur faces. When you overcome one challenge, there's always going to be another problem, another challenge around the corner. You have to just to suck it up, solve the problem, then move on."

The third P is perseverance. Where persistence is continuing to do something despite difficulty or opposition and maintaining a single-mindedness for achievement of a particular goal, perseverance is continuing a course of action despite a lack of success.

Or as Tyson says, "It's getting over the gut-punch that you're bound to get and learn from it."

The last P is patience, which is defined as *the capacity to accept or tolerate delay, trouble, or suffering without getting angry or upset*. For an entrepreneur, patience is the foundation for building a business the right way, with no cut corners.

"You have to be patient because growing a business it will almost always take longer than you want; it's not built overnight. It takes time. That doesn't mean you get to sit back on your hands and wait for it to come. You have to work really hard, and you can't get discouraged. It's hard to be patient through the process for a lot of reasons beyond that like finances or competition or even ego. I think a lot of entrepreneurs are really hard-charging people who expect things to happen quickly and when it doesn't, they see it as some kind of failure."

Tyson also observes that our technology-fueled, instant gratification world has made everyone less patient. We press a button or click a link and get anything we want. While different people are driven by different motivations and come from different circumstances, patience is a crucial, universal truth for all entrepreneurs while working through their unique start-up experiences.

"You're going to have high highs and low lows," Tyson says. "So you need to find a medium spot to rest in where you can control those emotions and take advantage of your opportunities when they present themselves. There are always opportunities; you just need to be able to be see them and capitalize on them."

Or be ready to capitalize on them. Tyson says that for now he's where he should be.

"I like building companies, but what I really like is being able to strategize and organize the company to be not only successful for me but also the people that work for me. I like doing that. But eventually I would like to step away. I didn't necessarily choose this industry because I love it. I made the most of an opportunity that presented itself. I'm going to be forty-two in 2020 and am at a point in my life where I'd like to go do something I *want* to do. Something I don't *have* to do because of finances. But I still have a goal of where I want to get this business to. And I need to achieve that before I'll feel comfortable stepping away and doing something else. Until then I have a number of businesses and interests that I dabble in on the side, which helps me feel less restless."

But whatever direction his entrepreneurial journey takes him, it's probably a good bet it won't include law school.

Credit cards have been around since the early 1900s, when some department stores and oil companies started issuing proprietary cards. Those cards later introduced the idea of having a revolving balance and finance charges. Banks became players in 1966 when Bank of America's BankAmericard became the United States' first licensed general-purpose credit card. It would later be renamed Visa. That same year a group of California banks formed the Interbank Card Association and issued the nation's second major bank credit card, Master Charge, which became Mastercard.

Up through the early 1970s, payment-card transactions were processed largely without the benefit of computer technology. These early credits cards used a simple but effective paper system to process charges. Salesclerks conducted card authorizations either by telephone or by checking the consumer's card number in a directory of card numbers that were known to be invalid. Once transactions were authorized, the merchant used a manual machine to take multiple card imprints on a paper voucher using carbon paper. The merchant snail-mailed those paper drafts from the transaction to its acquiring bank, who then sent the drafts to the appropriate network. The drafts were sorted, bundled, and sent to the appropriate issuing bank to debit the consumer's account and then pay the merchant.

When credit card charges represented a minuscule percentage of transaction volume, manual processing was adequate. But as credit card use soared in the 1970s, the paper-based closed system became increasingly impractical. In 1979 Visa introduced the credit card terminal. This basic technology ruled the processing roost for a time, but credit card processing as we know it today was born in 1994 when Lipman Electronics Engineering created the first wireless terminal, which coincided with the arrival of the Internet. Online-based businesses required a virtual payment terminal that was compatible with the needs of online business.

Today the credit card industry is massive. People worldwide spend more than $7 trillion per year using credit cards with each transaction needing to be processed. While issuing banks still offer payment processing, businesses are more likely to use a third-party company such as technology start-up Universal Processing to handle credit card and debit card transactions.

Founded in 2003 by Saint Hung, Universal Processing now helps more than twelve thousand merchant partners across all fifty states process in excess of $1 billion in transactions annually through offices in New York, California, and Texas. Universal Processing made the 2019 Inc. 5000 list of fastest-growing companies in the United States, ranked #500, with a three-year growth rate of 869 percent.

Saint notes, "Universal Processing is not the overnight success that one hears about of contemporary unicorns and gangbusters start-ups, but a lesson in determination, focus, and perseverance over many years. Our organization tells a story of learning what to do right through earlier mistakes."

Not all payment processing systems and solutions are created equal and tend to vary depending on company size. For a small brick-and-mortar business owner, a standard point of sale system or credit card terminal is enough. If the business has an online presence, they will need a virtual

Saint Hung

terminal as well. Larger companies usually require an integrated payment solution that integrates credit card acceptance into the business management software driving the enterprise.

Merchants large and small face any number of fees associated with processing. Costs can include per-transaction fees the bank charges, the bank's card processing network, established fee structures with the network of card processors, and any monthly or annual fees the bank charges for various services.

Larger companies are big enough to absorb the fees—or pass along the cost to consumers. For smaller businesses surviving on razor-thin margins, the fees can be a hindrance to growth as well as their ultimate sustainability. So Saint founded Universal with a mission to work with small to medium business owners rather than against them by providing open communication, minimal rates and fees, efficient and simple credit card processing, and high-quality customer service.

"We believe in putting people before profits," Saint says. "We keep costs low to ensure clients keep more of their hard-earned money, and we perform our business in a way that puts our clients' best interests at the forefront. We work hard to maintain an open, honest, and ethical business that is transparent with our costs so clients are spending more time on their business and less time worrying about any mysterious charges or unexpected new fees. We have solidified our growth and scale over these last seventeen years by providing incomparable service to small- and medium-sized minority business owners as well as by hiring professionals of all races, ethnicities, beliefs, and lifestyles and providing them careers with unlimited potential."

Much of Saint's business philosophy was forged working for large merchant service providers. The summer before his senior year in high school when Saint was sixteen, he landed an internship at Morgan Stanley Dean Witter (now Morgan Stanley), and says he took an immediate liking to the financial services industry, particularly cold-calling, sales, and business development.

"I didn't do too well my senior year of high school because I was not a good student," Saint admits. "I probably would have been a high school dropout, but thankfully I only needed to pass my gym classes."

His superior from Morgan Stanley had moved over to Merrill Lynch, and in the summer of 1997, following his graduation, Saint started working at Merrill Lynch and says that's when he transitioned into payment processing. While most employers today in the finance industry put great emphasis on applicants having a college degree, Saint thinks it simply depends on the applicant.

"I think many people overestimate the value of a college education or it's used as a social tool. I think it's about how you conduct yourself. If I were to go anywhere and look for a sales job now, even without a college degree, I don't think I'd have a problem. So it depends on the person, and it depends on the perspective. I do consider myself lucky having had experience at Merrill Lynch and Morgan Stanley prior to getting my first full-time, serious job at JPMorgan Chase when I was twenty. I was hired with just a high school diploma and about four years of hands-on work experience and was the youngest person in my department across the country. I think that's one of the great attributes of America and the American dream: you can make it from anywhere. Hopefully I'm a testament to that for others."

Saint says he enjoyed the first couple years at Chase. "I mean, it was great to be making full-time money, and everything was new. I'd go to annual events, and every day I was meeting business owners, working with new customers, and acquiring big-dollar businesses for Chase. But no matter how much business you do or what you accomplish, everything resets at the beginning of the next month, and over time my contributions to the company seemed to mean less and less even as I attained ever-higher marks. I did about $600 million in business for Chase but never got so much as a pat on the back. Whether because of my age or my ethnicity or because I was too much a straight shooter or I didn't kiss enough butt, I kept getting overlooked for promotions in favor of less qualified, less merited individuals. So pretty soon you start seeing the writing on the wall of what a future in Corporate America looked like."

The view was not particularly egalitarian.

"You'd go to annual events and our executive management or board of directors would say: *Our numbers aren't looking good. I'm sorry, but we're going to have to cut back.* And the ones who took the hit were the sales teams, the operations teams—the employees—whether through layoffs or a reduction of benefits. But upper management though didn't feel the need to sacrifice executive perks like private jets, vacations, and bonuses. I could not give another quarter-century or half-century of my life to an organization I felt was not appreciative of its rank-and-file's contribution. So after about four years, I thought: *There's got to be a better way.* So with little more than a couple of dollars in my pocket and some shares of employee stock, I decided to leave and do it my way."

Saint assumed that he could grow his client base using some of the relationships he had built while at Chase. "Not to solicit them out of their contract, but to talk to them once their contract was up. But after leaving I immediately received a cease-and-desist letter telling me that I'd get sued from here all the way across the world for talking to anybody—any client of Chase or even any employee of Chase."

The threatening legal letter stated Saint could have no contact with anybody having to do anything with Chase for the following five years minimum. In some situations the term was for ten years.

"So I said: *Whoa. Well, there's only one way to do this, which is roll up my sleeves and go knocking door-to-door.* Which basically is what I did when I started with Chase. So that's how I grew Universal Processing, by trying to convince other people that my mission was better than any other company in existence—definitely better than Chase's," he says with a laugh. "I suppose the jury's still out. But I believe—and my workers and colleagues believe—that we do things better than the big banks out there do."

During his experience in Corporate America, Saint noticed that minority and underserved business owners who sought to advance their businesses with payment processing technology were often neglected. Corporate America disregarded those minority and underserved business owners if there was a language barrier or they didn't have enough zeroes in their bank accounts. Offering ethnic minorities, women, the LGBTQ community, immigrants, mom-and-pop business owners, and any other underserved community access to payment processing tools and support was another impetus for Saint to start his own company. That embrace of diversity holds true for his own company as well.

"My company is 70 percent female, and they get paid the same—if not more—than the men in the company. All of those underserved, under-represented markets get represented at Universal Processing. And since I was effectively a near-high school dropout, I give GED holders, high school graduates, and community college students the same opportunity I would give a college grad."

Mentoring is an important part of Saint's philosophy. "I find that anybody can mentor anybody else as long as they have experience in the field that others will find valuable. And I do my best to spend my time with people that are appreciative of that time and to focus on the individuals that give the most to the company and have the most potential and ability. The ones that are most loyal. And I also do that with my subsidiary and affiliated companies. We have spin-off companies that have their own CEOs and their own executive team, and nowadays I need to advise them. I need to advise the leaders within our company. I need to advise the leaders of the other companies that we own small stakes of. They in turn need to understand that in order for their companies to succeed they need to foster and nurture their key people and teach them how to be fostering nurturing leaders of their own. It might sound like a platitude, but you build your relationships one-to-one, and that's what a mentor-mentee relationship really is at the end of the day. Similar to a master craftsman-apprentice type of mindset."

That company culture brings the best out of Universal Processing's employees. "The lives of the hundred or so people under our roof have been effectively changed," Saint says. "Most of our employees are minorities, and they make a great living. They are land-owning individuals in America, and I couldn't be prouder. I try to give every single person that walks into our doors the ability to be as successful as any other American. Even though that message hasn't necessarily been too popular these past two or three years toward certain demographics in America, that's always been my goal since day one."

Universal Processing took the better part of a decade to get to the point of being able to offer

Halloween costumes contest

those opportunities. He says the early years were a series of one step forward, two steps back. "A couple of the processing companies we used decided not to honor their contracts and liquidated. And I couldn't afford a legal department to fight it. So twice in six years we were wiped out and had to go back to zero and start over."

Undaunted, Saint kept going. He pursued an associate degree in business administration to navigate the landmines of entrepreneurship. For someone who jokes he was a borderline high school dropout, Saint excelled at the Borough of Manhattan Community College, where he was an honors student and a member of the Phi Theta Kappa Honors Society and selected by *USA Today* as a member of the All-USA Academic Team.

"BMCC helped me to develop my work ethic," he says. "I still apply that each day in my business, and it afforded me the opportunity to lead other talented individuals through the multitude of leadership positions and extracurricular activities that were available."

After two fitful starts, the third time around Universal Processing finally had a breakthrough when a mentor from Saint's internship days opened up his own processing company.

"He walked into my office and said: *I know you've really hustled hard and taken your lumps, but if you just give me one deal, I promise that we'll grow rich together.* I decided to trust him, and for the past thirteen years, we're still doing business together. That was likely the difference-maker."

Today the core of Universal Processing's business is handling electronic payments for small businesses through his former

Operation department

mentor's third-party processor. They also do point of sales systems as well as marketing, funding, and consulting for small businesses. "We're part of that electronic payment processing, credit card processing, debit card processing ecosystem, conveniently bundled together as FinTech, or financial technology."

To handle the back-office operations, which includes a customer service department that can field calls in whatever language that their clients speak, Saint says his team is comprised of professional, college-educated individuals—the only positions in his company he does require a college degree.

"For our sales and more entrepreneurial-focused team, we don't have any education requirements for all the reasons I mentioned before. And to be honest, when it comes to sales we sometimes prefer not having someone from an elite or Ivy League school. Don't get me wrong; I love education. I love having sophisticated conversations with educated folks. But sometimes I think that college makes you lose your get-up-and-go. I think it can breed entitlement rather than hunger and determination and perseverance. Many people coming out of an elite college feel professionally entitled. They're young, and they have a full head of steam, and come here to apply for entry-level positions and ask for a quarter-million-dollar package and the golden parachutes. They don't get a second interview. They don't realize they still have a lot to learn about people. About company culture. About business relationships. Academic learning is all very important and builds you as a person, but it doesn't make you better than other people or more entitled to certain benefits than other workers. I think that's the dark side of education. And it's an institutional thing; it has nothing to do with the subject matter studied."

From the days of pounding the pavement looking for clients, Saint's role at Universal Processing has evolved from a jack-of-all-trades bootstrapping founder to the big picture visionary, which includes establishing several vertical businesses as part of the overall ecosystem.

"It's usually out of necessity," he says. "My attitude is, if nobody does it better than us, then we need to do it. The grim reality is that most people today are out for themselves, which is the antithesis of our mission statement. Not many people honor a handshake, and too few people have integrity. Getting shafted by people not fulfilling their contract or promises made us realize we needed to build our own software company. We needed to build our own marketing company. We needed to build a plethora of companies to support our own companies."

Saint approaches his company as a family.

"Like any family, we take care of our own. Our friendly and knowledgeable staff is standing by twenty-four hours a day, seven days a week, 365 days a year to provide support in eight different languages. We provide dedicated relationship managers who are ready to support clients' individual needs. In order to keep your business running smoothly, you need strong, reliable tools, but as a business owner, your time is limited. This is why Universal Processing offers durable, easy-to-use terminals, and fast, powerful online reporting tools. We also provide the convenience and experienced technicians who personally install and train clients, free of charge. We also understand that identity theft and fraud protection is a major concern for any customer or company doing business with credit cards. We want to help you focus on growing your business, and not what can hurt it, so we chose First Data as our electronic payment platform based on their experience, clean record of breeches, and reputation as the most secure processor in the payments industry."

There's an old adage that imitation is the sincerest form of flattery.

But Saint says over the years the competition has changed because the processing industry has changed.

"I would say this industry was emerging from the '90s to the early 2000s and experienced very rapid growth. Then in 2015 it went the other way because of mass consolidation. The big guys with the big money got involved and bought up as many companies as they could. So while we now have fewer competitors, we have bigger competitors. But we have managed to maintain growth because consolidation has underscored what we offer compared to our conglomerate competition, not the least of which is personal relationships."

Even though Universal Processing is no longer a struggling start-up and has emerged as a processing industry innovator, Saint still relies on personal relationships forged when the future was uncertain.

"I have some personal client relationships of twenty-plus years that I still maintain, people who sought me out after my non-compete expired. They still call me, and I still thank them for their business. And the reason why they've stayed with us for seventeen-plus years—and some have even passed their companies on to their children, who still do business with us—is because I took the time to develop a one-to-one relationship. I did that the first day, and I've never stopped. I still take phone calls from new clients who literally don't know how to turn the power on and off on their machine. So I walk them through rebooting the machine. I don't care what my title is. The most important thing is being a down-to-earth individual who is willing to help a client, whatever the problem. And you better believe my executives understand that if I'm doing it, they better be doing it. And those executives teach their managers."

He likens it to a Russian doll, with each new layer identical to the one before. "I feel we go several layers deep. As long as the imprint and the values are passed on level-by-level, layer-by-layer, generation-by-generation within our company, then at the end of the day, the final relationship is still a one-to-one relationship between a sales executive and their client."

Looking back over the struggles and accomplishments to get to where Universal Processing is today, Saint says a lesson he learned he would pass on to the next generation of entrepreneurs is to be smart with your cash and have legal representation.

"Every intelligent legal dollar that is spent can save you hundreds of dollars in the future. Consider my first four years. I can't get that time back. And even if I could, I wouldn't because the lessons learned were so valuable that I couldn't even quantify it. That said, if I had spent even as little as $1000 or $3000 on legal representation back in the early 2000s, I could've saved myself a few years of work and from half a million to $1 million that I was effectively screwed out of. But that's life. That's business. You can't feel sorry for yourself. But understand that if you don't know how to manage your contracts and you're just a bright-eyed, bushy-tailed green start-up into the business world, you will be fresh meat for the predators out there. So find the money to get legal representation because it will pay for itself in spades."

Annual gala group photo

For thousands of years most entrepreneurial service businesses ran fundamentally the same way. The professional would secure a shop or office, hire local help, and open for business, attracting customers from that town or one nearby. The enterprises themselves remained largely unchanged over the years, sticking to time-honored practices.

Over the last half-century or so, modern telecommunications and digital technology have made that traditional method obsolete. Businesses are no longer limited by geography or the local talent pool, and there are many new avenues for reaching potential customers and clients. But the flip side is a marketplace that is fluid and competitive, with consumers having expanded choices and being proactive about asserting their wants. The traditional methodologies for branding and building market appeal have been challenged by the fast-moving global economy.

Today some of the most innovative companies embrace an agile approach, which promotes collaboration, flexibility, and adaptability. Originally designed for software development, the agile method improves productivity and the speed of decision-making, taps into the creative energy of an organization's talent, and minimizes the time needed to achieve sought-after results.

Sunny Beth White founded Philadelphia-based Xavier Creative House (XCH), a healthcare creative agency, with a distinctive agile business model, so it could quickly adapt to market changes. At a time when brick-and-mortar agencies dominated the healthcare space, XCH benefitted from launching as a virtual operation. It took extreme discipline and coordination to set up an effective model. The firm uses digital and cloud technologies to facilitate seamless collaboration for contributors around the world, and that has paid off. XCH tripled in size between 2016 and 2018 and has been honored with numerous awards.

Sunny says, "XCH specializes in creating healthcare marketing strategies for pharmaceutical, biotech, medical device, and health system brands that thrive in today's multichannel world. We build healthcare brand stories from the ground up with bold and evocative creative paired with meaningful technology. The team at XCH is a group of experienced and talented brand experts from all healthcare marketing backgrounds and disciplines. They are master craftspeople who have earned their reputations by constructing exemplary healthcare brand marketing solutions."

Since its launch in 2013, XCH has used that foundation to go from start-up to upstart. The business achieved WBENC certification in February 2015 from the Women's Business Enterprise National Council, the largest third-party certifier of businesses owned, controlled, and operated by women in the United States. Fast-forward to 2019, when Xavier made the Inc. 5000 list of fastest-growing privately held companies by posting a three-year growth of 416 percent. It also ranked #2 on both the Philadelphia100 and the Philly Soaring 76 lists of the region's fastest-growing companies. The year concluded with Sunny being honored by the *Philadelphia Business Journal* as one of Philadelphia's Most Admired CEOs.

Sunny credits the creative team for the Xavier Creative House's award-winning pedigree. "We purposefully assemble our talented healthcare marketing experts based on the nature of the brand, therapeutic areas, and the demands of the project. XCH's global team of brand builders

Sunny White

and healthcare marketers, tech-savvy go-getters, and innovative dream-vetters are passionate about the big idea that changes behavior in the healthcare marketplace."

Sunny was born into an entrepreneurial family in which business was a frequent topic of conversation at the dinner table. "My mother is a serial entrepreneur and dad was a partner in a property tax consultancy," Sunny says. "They would always talk about their work, so at a very young age, my siblings and I were exposed to these conversations. It shaped my vision of what it means to be successful in business, and I imagined myself following in my parents' footsteps. Naturally it further manifested in college. I attended St. Michael's College for a liberal arts education that would allow me the flexibility to explore multiple majors to understand the interdependencies of courses. Abnormal psychology fascinated me, but when I took my first business course, it was a revelation because it was so easy and felt so right; I knew it was my future."

After college, Sunny was determined to strike out on her own and use her education in Corporate America. She started out in finance and quickly learned she preferred marketing and sales. To help give Sunny the space to make a transition to a more suitable career track, Sunny's mother invited her to work in the family business and introduced her to an executive coach.

"That's when I first learned the value of mentorship," Sunny says. "In addition to having a sounding board for ideas and a resource for questions, my coaching sessions led me to identify the core competencies needed to progress into a leadership role."

While her mother focused on the bigger picture of what was then a

$10 million company, Sunny set out to improve operational efficiencies. She devised a plan to bring the compliance services in-house and bill it back to the clients, saving the company thousands of dollars a month. Once the new processes were running smoothly, Sunny's mom assigned her to run the human resources department. One minor detail: Sunny says she knew nothing about HR.

"My reaction was: *How can I be put in charge?* That was the beauty of working for a rapid-growth company. There was always an opportunity to try something new in a supportive environment. I gained a real appreciation for the leadership team at the contact center, the trust we placed in each other, and the collaboration we employed to cross-train and cover all the functional areas. Their culture influenced my transformational leadership style, which engages everyone on the Xavier team to be fluent in all functions and stretch themselves to achieve beyond their existing skill level."

Sunny also joined an industry association to gain expertise from people who had decades of experience. It was the beginning of Sunny's professional development strategy to surround herself with leaders who inspire her to raise the bar.

Eventually Sunny's mom rotated her through the other departments, from operations to sales and marketing, essentially giving her an all-out hands-on education on running a business. Think of it as an entrepreneurial tough love.

"Her style was very much: *You need to dive in and learn.* She wasn't there to hold my hand and that built my confidence and independence. I now think that was my mom's master plan to rope me into the family business," Sunny laughs.

During that time, Sunny completed an MBA program specializing in international marketing. Her goal was to earn a degree in less than a year and a half.

"When everyone told me that was impossible, I proved myself by completing the program in fourteen months."

When Sunny was ready to move on, she thoughtfully considered how to broach the topic with her mom. "I had to have a difficult conversation to let her know it was time for me to see what else I could do."

Her mom's practice of building a company then selling it offered Sunny a graceful exit when the timing of the contact center sale coincided with Sunny's next opportunity. She accepted a role to help an insurance brokerage company out of Arizona create an East Coast presence in Pennsylvania. It was approaching the open enrollment season, and the operation needed to be up and running within sixty days.

"I walked into an office space that didn't have any pens, paper, or people," Sunny recalls. "And we did it. It was really stimulating to have been given the opportunity to build something from nothing. I think running a company is in my DNA, and this role proved I was ready to do it my way."

Sunny decided to follow in the footsteps of her brother, who was president of a healthcare advertising agency. The name of Sunny's company has a double significance.

"Xavier is my brother's middle name," Sunny explains. "He encouraged me to take that leap of faith to open the business, so I will always be grateful for that." Also the name Xavier, which is of Basque origin, means *new house*, hence Xavier Creative House.

Once again, Sunny was building a business. "I had never stepped foot in a pharmaceutical company or an advertising agency. And there I was the CEO of a healthcare creative agency."

Rather than worry about what she didn't know or how her competitors conducted business, Sunny built the agency her own way.

Sunny looks at the industry through a fresh lens focused on making a difference in the lives of others by offering brand strategies that influence the behaviors of patients, caregivers, and healthcare professionals (HCP).

"I know what makes us different from the competition is the fact that I'm not limited by the knowledge of how healthcare agencies have always operated."

The Xavier X-factor is bold and evocative creative solutions with a focus on stellar customer service that goes beyond what people expect. Feedback from XCH clients is that the agency surprises and delights them with its unique approach. Clients have even given it the nickname *Xavier-fy*.

Another priority for Sunny is making sure the agency maintains a supportive, nurturing work environment and collaborative culture. "Even though I didn't know what direction my career was going, I always had a vision of creating a company that others would want to work for. So I made XCH a firm that people aspire to join and want to stay with long-term."

Sunny notes that when they recently posted a position for graphic designer, more than 125 people applied. "That was really exciting for me because it fulfilled my goal that exceptional talent would be drawn to my company."

Part of the XCH culture is to encourage a work-life balance. Sunny believes that what's good for the team is good for the company, and Xavier keeps a global calendar for employees to block time when they need to unplug.

"Time off should not be spent answering emails. It's the opportunity to recharge your creativity. We want our employees to create a space for themselves so that they can be happier doing the work they love and building brands that make our clients proud. We consider it a win-win."

Currently XCH specializes in four markets: pharmaceuticals,

medical devices, biotech, and health systems. "Our verticals appreciate how we explore unconventional approaches that differentiate and elevate their brands. Advances in healthcare like artificial intelligence, have become ingrained in how we help our clients from a marketing perspective."

While the cliché *Think outside the box* has clearly seen its day, one of Sunny's favorite marketing entrepreneurs, Seth Godin, has reworked the phrase as: *Thinking on the edges of the box.* Sunny says that perfectly describes the way Xavier balances edgy creative for clients in highly regulated industries.

"Our first big pharmaceutical client came from a referral, proving our theory that there is value in every relationship. At Xavier, we believe life is about connections and healthcare is about life, hence our tagline: Where Healthcare Brands Live.

Sunny enjoys learning about new therapeutic areas and diving into clients' brands to fully understand their impact in the market and how it influences HCPs and patients. "That's what we do as marketers; we tell those stories," she says. "By working closely with healthcare professionals, we can make a difference. We offer physicians a view through a new lens. We did an inspirational engagement where we put doctors in the shoes of a patient through an immersive experience. It altered their perspective by helping them think differently about the patients they were treating and by promoting strong feelings of empathy. The engagements we do stand out because we think through things. It just feels different. We don't play the safe card, and that's why people love us."

As XCH has grown, Sunny's responsibilities and role in the company have changed. Some entrepreneurs resist delegating their founder duties to make time to focus and concentrate on the company's big picture as CEO. Sunny understands the angst, but it is tempered by her commitment to developing her team to work at the highest possible level.

"I'm a very big advocate for continuing education. I always have my staff engaged in growth activities that stretch them beyond their core competencies. This year our creative director is taking a leadership class, and our vice president is leveling up in the Seth Godin alt-MBA."

Sunny says she stays sharp by interacting with mentors and fellow business owners, including a CEO peer-to-peer group called the CEO Think Tank.

"Many members of the group own much larger companies than I do," she says with a laugh. "I think a key to learning to scale and being successful is surrounding yourself with smart people with big visions. There's a saying that you start becoming the five people you are around the most. So I try to associate with people who think big but also those who are good-hearted.

For Sunny it's all about enlightened leadership. "That is super important to me. It's not about my success; it's about the team's success. It's about giving back to the world and paying it forward. That's been my life, and as I progress in my career, supporting the next generation of leaders has become my philanthropic platform. Mentorship goes full circle when I pass along my lessons to someone who is just starting out. I find it very fulfilling."

Even with all her achievements, Sunny believes XCH is just getting started, and it hasn't gone unnoticed within the industry. She says various people have approached her with offers to buy the company.

"I always entertain those offers, but when it comes down to it, I love what I do every day, sometimes to the detriment of other things. And that's probably the hardest part about being an entrepreneur because we're wired for success. I'm not sure I really believe in the word *balance*; it's more like putting things in perspective and prioritizing by the order of importance. I make time for my two children, my husband, and self-care to stay grounded and embrace each day, creating a rewarding personal life.

"I'm fulfilled in business when I use my brain to create complex, creative solutions that add to advancements in healthcare marketing. The industry is evolving significantly. The day is coming where when we call 911, instead of an ambulance coming, a drone might show up, depending on the issue. For example, if you need an EpiPen or snake antivenom, it'll be easier and quicker to send a drone. I'm drawn to this industry because those kinds of advances are innovative and impactful, and I'm proud to be part of it."

Sunny wants to be known for elevating the relationship between patients and HCPs. She gave her legacy a great deal of thought after hearing Jeff Hoffman, the CEO of Priceline, speak on the topic.

"He inspired me to be proud of my drive to succeed. For me success increases my ability to access more resources to help others, especially my team and my clients. A major focus of my outreach this year is to support the up-and-coming entrepreneurs who are watching my example. I'm a philanthropist at heart, with a commitment to make a difference. The impact of Xavier Creative House on healthcare is made possible by the way the dedicated team authentically connects with patients and HCPs through a collaborative process that creates trust and enduring relationships. We can expect big things over the next decade in healthcare and this is our formula for relevant brand promotion."